Applied Public Relations

With its practical orientation and scope, *Applied Public Relations* is the ideal text for any public relations case studies or public relations management course that places an emphasis on stakeholder groups.

Through the presentation of current cases covering a wide variety of industries, locations, and settings, Kathy Brittain Richardson and Marcie Hinton examine how real organizations develop and maintain their relationships, offering valuable insights into business and organizational management practices. The book's organization of case studies allows instructors to use the text in several ways: instructors can focus on specific stakeholders by using the chapters presented; they can focus on particular issues, such as labor relations or crisis management by selecting cases from within several chapters; or they can select cases that contrast campaigns with ongoing programs or managerial behaviors.

A focus on ethics and social responsibility underlies the book, and students are challenged to assess the effectiveness of the practices outlined and understand the ethical implications of those choices.

This Third Edition features:

- Twenty-five new and current domestic and international case studies specifically chosen for their relevancy and relatability to students.
- New "Professional Insights" commentaries where practitioners respond to a set of questions relating to their work.
- Increased emphasis on ethics and social responsibility.
- Fully enhanced companion Web site that is connected with the text, including a test bank and PowerPoint presentations for instructors, and chapter-specific discussion questions and additional readings for students.

Kathy Brittain Richardson is a professor of communication at Berry College, Rome, Georgia, where she has served as provost since 2013.

Marcie Hinton teaches public relations in the journalism/mass communication department at Murray State University.

ROUTLEDGE COMMUNICATION SERIES

Jennings Bryant/Dolf Zillmann, Series Editors

Selected titles include:
Moore et al: ***Advertising and Public Relations Law***
Bardhan et al: ***Public Relations in Global Cultural Contexts***
Stromback et al: ***Political Public Relations***
Sriramesh et al: ***Culture and Public Relations***
Holtzhausen: ***Public Relations As Activism***
Richardson et al: ***Applied Public Relations: Cases in Stakeholder Management***

Applied Public Relations

Cases in Stakeholder Management
3rd edition

Kathy Brittain Richardson
Marcie Hinton

Routledge
Taylor & Francis Group
NEW YORK AND LONDON

Please visit the companion website at
www.routledge.com/cw/richardson

This edition published 2015
by Routledge
711 Third Avenue, New York, NY 10017

and by Routledge
2 Park Square, Milton Park, Abingdon, Oxon, OX14 4RN

Routledge is an imprint of the Taylor & Francis Group, an informa business

First edition published by Lawrence Erbaum Associates Inc. 2005
Second Edition published by Routledge 2009

Library of Congress Cataloging in Publication Data
McKee, Kathy Brittain.
Applied public relations : cases in stakeholder management / Kathy Brittain Richardson, Marcie Hinton. — 3rd edition.
pages cm
Includes bibliographical references and index.
1. Public relations—Case studies. I. Hinton, Marcie. II. Lamb, Larry F. Applied public relations. III. Title.
HD59.L36 2015
659.2—dc23
2014036972

ISBN: 978-0-415-52658-6 (hbk)
ISBN: 978-0-415-52659-3 (pbk)
ISBN: 978-0-203-43663-9 (ebk)

Typeset in Sabon
by Swales & Willis, Exeter, Devon, UK

Printed and bound in Great Britain by
CPI Group (UK) Ltd, Croydon, CR0 4YY

CONTENTS

CASES

PREFACE

Applied Public Relations: Cases in Stakeholder Management offers readers the opportunity to observe and analyze the manner in which contemporary businesses and organizations interact with key groups and influences. A basic assumption of the text is that principles of best practice may best be learned by examining how real organizations have chosen to develop and maintain relationships in a variety of industries, locations, and settings.

We seek to offer insights to readers into contemporary business and organizational management practices. Some of the cases detail positive, award-winning practices, while others provide an overview of practices that may have been less successful. Some target specific public relations campaigns, while others offer evidence of broader business and organizational practices that had public image or public relations implications. Readers should be prompted not only to consider the explicit public relations choices but also to analyze and assess the impact of all management decisions on relationships with key stakeholders, whether they were designed, implicit or even accidental.

Pre-professional programs in schools of business, law, and medicine commonly include case-study courses because they encourage students to use both deductive and inductive reasoning to sort through the facts of situations, propose alternatives, and recommend treatments or solutions. For the same reason, academic programs in public relations usually offer courses that teach reputation and relationship management through the case-study method. In fact, the Commission on Public Relations Education has specifically recommended the use of case-study teaching to provide undergraduates with a bridge between theory and application.

The strategic use of public relations is expanding in business, government, cultural institutions, and social service agencies. According to the U.S. Bureau of Labor Statistics, public relations continues as one of the fastest growing professional fields in the nation, and its practice is spreading rapidly throughout the rest of the world as well. Paralleling this growth, the complexity of public relations has increased with globalization of corporate enterprise and the application of new communication technologies. Social movements and activist organizations now cross borders easily by using public relations strategies to influence a public that is connected by satellites and the Internet. Through case studies throughout the book, readers can examine these changing stakeholder relationships from several perspectives.

This book is appropriate for use as an undergraduate text for courses such as public relations management, public relations cases and campaigns, business management, or integrated-communication management. A commitment to the ethical practice of public relations underlies the book. Students are challenged not only to assess the effectiveness of the practices outlined but also to consider the ethical implications of those choices. We have placed special emphasis on public relations as a strategic management function that must coordinate its planning and activities with several organizational units—human resources, marketing, legal counsel, finance, operations, and others.

The first chapter provides a review of the public relations landscape: the basic principles underlying effective practice. It also offers a method for case analysis, pointing to an understanding of the particular case and leading students to assess the more comprehensive implications for best practices and ethical practices.

This chapter is followed by nine chapters, each of which offers an overview of principles associated with relations with the particular stakeholder group and supplemented with suggestions for additional readings. Then, within each chapter, four to six case studies are presented, to offer sufficient information for analysis and to provide opportunities for students to engage in additional research that would support their conclusions. Reflection questions are offered to help prompt thinking and focus discussion.

Chapter 2 examines relationships with employees, posing such questions as how employee satisfaction is vital to customer service, financial results, recruiting, and compensation. How do high-performing organizations use employee communications in a mutually beneficial manner?

The third chapter explores relationships with community stakeholders. What obligations or duties do organizations have to act as good citizens? What are the appropriate means of publicizing organizational activities as a community citizen? How do companies define their "communities"?

Relationships with consumers are probed in Chapter 4. What are the most effective means of communicating with this group? How are new fusions of marketing, public relations, and advertising working together to reach this group? What duties do businesses owe their customers? How can strong relationships be developed and maintained?

What is news and what motivates reporters to cover it are some of the concerns raised in Chapter 5, which addresses media relations. Cases explore both planned and unplanned interactions with reporters and raise issues of traditional and emerging media formats. What are the most effective means of countering negative publicity?

Chapter 6 focuses on priority stakeholder groups for public companies: shareholders and investors and those who offer advice to them. Examining the cases presented in this chapter yields insight into issues such as the importance of timely and truthful material disclosure and the implications management decisions have on subsequent stock values. In contrast, Chapter 7 focuses on building and maintaining relationships with the stakeholders of nonprofit organizations, their members, volunteers, and donors. The unending need to raise funds is addressed, as is the ongoing need to keep members and volunteers satisfied and to attract new members and volunteers.

Relationships with government regulators are addressed in Chapter 8. Cases examine how governments seek to influence their constituents and how organizations seek to influence regulation.

Chapter 9 examines activist stakeholder groups and how they use public relations strategies to grab attention, win adherents, and motivate change. It also considers how targeted organizations may establish and maintain effective communication with them. The impact of public demonstrations and of media coverage is examined. Principles of cooperation are explored.

The final chapter looks at relationships in the global community, focusing on the many ways in which media practices, cultural mores, and political differences may affect relationships that cross borders and languages.

Professors may approach the cases within the book in several ways. A focus on specific stakeholder groups would be easily possible, using the chapters as presented. However, one might also focus on particular issues, such as labor relations or crisis management, by selecting cases from within several chapters. One might highlight the operations of agencies, corporations, and nonprofits in the same manner. One might also select cases that contrast campaigns with ongoing programs or managerial behaviors.

Additional materials for faculty and students are available in the book's companion Web site at routledge.com/cw/richardson. Outlines of key chapter concepts are provided in PowerPoint slides. Faculty will find suggested in-class activities for each chapter; suggestions for types of guest speakers, career-related exercises, and group assignments are outlined. Sample course syllabi, case presentation assignments, grading rubrics, and a test bank are available. Students will find study and reflection questions provided for each chapter, a list of the key terms used in each chapter, and suggestions for additional readings available through the Web site.

We acknowledge with deep gratitude the contributions to the text offered by the co-author of the first two editions, Larry F. Lamb. Some chapter introductions and several classic cases written by Mr. Lamb are included in this edition, and his experience and expertise in the practice of public relations continue to undergird the text. The copy-editing skills of our colleague, Martha Van Cise, are deeply appreciated. Ten guest commentaries are included, each answering a question about the practice of contemporary public relations. We thank practitioners Paul Bernadini; Brian Brodrick; Shana Glickfield; Sharon Shaffer Guess; Amber Hurdle; Dwain McIntosh; James E. Moody; and Jason Rudd for their professional contributions, and scholars Dr. James Grunig and Dr. Carol J. Pardun for sharing their insights. Our thanks as well to the International Association of Business Communicators and the Public Relations Society of America for granting the rights to include their professional codes of ethics in this edition—codes that we hope will help young practitioners better understand the obligations of public service accepted by those who practice public relations in a democracy.

CHAPTER 1

Public Relations

Mutually Beneficial Systems of Stakeholder Relationships

No formal organization is an island. Each is composed of an internal system of social networks, and each exists within a framework of interrelated systems of relationships with key stakeholders such as consumers, shareholders, competitors, donors, regulators, the media, and so on. Some organizations may prefer to think of themselves as islands or as floating battleships equipped with all the resources necessary for their own sustenance. In reality, such a view is too shortsighted for success. In an era when a tweet about an organization's poor service or a nine-second complaint video can be uploaded to the Web while someone waits in a checkout line, understanding how to participate in the global conversation quickly and appropriately is vital—and underlies the need for businesses, corporations, and nonprofits to understand and apply the principles of effective public relations practice.

PRACTICING PUBLIC RELATIONS

Public relations is thought of here as *the communication and action on the part of an organization that supports the development and maintenance of mutually beneficial relationships between the organization and the groups with which it is interdependent.* This text is written overtly from a systems theory perspective, which suggests that without such adaptation, units in an environment will wither and fade, as they will not be able to exchange vital information with other units in the environment. Such a balanced flow of information creates an *open system*, one that is responsive and adaptive to changes within the environment and its internal and external systems and subdivisions. In public relations terms, we think of this exchange as occurring through the building of mutually beneficial relationships based on an active flow of information from and to the organization and its key publics. Thus, effective public relations practice underlies the maintenance of an open system. Conversely, when public relations is not an integral part of the organization and balancing internal and external communication with the environment and other systems and subsystems is not a basic function for the organization and its management, then the system is described as closed, one subject to restriction and decline because it will not or cannot change or respond to its environment. Thus, the effective practice of public relations is integrally bound to the health of an organization or institution. As such, it provides the avenue for the organization to monitor, interact, and react effectively with other key groups in the organizational environment.

Clearly, for the practice of public relations to ensure openness, it requires the support and involvement of management. To use a crude human systems example, the nervous system within one's leg or arm cannot truly function without support and direction from the brain. Although some movement or reaction may occur, the functioning of the limb is dependent on coordination with all other internal systems triggered by the brain through the central nervous system. Public relations practitioners may be assigned duties or activities, but unless these are coordinated with the "management brains" of the entire organization, these actions may produce little that is truly functional for the organization or its interrelated systems.

PUBLIC RELATIONS PROCESSES WITHIN SYSTEMS

With the assumption that effective public relations promotes a healthy, open system for an organization and its interrelated systems and environment comes certain other suppositions. First, an organization must be able and willing to identify who or what these key interrelated systems are. Because the health of other units within a system is also dependent on a mutually beneficial relationship and exchange, as is that of the central unit, they have a mutual stake in each other's well-being. Thus, these groups are often identified as *publics* or *stakeholders*. The process of coming to know and continuing to understand the concerns, needs, priorities, media habits, communication patterns, and social commitments of those key stakeholder groups requires effort, resources, and knowledge. Although it may be sometimes frustrating, such research is an ongoing process; one never can "know" all one needs to know about a stakeholder. Thus, the practice of public relations requires continuing efforts at research, planning, executing, and evaluating in order for organizations to remain open for new input and output. This text seeks to explore how the relationships with those stakeholders may best be managed through appropriate public relations practices.

Stakeholder theory takes a similar approach in understanding how business and corporate "firms" relate to their stakeholders—defined as those with the power to affect or be affected by a firm's performance.

From this theoretical standpoint, the relationships between and among stakeholders and the organization are metaphorically described as "contracts," which "can take the form of exchanges, transactions, or the delegation of decision-making authority, as well as formal legal documents" (Jones, 1995, p. 407). Managers within firms make decisions that may not necessarily be the most efficient in advancing the interests of all stakeholders, and some decisions or contracts may be more ethical than others. Stakeholder analysis, then, seeks to understand how the contracts can become more efficient, ethical and effective in advancing the interests of the firm and its stakeholders.

Although different writers and organizations may describe the process differently, systems theory suggests that the practice of public relations requires systematic, ongoing environmental monitoring. Plans should be based on solid and thorough research that explores the internal and external situation of the organization and its systems. Effective public relations departments or firms lead their businesses and clients to engage in *issues management*, a systematic environmental analysis that helps identify potential problems and potential ways of responding to or avoiding them. Such research should guide organizations to define carefully the problem or opportunity within the environment that should be responded to. Setting a goal or goals relating to the problem or opportunity establishes the environment for planning. In turn, plans are only as good as their execution, and systems theory again would suggest that such execution should be carried out while the organization is maintaining active environmental monitoring. Finally, input regarding successes and weaknesses should be sought out deliberately at the end of a program and plan. That way, important feedback may become part of the next system action or program and perhaps shared with other linked systems as appropriate to help foster their health.

On occasion, however, organizations may find themselves in crisis situations, some anticipated through scenario planning, others because of sudden internal or external changes in the environment. Public relations practitioners have important responsibilities in helping organizations craft solutions and communications in those instances. While particular responses may vary, organizations that continue to communicate clearly, carefully, compassionately, and accurately with their stakeholders usually find those relationships endure beyond the crisis.

It should be acknowledged that effective analysis, planning, executing, and evaluating of both the environment and relationship management may be approached from other theoretical perspectives. Additionally, other theories and constructs may inform the assumptions of systems theory. Persuasion theory suggests that the motivations and needs of those communicating—both the speaker and the receiver—should be considered when shaping strategies. Members of different publics judge the credibility of the communicator differently, based not only on the communicator's perceived characteristics, but also on their own social and psychological attributes.

Practitioners and managers within organizations would be well advised to come to understand some of the other dominant communication and social-psychological constructs as they seek to provide strong counsel to employers and clients. Classical rhetoric stresses the importance of credibility and character, concepts as important in the 21st century as they were 25 centuries earlier. Social exchange theory stresses the importance of understanding the ways in which people use variations of cost–benefit analyses to make decisions about relationships. Agenda setting theory offers insights into the many ways in which media coverage affects public awareness and opinions about issues and personalities. Similarly, social learning theory stresses the many ways in which observing models shapes subsequent behavior. Other perspectives—from the elaboration-likelihood model to the diffusion of innovations theory—help practitioners better understand how to affect the attitudes, opinions, and behaviors of critical stakeholders. Knowledge of traditional business fields such as marketing and management provides a solid underpinning for effective communication within and throughout organizations. And, an understanding of the ways in which contemporary mass media and social media practices are changing is vital for practitioners.

ETHICAL AND LEGAL PERSPECTIVES

A plethora of laws, regulations, and torts may govern the relationships of organizations with various publics. In the United States, the framework of the First Amendment to the Constitution provides for the free practice of public relations, yet certain practices may be either restricted or required by statute or regulation. For example, businesses and organizations are as affected by concerns regarding libel and privacy as any individual or media group. Copyright and trademark regulation may, in fact, promote and protect the interests of organizations over the interests of individuals. Publicly traded companies face specific regulation of market communication activity, ranging from required speech dealing with quarterly and annual statements, to prohibited or premature information sharing among insiders. Clearly, the practitioner must consider the legal environment as a key component that affects relationships with stakeholder groups.

The social and economic power of public relations practices today should also be grounded in a foundation of social ethics. Professional associations such as the Public Relations Society of America (PRSA) and the International Association of Business Communicators (IABC) have endorsed principles that should underlie practice: advocacy of free speech and communication; commitment to disseminating truthful and accurate information; respect for the dignity and value of all individuals; and the maintenance of independence from undue conflicts of interest or allegiance. (Statements of these principles are included in Appendix A and Appendix B.) Systems theory suggests that the good of the whole is supported by the good of the parts, so behaviors that promote mutual benefit are not only ethical but even essential for the ongoing growth and success of an organization or business. As the communications conduit between and among systems that may have competing interests, determining what choices offer the most effective ethical alternatives requires reflection and introspection, rather than just reaction and response. Practitioners must discern what is the best choice for behavior—that which most effectively promotes the principles of human dignity, social responsibility, and truth telling.

CASE-STUDY ANALYSIS

This book addresses nine key stakeholder groups with which many businesses and organizations interrelate and offers contemporary case studies for analysis. Some of these cases exemplify the very highest standards of public communication, mutual benefit, and business savvy. Others may raise questions about performance and benefit. Chapter 2 investigates relationships and communication with employees as exemplified by national and international firms such as Zappos, McDonald's, and Southwest Airlines. Chapter 3 presents examples of community stakeholders from the perspective of for-profit corporations such as PepsiCo and nonprofit groups such as the Make It Right Foundation. The ways in which corporations seek to foster healthy relationships with consumers may be examined through cases in Chapter 4 involving crisis communication, branding, and product publicity.

The important role played by media relations is explored in Chapter 5 where health care, sports, religious, and social issues arouse media coverage to which organizations had to react and respond. Chapters 6 and 7 address special stakeholder groups, investors, members, and volunteers. From crises of financial reporting to efforts to diversify memberships, these cases raise issues for publicly traded and nonprofit organizations.

Chapter 8 investigates the relationships between governmental organizations and their publics or organizations and regulatory agencies. Critical questions about the role of public relations within public affairs are explored. Chapter 9 addresses critical questions from another perspective—those raised by activist groups seeking to affect change in environmental or social practices. Last, Chapter 10 raises the issue of the expanded international environment in which organizations and businesses now operate. How does one successfully build and maintain relationships in varied settings with diverse stakeholders?

Although there are many ways to approach case studies as a learning tool, the following method may prove helpful and direct. It suggests three layers of analysis that might be used:

- Analyze the Problem: How fully do you understand the situation described here? Note the various stakeholders that may be involved in each case, and how the issue raised in the case is affecting them. Through additional research, what more can you learn about the organization in question, its stakeholders and publics, this situation, or other organizations that have faced similar situations? Seek to articulate the public relations problem or opportunity faced by the organization and/or its key stakeholders in one or two sentences.
- Understand the Practices: Critique the actions or reactions undertaken by the organization and its publics described here. Identify the phases of the communication or campaign cycle—the research, the strategies, the actions and communication tools, and the evaluation processes—and judge the strengths and weaknesses of the plan and actions. Are they in line with accepted best practices? In your opinion, were actions taken that were not necessary? Were other appropriate actions not included? Were there factors of timing and budgeting that affected actions, or that could have been exploited to better advantage?
- Identify the Principles: What long-term principles seemed to underlie the decisions made by the organizations and groups in each case? What did each value? What are the implications of this case for developing, maintaining, or restoring mutually beneficial relationships with the key stakeholder identified, or with other strategic stakeholders? How does this case illustrate, either positively or negatively, common ethical principles for effective practice? What does this case suggest in terms of effective principles for public relations practitioners in other situations with the same stakeholder or others?

The following questions may help you to clarify aspects of the cases as you analyze these levels:

- What is the environmental situation for the organization in this case? Is it economically healthy? Is the organization in a stable or changing environment?

- What goal(s) and objectives do you think this organization is attempting to achieve through its actions or reactions?
- What communications or actions would characterize a mutually beneficial relationship with this particular public or stakeholder? What would motivate members of that stakeholder group to enter into or to maintain a relationship with this organization? What might cause the relationship to deteriorate?
- Do this organization's actions demonstrate open- or closed-system practices and philosophies? What type of research do you believe was used to develop this plan of action—or should have been used? What more should the organization have known to more effectively plan and execute its communication program or campaign?
- What ethical philosophies or precepts are demonstrated by the organization in this case?
- Are there other examples you can cite of organizations that have faced similar challenges? What do those examples tell you about how this organization might have improved its relationships and its outcomes?
- What style of internal management does this case illustrate? Does it appear that public relations practitioners within the organization are taken seriously? Is public relations a management function within this organization?

ADDITIONAL READINGS

Broom, Glen M. (2012). *Cutlip and Center's effective public relations.* (11th ed.). Upper Saddle River, NJ: Prentice Hall.

Caywood, Clarke L. (Ed.). (1997). *The handbook of strategic public relations & integrated communication.* Boston: McGraw-Hill.

Freeman, R.E. (1984). *Strategic management: A stakeholder approach.* Boston: Pitman.

Grunig, James E. (Ed.). (1992). *Excellence in public relations and communications management.* Hillsdale, NJ: Lawrence Erlbaum Associates.

Ihlen, Oy., Ruler, Van., & Fredrickson, M. (2009). *Public relations and social theory: Key figures and concepts.* New York: Routledge.

Jones, T.J. (1995). Instrumental stakeholder theory: A synthesis of ethic and economics. *The Academy of Management Review, 20*(2), 404–437.

Marsh, Charles. (2012). *Classical rhetoric and modern public relations.* New York: Routledge.

Sriramesh, Krishnamurthy, Zertass, Ansgar, & Kim, Jeong-Nam. (2013). *Public relations and communications management.* New York: Routledge.

Wilcox, Dennis L., & Cameron, Glen. (2011). *Public relations: Strategies and tactics.* (10th ed.). Boston: Allyn & Bacon.

PROFESSIONAL INSIGHT Why do so many college students major in public relations?

Figure 1.1 Dr. Carol J. Pardun, Professor, University of South Carolina School of Journalism and Mass Communication

The Journalism School at the University of South Carolina where I am a professor enrolls 1,517 undergraduate students. The J-School students can choose from four majors: journalism, advertising, visual communications, and public relations. We have 610 students who have chosen public relations—fully 40 percent of the enrollment. These numbers are consistent with journalism schools across the country.

Why?

During the years I have been in academe, I have asked hundreds of students why they picked public relations as a major. Occasionally, they answer with a clear vision of what a public relations major entails and they understand how the major celebrates much of what a truly liberal arts education (critical thinking, strong writing, and analytical skills, for example) can provide. But that's the exception.

More often they say something along the lines of "I'm creative, but I can't draw," or "I'm a people person," or "I don't know, but it sounded fun." We professors typically go a little nuts with the "I like people" mantra, but rather than criticize the students for their lackadaisical responses, these comments actually get at the heart of what makes public relations such a popular (and worthwhile) major. College students pick public relations as a major because even if they don't really understand all that the major encompasses, they know that this major will give them options when they graduate.

What other major offers these promises?

1. Work with, in, or for the media.
2. Write. (Oops, don't like writing? Don't major in PR.)
3. Learn about strategy, history, budgeting. (Oops, don't like numbers? Don't major in PR.)
4. Learn about marketing. (It's a whole lot more fun to learn about marketing from a communications perspective than it is from a business school!)

5. Be creative. (The major will teach students all sorts of ways to increase their creativity.)

In other words, when students major in public relations, they don't have to decide which specific job they're going to pursue when they graduate. I like to tell students that if they work hard in college, they'll find a job when they graduate—and even if they don't know what that job looks like during their student years, they'll discover that the career they enter is most certainly appropriate for the public relations skills they developed in college.

Former students in our school have become lobbyists, nonprofit communication managers, corporate spokespeople, educators, social media gurus, lawyers, and yes, even the occasional wedding planner.

So many college students pick public relations as a viable major because they intuitively sense that it is an area of study that is broad enough to open up the professional world in ways that they can only begin to imagine.

In many schools of journalism across the country, the public relations major has melded with advertising to become a strategic communication major. This is all done in the name of progress, but I worry that the damage to the benefit of choosing public relations as a stand-alone major is far reaching. The danger of the strategic communications major is that too often public relations is viewed narrowly—only as a support function for advertising. While public relations does, indeed, support the promotional aspect of marketing, that is only one small part of what public relations entails.

The public relations major provides a background for just about any area of communications. I have a student who graduated last semester and is in charge of new product development for a start-up company. I know another student who, after teaching English as a second language in South Korea for a year, is a master's student in public health. I also know plenty of former students who are working at stand-alone public relations agencies, advertising agencies with public relations departments, and at strategic communications corporations. And for the record, I have plenty of former journalism/news editorial students who eventually found their life-long passion in the world of public relations rather than in the news industry.

The point is that the public relations major prepares a student for all of this. The curriculum typically focuses on writing, systematic analysis, and creative solutions for all sorts of communication challenges. Those advocating for more innovation in journalism education often tell anyone who will listen that we need to prepare students for careers that don't yet exist.

Of all the majors typically housed in schools of journalism across the country, public relations majors are the best poised to do this—not only in the future—but right now.

Dr. Carol J. Pardun is a professor of journalism and mass communications at the University of South Carolina. She holds a Ph.D. in mass communication from the University of Georgia. She has served as the director of the School of Journalism and Mass Communication at the University and as director of the School of Journalism at Middle Tennessee State University. She was president of the Association for Education in Journalism and Mass Communication in 2009–2010 and serves on the Accrediting Council for ACEJMC.

CHAPTER 2

Stakeholders

Employees

The first day of a new job often includes an employee's initial contact with the public relations department, though the employee may not realize it. Part of the day is spent in the human resources office, completing paperwork and an orientation program, and part is usually spent with the employee's new supervisor. During these visits, a new employee may receive printed material about the organization, see an orientation video or animated tutorial, and learn how to use the intranet to get news and information. The printed, visual, and online materials very likely were prepared by or with help from a public relations professional. Through a variety of media channels, this connection to public relations will continue, directly and indirectly, until the individual retires or leaves the organization.

Employee relations responsibilities cut across many departments. Human resources focuses mainly on recruiting, pay and benefits, training programs, employee appraisal systems, and similar concerns affecting all jobholders. The marketing department wants to keep employees up to date on products and services offered to customers. In every department, individual supervisors handle employee relations needs that are specific to the people in their work groups, such as linking an organization's overall mission and goals to the everyday reality of the job.

Public relations professionals work in close partnership with these human resources managers, individual supervisors, and others to foster good employee relations. In fact, public relations professionals seldom undertake employee relations programs without input from human resources and other departments. This partnership aims to create conditions where all employees, individually and as a group, can get the greatest reward from the human capital they invest in the job and where the organization can gain the highest value from the resources it uses to reach its goals.

All of us invest varying amounts of human capital in work. Human capital is the combination of talents and skills, knowledge, behavior, effort, and time that an individual commits to the job. In turn, an organization pays its workers for their human capital and also provides capital of its own—machinery, office space, computers, and so on—for each of us to use on the job.

EMPLOYEE SATISFACTION PAYS MEASURABLE RETURNS

Everyone, individuals and the organization, will get the most from an enterprise when all commit as much human and hard capital to the endeavor as they can. Satisfied employees care more about customer satisfaction, cooperate more with each other, and apply more effort, so employees are most likely to invest more human capital when they are satisfied with their jobs. They are more productive.

Employee satisfaction has tangible benefits for all organizations, but the results may be most easily measured in for-profit businesses. Satisfied employees are associated with higher revenues (the dollars that businesses receive from their customers), lower costs (the dollars that businesses spend to provide customers with products or services), and greater profitability (the revenues that remain after all costs are met). The reasons for the positive payback from employee satisfaction are self-evident. Not only do they appeal to our common sense, but they also have been examined by researchers and found valid. Here are a few examples:

- Employee retention: Satisfied employees are less likely to look for or accept new jobs with other organizations, which might be competitors. As workers stay longer at one employer, they become more proficient, building up their human capital in ways that benefit both employee and employer. Turnover, replacing employees who quit, is expensive; some say it may cost up to 250 percent of the employee's annual salary. It entails not only the visible costs of recruiting new workers but also the invisible costs of a lower level of human capital offered by a new employee.
- Customer satisfaction: Each of us, as consumers, has encountered unhappy employees, surly or slow or sour, who can make a sales transaction or a meal away from home an unpleasant experience that we vow never to repeat. On the other hand, satisfied employees create a detectable climate of care to which customers respond. It may lead to a bigger purchase and to repeat business. Similarly, customer satisfaction appears to have a reciprocal effect on employees. Imagine how much more pleasant a job can be when customers are happy.
- Productivity: Employees generally must interact with coworkers and managers to make a product or provide a service; few create output entirely on their own. When individuals actively cooperate with each other, more work gets done in less time, often

> using fewer resources. Similarly, satisfied employees put more "discretionary effort" into the job, making the difference between average and superior performance.

Considering the pay-off that is available to employers from taking steps to assure employee satisfaction, what's surprising is how many organizations neglect the things they could be doing, big and little, to make employees happier.

EFFECTIVE LEADERS INSPIRE TRUST AND CONFIDENCE

Some things that might improve employee satisfaction are beyond the influence of public relations professionals—for example, better pay and benefits. Yet, there are many areas where public relations professionals, in partnership with others, can and should apply their expertise: Feedback mechanisms that give employees a voice and an opportunity to raise questions; "open-book" management that shares details on current results; reports on goals and plans that are expressed in language everyone can understand; and more.

Perhaps the best place to begin is employees' desire to know where the organization is going, how it's going to get there, and when it will arrive—goals, strategies, and timetables. These subjects constitute leadership responsibilities, and there may be nothing more important to employees. Coincidentally, these subjects also give public relations professionals the opportunity to make their greatest contributions.

Research shows that employee satisfaction depends on the qualities of trust and integrity that bind individuals to organizations. Yet, investigators have learned that workers are most disappointed in employers' efforts to achieve open and honest communication; surveys of employees consistently suggest that only 1 in 5 indicate that they trust their organizations and about 1 in 10 say their managers do what they say they do.[1] Employees also noted disappointment in the willingness of managers to share information.

The Hay Group, international consultants on human resources, says that its studies have shown that trust and confidence in top leadership constitute the single most important predictor of employee satisfaction. Moreover, a Hay study found that leaders can get trust and confidence through effective communication programs that:

- Help employees understand the overall strategy of the organization.
- Help employees see their role in achieving key objectives.
- Update employees regularly on progress that's made toward the objectives.

SOURCE OF SATISFACTION: OPEN AND HONEST COMMUNICATION

Because key indicators of an organization's success depend on employee satisfaction and, in turn, satisfaction depends on trust and confidence in leadership, public relations professionals should develop programs that help leaders win trust and confidence as well as show respect and appreciation for employees. In some cases, these programs will involve giving employees valid reasons to extend trust; in others, programs will help leaders earn it. In all cases, trust cannot exist without open and honest communication.

Of course, communication should be two-way—not simply the top-down, here's-what-you-need-to-know approach used in too many employee relations programs. Instead, it should provoke a dialogue that will help employees gain satisfaction from their work life and support the overall goals of the organization.

When Towers Watson, a global human resources consulting firm, examined 41 global companies to learn how they foster success, they found that the high-performing companies have developed ways of fostering and sustaining high employee engagement—and internal communication is a critical aspect of developing such engagement. Companies with highly engaged employees financially outperformed other companies in their sectors by an average of 18 percent. Towers Watson found that high-performing organizations:

- Provide channels for upward communication and involve employees in decision making early in the process.
- Recognize the critical role internal communication plays in helping the organization adapt to change.
- Focus on helping employees understand the business, its values and culture, goals and progress, and ways for employees to improve performance.
- Clearly communicate the career paths available to employees within the organization, and support them in finding a balance between work and personal lives.

MEDIA CHANNELS FOR EMPLOYEES

Organizations use a variety of media to reach employees, including the traditional methods of newsletters and employee newspapers, posters, and bulletin boards. Increasingly, organizations are turning to social media tools, from instant messaging and streaming audio and video to voicemail announcements, e-mail, intranets, blogs and vlogs, social media networks, YouTube channels, video sharing, and organizational apps. The live, interactive communication available through digital audio and video tools can help promote engagement across numerous domestic and international organizational sites as employees participate in discussions in "virtual meetings."

Intranet communication has been growing fastest because it offers the advantages of speed, flexibility, color, interactivity, and ease in updating. However, experts advise public relations professionals to use intranet communication for its special capabilities rather than treat it as if it were print projected on a screen. Intranets can offer multimedia, chats and bulletin boards, previews of ad campaigns and commercials, breaking news, and more, but people don't read intranet screens as if they were the printed page. Communicating through phone and tablet screens offers new design and writing challenges for professionals. Messages must be concise and clear.

Public relations professionals often play an important role in the success of such meetings even though they may not be visible during videos or presentations. To introduce major policy changes and the like, materials for the meetings are prepared in advance by public relations practitioners: an agenda, skeleton remarks for the supervisors to adapt, short videos or slideshows, handouts for participants to download, feedback forms, and similar items. The purpose is to give the supervisor useful materials, minimize preparation time, keep the message consistent, and achieve communications objectives. Following the videoconference, these materials may be maintained on the intranet for later reference.

Yet even with all the advanced technology available today, one of the most effective media channels is an old standby used in offices and retail establishments and on the plant floor for generations: the small-group meeting where the boss and team get together for a 10- or 20-minute discussion. There are two main reasons for the continued popularity of on-site small-group meetings:

- Face-to-face discussion is the most effective form of communication.
- Employees prefer to get job-related news from their immediate supervisor.

The cases in this chapter provide opportunities to discuss some of the opportunities and challenges faced by practitioners communicating with or about employee stakeholders. As you consider these cases, seek to identify the public relations problem or opportunity, the methods and tools used to resolve the situation, and how one might evaluate the success or failure of the public relations efforts. Ask yourself: What are the issues employees care about in this case? How might management communicate its goals, strategies and progress more effectively? How might employee viewpoints be sought out and responded to in a timely manner? Are the communicators engaging in open and honest dialogue?

NOTE

1. Blanchard, K. (July 2013). Trust. www.trainingjournal.com, pp. 55–58.

ADDITIONAL READINGS

Becker, Brian E., Huselid, Mark A., & Ulrich, Dave. (2001). *The HR scorecard: Linking people,strategy, and performance*. Boston: Harvard Business School Press.

Beitler, Michael A. (2003). *Strategic organizational change*. Greensboro, NC: Practitioner Press International.

Catlette, Bill, & Hadden, Richard. (2012). *Contented cows still give better milk, revised and expanded: The plain truth about employee relations and your bottom line*. Hoboken, NJ: John Wiley and Sons.

Koys, D.J. (2001). The effects of employee satisfaction, organizational citizenship behavior, and turnover on organizational effectiveness: A unit-level, longitudinal study. *Personnel Psychology*, *54*(1), 101–114.

Schade, J. (2011, Winter). What the best leaders say and do. *The Strategist*, 36–37.

Towers Watson. (2013). The power of three: Taking engagement to new heights. www.towerswatson.com.

CASE 1: "CREATE FUN AND A LITTLE WEIRDNESS" AT ZAPPOS

Figure 2.1 Zappos promotes a culture of informality to inspire creativity and collegiality that will result in employees providing excellent customer service. (Photo: ©Zappos IP, Inc. 2014.)

No dress codes. No job titles. Shadowing sessions where customer loyalty team members explore job responsibilities in other areas. An intensive new employee training program. Life coaching. Blogs. On-site fitness center.

One hundred percent coverage of health benefits. Bonus of Amazon.com stock worth 20 percent of the employee's wages. Domestic partner benefits. With these characteristics, Zappos' listing as one of the "100 Best Companies to Work For" in 2013 (and 2009, 2010, 2011, and 2012) is no surprise. Its more than 1,700 employees seem to find the online shoe retailer an unusual but engaging place to work.

Only Friends Can Apply

In fact, Zappos has decided it no longer needs to advertise its job openings. *The Wall Street Journal* reported that the corporation received thousands of applications annually—more than 31,000 in 2013—and was able to hire about 1.5 percent of those. To make the application and hiring process more purposeful, Zappos announced in May 2014 that job openings would be made known to members of its social network, Zappos Insiders, where applicants can learn about the corporation and demonstrate their passion for working at Zappos as they communicate with current employees.

To become a Zappos Insider, one signs up for membership on the Web site to gain access to a wide variety of information about the corporation. According to Mike Bellen, senior human resources (HR) manager, in a May 27, 2014, blog post announcing the change: "Insiders have unique access to content, updates, tweetchats, online hangouts and back-and-forth discussions with recruiters and hiring teams." If invited to apply, then the prospective employees will get more attention from the corporate recruiters.

Once hired, the new employees are offered five weeks of training. At the end of the first week, Great Place to Work reports, the initiates are offered payment for the time spent training and a $2,000 bonus if they would like to quit—thereby allowing Zappos to retain employees who are fully engaged and committed to the corporation. As one employee noted on the Recruiter Spotlight blog on April 14, 2014: "you're welcomed with the opportunity to love the job you're doing."

A Culture of "Wow"

The employees, who sell more than 1,000 different brands of shoes, clothes, housewares, and other products through Zappos online, work in an intentionally unusual culture. The corporation, with revenues of more than $2 billion in annual sales, is a subsidiary of Amazon.com. It reorganized itself in 2013 into a system chief executive officer (CEO) Tony Hsieh calls a "holacracy," which seeks to do away with typical corporate hierarchies and integrate employees into some 400 circles in which individuals may have multiple responsibilities and opportunities for growth. The informality is designed to foster creativity and commitment.

Zappos culture rewards strong customer service and encourages its employees to do whatever it takes to make shoppers happy with their purchases and to seek their own happiness as well. Mig Pascual, one of the Zappos Insights content creators, explained in a October 30, 2012, *U.S. News & World Report* article that customer service representatives are given freedom to decide how best to address shopper concerns:

> If a customer loyalty team member needs to refund a customer's money, upgrade shipping, make that customer a V.I.P., or send a surprise WOW package of cookies or flowers to brighten a customer's day, they can do it. Empowering employees makes it feasible to scale the business to provide the highest level of service.

"Build a Positive Team and Family Spirit"

The corporate ethos of empowerment is based on 10 core values that include: deliver WOW through service; embrace and drive change; create fun and a little weirdness; be adventurous, creative, and open-minded; Pursue growth and learning; build open and honest relationships with communication; build a positive team and family spirit; do more with less; be passionate and determined; be humble.

A P.E.A.C.E. (Programs, Events, Activities, Charity & Engagement) team plans and executes numerous employee events each year, ranging from monthly birthday parties and recognition programs to workshops to parades to 5K races. A corporate fact sheet explains: "The theme behind everything we do is engagement."

Community engagement through charitable events is highly encouraged. In fact, CEO Hsieh has been actively investing to help revitalize downtown Las Vegas through the Downtown Project (downtownproject.com) that has fostered renovations, new business starts, and civic events. Zappos headquarters has moved to occupy a renovated building there.

Questions for Reflection

1. How successful do you think Zappos will be in attracting talented employees without direct advertisements?
2. Discuss the strategic purposes in engaging prospective employees through social media before they even apply for a position.
3. As you consider Zappos corporate values, discuss how they would contribute to a distinct culture for employees and customers. Would any or all of these values be transferable to other businesses or nonprofits?

Information for this case was drawn from information from the Zappos corporate Web site and Auriemma, Adam. (May 28, 2014). Zappos

zaps its job postings. *The Wall Street Journal.* http://online.wsj.com/news/articles/SB100014205270230481190457986300322355082;
Bellen, Michael. (May 27, 2014). Goodbye job postings! Zappos Blogs. http://blogs.zappos.com/blogs/inside-zappos;
Corbett, Sara. (January 21, 2014). How Zappos' CEO turned Las Vegas into a startup Fantasyland. Wired. http://www.wired.com/2014/01/zappos-tony-shieh-las-vegas/;
Erb, Marcus. (2011). How Zappos creates happy customers and employees. Great Place to Work. www.greatplacetowork.com/storage/documents/Publications_Documents/Zappas_How_Zappos_Creates_Happy_Customers_and_Employees.pdf;
Hochman, David. (April 16, 2014). Playboy Interview: Tony Hsieh. *Playboy.* http://www.playboy.com/playground/view/playboy-interview-tony-hsieh-zappos;
Pascual, Mig. (October 30, 2012). Zappos: 5 out-of-the-box ideas for keeping employees engaged. *US News & World Report.* http://money.usnews.com/money/blogs/outside-voices-careers/2012/10/30/zappos-5-out-of-the-box-ideas-for-keeping-employees-engaged.

CASE 2: MCDONALD'S TRIES TO DRIVE THROUGH EMPLOYEE CRISES

In October 2013, Nancy Salgado, who had worked at a Chicago McDonald's for 10 years, called McResource, a helpline the fast-food corporation developed to help its employees cope with personal and family issues. The McResource Web site explained: "You can find practical solutions to many of life's problems and challenges with McResource Line, a benefit for McDonald's restaurant employees and their immediate family members." As "Easy as 1-2-3." "Your McResources Line consultant will make sure that you have what you need and find out if you need any additional information or assistance."

Human Resource Line Offers Unpopular Advice

Ms. Salgado makes $8.25 an hour working at the restaurant. According to a recording of the phone conversation, after she asked for assistance managing her expenses, Ms. Salgado was advised to go to food pantries, to ask for help with her heating bills through the government-funded Low Income Home Energy Assistance Program, and to apply for food stamps and Medicaid to supplement her restaurant wages. She was then given the local phone numbers to call to sign up.

A labor advocacy group called Low Pay is Not OK released an edited version of the taped phone call. The video prompted debate and criticism in the media and on Internet sites, which prompted a corporate statement.

Many questioned why the employees were being referred to federal and state agencies to receive aid.

As reported by the *Los Angeles Times* on October 13, the corporation responded:

> This video is not an accurate portrayal of the resource line as this is very obviously an edited video. The fact is that the McResource Line is intended to be a free, confidential service to help employees and their families get answers to a variety of questions or provide resources on a variety of topics including housing, child care, transportation, grief, elder care, education and more.

The McResource Line continued to gain the corporation unwanted attention. In December 2013 several posts on the line warned of the dangers of eating fast food, calling a cheeseburger and fries an "unhealthy choice." Critics noted the incongruity between the advice and McDonald's menu options. In response, CNBC reported on December 28 that the Web site was closed, although employees could still phone for assistance.

The corporation explained:

> We have offered the McResource program to help our valued McDonald's employees with work and life guidance created by independent third party experts. A combination of factors has led us to re-evaluate, and we've directed the vendor to take down the website. Between links to irrelevant or outdated information, along with outside groups taking elements out of context, this created unwarranted scrutiny and inappropriate commentary. None of this helps our McDonald's team members. We'll continue to provide service to our folks through an internal telephone help line, which is how the majority of employees access the McResource services.
>
> (http://news.mcdonalds.com/Corporate/Media-Statements/McResource-Statement)

Web Site Suggests Getting a Second Job

Another McDonalds's Web site that offered advice for its employees had garnered public criticism several months before. McDonald's offered employees a "Practical Money Skills Budget Journal" Web site that had been prepared by Visa Inc. and Wealth Watchers International in July 2013. Income created for the sample monthly budget indicated that minimum-wage employees who worked 35 hours a week at McDonald's (earning a monthly income of $1,105) would need a second job to get to a monthly income total of $2,060. The sample budget then showed expenses such as mortgage/rent of $600, health insurance of $20 monthly (although McDonald's charges its employees $14 a week), and omitted funds for gas, food, child care or clothing in order to arrive at a monthly expenses total of $1,510.

Such corporate-sponsored advice for its employees' financial health was hotly debated by some media outlets, spoofed by Stephen Colbert, and criticized on the Internet, with many commenting about the unworkable nature of the sample monthly budget provided.

The debate highlighted an employee relations concern of many fast-food restaurants whose employees were lobbying for an increase in wages. McDonald's prominence in the industry likely garnered it special attention as part of a larger movement of fast-food workers and others employed at the federal minimum wage of $7.25 who were seeking an increase in base pay to $15 an hour. Heidi Barker Sa Shekham, of McDonald's Global External Communications, posted the corporation's response in a statement of their position on the issue on its Web site:

> At McDonald's, we offer part-time and full-time employment, benefits and competitive pay based on the local marketplace and job level. McDonald's and our owner-operators are committed to providing our respective employees with opportunities to succeed, and we have a long, proven history of providing advancement opportunities for those who want it. We invest in training and professional development that helps them learn practical and transferable business skills whether at McDonald's or elsewhere. It's important to know approximately 80% of our global restaurants are independently owned and operated by small business owners, who are independent employers that comply with local and federal laws.
>
> This is an important discussion that needs to take into account the highly competitive nature of the industries that employ minimum wage workers, as well as consumers and the thousands of small businesses which own and operate the vast majority of McDonald's restaurants.
>
> We respect the right of employees to choose whether or not they want to unionize.
>
> (http://news.mcdonalds.com/Corporate/Media-Statements/Statement-on-Minimum-Wage)

The employees used various techniques to communicate their messages, from protests outside restaurants to short-time strikes. The Low Pay is Not OK group presented their cause on its Web site (http://FastFoodGlobal.org/), and offered information about protests and an online petition that workers could sign. After an initial one-day strike in November 2012, the group planned four other one-day walkouts at U.S. restaurants and businesses in 2013 and 2014.

The Service Employees International Union, which advocated for fast-food workers to unionize and to ask for $15 an hour as a starting wage, organized a strike against McDonald's on May 15, 2014. *The Wall*

Street Journal reported that McDonald's had been targeted by workers' groups that were supported by the union since November 2012. After demonstrators seeking higher wages marched on the corporate headquarters in Illinois, one of the corporation's headquarters buildings in Illinois was closed the day before its shareholder meeting was scheduled to meet there. *USA Today* described protesters outside McDonald's restaurants in Switzerland, New Zealand, the Philippines, Japan and at Seoul, Korea, where one protester wore a Ronald McDonald costume.

The corporation issued a statement on its Web site:

> We respect everyone's right to voice an opinion. McDonald's respects our employees' right to voice their opinions and to protest lawfully and peacefully. If employees participate in these activities, they are welcomed back and scheduled to work their regular shifts. We value our employees' well-being and the contributions they make to our restaurants, and thank them for what they do each and every day. Our restaurants remain open today and every day thanks to the dedicated employees serving our customers. We respect the right of employees to choose whether or not they want to unionize.
>
> (http://news.mcdonald's.com/Corporate/Media-Statements/Statements-on-May-15th-Rallies)

However, workers at other restaurants including Burger King, Wendy's and KFC in 150 U.S. cities and 80 cities in more than 30 countries from Ireland to Korea to India joined in the one-day action, supported by the International Union of Food, Agricultural, Hotel, Restaurant, Catering, Tobacco and Allied Worker's Associations labor federation that represents 12 million workers in more than 120 countries, according to *The New York Times*.

The corporate Web site (http://www.aboutmcdonalds.com/mcd/our_company.html) describes the corporation as "the leading global food-service retailer with more than 35,000 local restaurants serving nearly 70 million people in more than 100 countries each day." More than 1.9 million people work for the corporation. One of the corporate values noted on the Web site describes its human resource philosophy:

> We are committed to our people. We provide opportunity, nurture talent, develop leaders and reward achievement. We believe that a team of well-trained individuals with diverse backgrounds and experiences, working together in an environment that fosters respect and drives high levels of engagement, is essential to our continued success.

Questions for Reflection

1. How might management have communicated its messages through the McResource Web site more effectively?
2. Evaluate the statements McDonald's issued addressing employee and media concerns. How do they attempt to balance corporate priorities with those of their employee stakeholders?
3. What legal and ethical issues must be confronted by a corporation or business when its employees are considering union representation?

Information for this case was drawn from the corporate Web site and from Gasparro, Annie. (May 21, 2014). Protesters shut down McDonald's HQ—And they'll be back on Thursday. *The Wall Street Journal*. http://blogs.wsj.com/corporate-intelligence/2014/05/21/protesters-shut-down-mcdonalds-hq-and-theyll-be-back-on-thursday; Greenhouse, Steven. (March 14, 2014). McDonald's workers file wage suits in 3 states. *The New York Times*, B8; Greenhouse, Steven. (May 15, 2014). Fast food protests spread overseas. *The New York Times*, B1; Horovitz, Bruce, Alcindor, Y., Woodyard, C., MacLeod, C., & Hjelmgaard, K. (May 15, 2014). Fast food workers rally for higher wages. *USA Today*. http://usat.ly/1lshmgA; Jargon, Julie. (May 7, 2014). McDonald's prepares for another day of protest. *The Wall Street Journal*. http://blogs.wsj.com/corporate-intelligence-2014/05/07/mcdonald's-prepares-for-another-day-of-protest/; Little, Katie. (December 26, 2013). McDonald's removes worker site after fast food flap. CNBC. http://www.cnbc.com/vid/101296435; McDonald's shuts down employee site following scrutiny over posts that told workers to avoid fast food. (December 26, 2013). FoxNews.com. http://www.foxnews.com/health/2013/12/26/mcdonald-shuts-down-employee-site-following-postings-that-told-workers-to-avoid/; Peterson, Hayley. (October 24, 2013). McDonald's hotline caught urging employee to get food stamps. Business Insider. http://www.businessinsider.com/mcdonalds-mcresources-hotline-tells-nancy-salgado-to-get-on-food-stamps-2013-10; Philpott, Tom. (July 20, 2013). McDonald's to employees: Get a (second) job. Mother Jones. http://www.motherjones.com/tom-philpott/2013/07/mcdonalds-budget-mcwrap; Shin, Laura. (May 15, 2014). Fast food worker protests over minimum wage spread across the globe. Forbes.com. http://www.forbes.com/sites/laurashin/2014/05/15/fast-food-worker-protests-over-minimum-wage-spread-across-the-globe/; Velasco, Schuyler. (October 24, 2013). McDonald's helpline to employee: Go on food stamps. *The Christian Science Monitor*. http://www.csmonitor.com/Business/2013.1024/McDonald's-helpine-to-employee-Go-on-food-stamps.

CASE 3: "'YOU CAN'T BUY THAT KIND OF PR" FOR SOUTHWEST AIRLINES

Perhaps the most telling evidence of the relationship between Southwest Airlines and its most important publics lies in the capitalized words within the corporate mission statement:

> The mission of Southwest Airlines is dedication to the highest quality of Customer Service delivered with a sense of warmth, friendliness, individual pride, and Company Spirit.

To Our Employees

> We are committed to provide our Employees a stable work environment with equal opportunity for learning and personal growth. Creativity and innovation are encouraged for improving the effectiveness of Southwest Airlines. Above all, Employees will be provided the same concern, respect, and caring attitude within the organization that they are expected to share externally with every Southwest Customer.
> (https://www.southwest.com/html/about-southwest/)

Employees, Customers and Company: Integral relationships for the consistently profitable airline. This commitment to emphasize these relationships was evident in the low-cost airline's participation in the reality program, "Airline," that aired for three seasons, 70 episodes, during 2004 and 2005 on the cable TV A&E network and on the second reality program, "On the Fly," that offered 13 half-hour episodes on TLC in 2011. The episodes typically followed multiple story lines as employees interacted with customers. Some customers were happy; others complained or coped with personal or travel issues.

On Air and In the Air

The idea for the first series was sparked by the success of a similar show in the United Kingdom, which had featured easyJet, a London-based airline, for more than six years, A&E officials told the Associated Press (AP, January 2, 2004). Colleen Barrett, then president and CEO of Southwest, said she approved the participation after consulting the British airline. "I started thinking . . . it's basically 18 hours of free publicity. You can't buy that kind of PR."

The series focused on the interactions of customers with customer service employees in the various airports. Episode titles describe the nature of the customer and employee interactions. "You Can't Take It With You," "Stormy Weather," "A Hard Day's Flight," and "Love at First Flight" illustrate the many stories captured by the television crew, who would show up at airports, Los Angeles International (LAX), Baltimore-Washington International, Houston Hobby and Chicago Midway, and film what they found of interest. Some customers also suggested story lines.

A&E's Web site described the episode "Spirit Party" in this way:

> The FAA rules are clear, alcohol and air travel simply do not mix. In LA, passenger . . . has been drinking and it's fallen to supervisor Yolanda to tell him he's too drunk to board the flight. It's the night of the Southwest Spirit Party—a vast annual staff gathering—and a huge occasion for supervisor Mike. He's invited a special guest he wants to introduce to his colleagues. Gospel group the Faithway Doves are on their way to Chicago to be honored by the American Gospel Society and surprise their fellow passengers with some remarkable spirituals.

Demonstrating Customer Service

Customer service supervisors and managers at the four airports became de facto cast members. Michael Carr, a customer service supervisor at LAX, told A&E that being a part of the "Airline" cast was "an honor. I feel very fortunate to demonstrate the excellent Customer Service Southwest Airlines prides itself on providing our Customers." The best experience he had filming the series, he said, was "Being able to show the daily challenges all airline employees deal with each day."

According to the AP, the airline received no compensation for participating in the show. Southwest could request a "voice-over narration to give 'context'" or explanation of how customer complaints were treated. Producer Chris Carey explained the relationship in *USA Today* after the first season:

> They clearly need to see the shows before they air to make sure we're getting facts right. . . . they have no editorial say. . . . Colleen Barrett only agreed to take part if it was real. They're proud of their airline and had the courage to step up to the plate and expose themselves.

Reactions were positive. Job applications at the airline rose from around 180 to 600 on the days following initial airing of the programs ("Job applications," June 18, 2004).

After its merger with Airtran Airways in 2011, Southwest Airlines offers service to 97 destinations in the United States, Puerto Rico, and Mexico. Based in Dallas, Texas, Southwest has more than 45,000 employees. The Associated Press reports that Southwest has been profitable since early 1991 and was the only major U.S. airline to earn a profit during the first six months of 2008. 2013 net income was more than $754 million.

Questions for Reflection

1. What were the benefits and risks faced by Southwest through its participation in reality television programming? What were the benefits and risks faced by its employees?
2. How has Southwest profited from its trust in its employees? How have the employees benefited?
3. A variety of businesses are now profiled on reality television programs that show employees behaving well and behaving badly. What legal and ethical considerations would impact participation in such a reality program?

Information for this case was drawn from: Associated Press. (January 2, 2004). Southwest Airlines stars in TV "reality show." *USA Today*. www.usatoday.com/travel/news/2004-01-02-southwest-tv_x.htm; Associated Press (August 27, 2008). Southwest to cut 196 flights in early 2009. *The Atlanta Journal-Constitution,* B3; Hodes, Chuck. (April 1, 2004). "Airline" TV show reflects airports, baggage and all. *USA Today*. www.usatoday.com/travel/news/2004-04-01-airline_x.htm; (June 18, 2004). Job applications for Southwest Airlines increase due to TV series. *Airline Industry Information.* http//www.lexisnexis.com; www.aetv.com/airline/airline_Episode_guide.jsp?/episode=150898); www.aetv.com/.airline/airline_castcrew_losangeles.jsp?index=1&type=character; www.southwest.com/about_swa/mission.html; TLC Release. "Buckle up! On the Fly is ready for Takeoff!" http://www.tlc.com/tv-shows/on-the-fly/about-the-show/about-on-the-fly.htm; http://blogs.star-telegram.com/sky_talk/2012/05/a-peek-behind-the-curtain-southwests-new-reality-tv-show-debuts-thursday.html.

CASE 4: AGENCY EMPLOYEES AFFECTED BY CONFLICTING CLIENTS

A presentation at a nonprofit group's meeting by a public relations agency employee apparently led an international corporation to drop the agency and a sister firm several weeks later. Felipe Benitez, an Ogilvy Public Relations employee, presented "Strategic Communications for Environmental Defense" before a nonprofit group, Amazon Watch, on May 9, 2012. *PRWeek* reported that before he became an Ogilvy employee in July 2011, Benitez had counseled the Ecuadorean government. Business Insider noted that the LinkedIn profile of Benitez indicated that he had worked with several Latin American organizations, including Amazon Watch, and the Ecuadorean government.

Clients with Conflicting Interests?

The Amazon Watch (http://amazonwatch.org/) Web site features a mission statement that explains that the nonprofit was founded in 1996 and "seeks to protect the rainforest and advance the rights of indigenous peoples in the Amazon Basin. We partner with indigenous and environmental organizations in campaigns for human rights, corporate accountability and the preservation of the Amazon's ecological systems."

Among its many projects is a targeted campaign named "ChevronToxico The Campaign for Justice in Ecuador" (http://chevrontoxico.com/). The campaign seeks to ensure that Chevron will pay a reported $27 billion judgment (Shan, 2009) that has been levied by an Ecuadorian court as compensation for environmental damage caused by oil drilling by Texaco, which became part of Chevron in 2001—the very same corporation that was a client of Ogilvy Public Relations.

Chevron had selected Ogilvy Public Relations as the agency to promote its Chevron, Texaco, and Caltex brands and its refining and manufacturing businesses in November 2008. But less than a month after the presentation by Benitez, Chevron severed its relationship with Ogilvy Public Relations and its sister firm Ogilvy Government Relations. *PR Week* reported that Dave Samson, the general manager of public affairs at Chevron, said the corporation had "uncovered a serious, material conflict of interest with Ogilvy," which prompted its action.

Lobbying Interests?

Ogilvy Government Relations had served as Chevron's lobbying firm since at least 2004, taking its $600,000 annual billings from the lobbying firm, according to Business Insider. The energy corporation was reportedly its third largest client. (Details of lobbying arrangements are usually public because of lobbying regulations.) *The Washington Post* described Ogilvy Government Relations as a "$20 million enterprise, the sixth highest grossing firm on K Street that, because of its relatively small size, was also raking in more revenue per lobbyist than almost any other shop." According to Politico, Chevron had been engaged in an ongoing lobbying campaign in the United States to find help in using the Andean Free Trade Agreement to pressure the government of Ecuador to intervene in the case (Vogel, 2009). The Huffington Post reported that representatives from Ogilvy Government Relations had worked with former politicians Trent Lott, John Breaux and former political staff members Mac McLarty, Brian Pomper, and Wayne Berman in the campaign.

After Chevron dismissed the agency, 12 employees—and the clients they represented, including Hilton Worldwide and the Goldman Sachs Group—left Ogilvy Government Relations, taking their billings with them (Ho,

2013). But within a year, the agency had hired new employees and acquired new clients. The firm's Web site (http://www.ogilvygr.com/) asserts:

> OGR represents dozens of large corporations and major trade associations with broad agendas. We also assist smaller companies and non-profits with very specific and target objectives. We have a proven track record of success affecting the decisions made by federal legislators and regulatory agencies.

Ogilvy Public Relations, Ogilvy Government Relations and Ogilvy Mather are owned by WPP, the world's largest communication services group with offices across the globe.

Questions for Reflection

1. Working for an agency presents different issues than when working for a particular corporation, business, or nonprofit. How might agencies work with their employees to identify potential conflicts of interest?
2. Should practitioners disclose their previous client list to all new clients? To their employers? If so, suggest some professional and ethical ways to do so.
3. What loyalty does one agency within a large holding company owe to another owned agency? How much disclosure is sufficient? Who within the agency has the responsibility for ensuring that potential conflicts are disclosed, discussed, and perhaps resolved?

Information for this case was drawn from Bloomberg News and Ad Age. (June 1, 2012). Ogilvy government relations lost Chevron over client conflict. *Advertising Age.* http:adage/com/article/agency-news/Ogilvy-government-relations-loses-chevron-client-conflict-235123/; Daniels, Chris. (June 8, 2012). Ogilvy's sacking by Chevron highlights conflict of interest issue. *PR Week.* www.prweekus.com/ogilvys-sacking-by-chevron-highlights-conflict-of-interest-issue/printarticle/244892/; Edwards, Jim. (June 1, 2012). Chevron fired its PR agency because ONE staffer spoke to environmentalists 4 years ago. *Business Insider.* www.businessinsider.com/chevron-fired-its-pr-agency-because-one-staffer-spoke-to . . . ; Ho, Catherine. (May 19, 2013). Ogilvy Government Relations eyes a comeback. *The Washington Post.* www.washingtonpost.com/business/capitalbusiness/ogilvy-government-relations-eye . . . ; Shah, Aarti. (November 24, 2008). Chevron taps Ogilvy PR for downstream business. *PR Week.* http://www.prweek.com/article/chevron-taps-ogilvy-pr-downstream-business/1249864; Shan, Han. (November 23, 2009). Oil giant Chevron accused of "extortion" on Capitol Hill. Huffington Post. http://www.huffingtonpost.com/han-shan/oil-giant-chevron-accused_b_368076.html; Snyder, Jim (May 31, 2012). Chevron fires Ogilvy as lobbyist over Ecuadorean dispute. Bloomberg. www.bloomberg.com/news/print/2012-06-01/chevron-fires-ogilvy-as-lobbyist-over . . . ; Vogel, Kenneth P. (November 16, 2009). Chevron's lobby campaign backfires. Politico. www.politico.com/news/stories/1109/29560.

PROFESSIONAL INSIGHT What's the best way to engage employees in a challenging economy?

Figure 2.2 Amber Hurdle, Moxie Internal Relations

Employee engagement is a trickle down effort that begins with a company routinely weaving cultural components such as vision, mission, values, and standards throughout all forms of employee communication, setting the tone for how all employees interact with each other and the company. During difficult seasons in company history or throughout a down economy, it is more important than ever to ensure the culture is stable, employees are invested in the common goals, and the company's most internal public is mirroring the messages being sent to the external publics. This is led by senior leadership guiding by example, then "trickling down" the effort through all levels of management to frontline employees.

Yet, while the company can drive the direction of the culture and frame messaging, it truly lives and breathes "live and locally," meaning from a direct supervisor, among the employee's peers. Investing time and energy into employees through sincere recognition, professional development and showing how each team member fits into the big picture are the best ways to engage talent in a challenging *or* healthy economy.

In fact, the most important recognition any employee can receive can be as simple as immediate and specific feedback for a job well done given in a way that is meaningful to that particular employee. While some may want public recognition, that could discourage others who would be instead motivated by a handwritten note. Knowing team members' unique personalities and triggers is key to an engaged, loyal team. Additionally, recognizing employees strengthens trust and encourages the two-way communication that is essential to any public relations effort.

Likewise, if a direct supervisor can further train or mentor a team member, that is an investment that pays dividends in a career that far surpasses a salary increase, while also giving the employee a deeper sense of empowerment. This could be cross-training or giving additional responsibility that can round out a resumé or support the promotion of a non-exempt employee to an exempt role.

Finally, when leaders show their employees how their contributions add value to the success of the company, it inspires them to continue to invest in the common vision and provide ongoing feedback for how operations can improve from their perspective. Activities like reading related customer feedback back to the team or talking about company accomplishments, then connecting the dots to how a particular department served the overarching goals of the organization are ways highly engaged leaders foster highly engaged employees.

While bonuses and raises are the easy answer, true employee engagement is sustained through people connecting with people and purpose in meaningful ways.

Amber Hurdle, CVACC, is the owner and lead executive coach of Moxie Internal Relations, home of Amber Hurdle Coaching & Training and the Mega Moxie Leadership Academy. Previously, she led the employee communications and events department at Gaylord Opryland Resort and Convention Center in Nashville, Tennessee. She also owned and operated Planit Nashville, where she worked with celebrities and record labels throughout the country music industry to engage their key stakeholders through experiential events.

CHAPTER 3

Stakeholders

Communities

What characterizes a good neighbor? In your neighborhood it may be someone who maintains a tidy lawn, or someone who has friendly children. It may be the homeowner at the end of the street with the beautiful garden or backyard pool. Yet what constitutes good neighborliness may also be conditional or contextual. The homeowner with the tidy lawn may also have a dog in the backyard that barks ferociously whenever anyone approaches its fence, or she may drive you to distraction during the holidays with an unapproachable standard of decorating. You may wish the friendly children were occasionally less so when you find their toys and playthings scattered across your yard or when their teenage son's car stereo wakes you up each Friday night when he comes home from a date. The level of familiarity you have with your neighbors may be based as much on your willingness to engage in a relationship as on their willingness to accept the responsibility of your friendship, and your satisfaction with the relationship may fluctuate depending on time and context.

COMMUNITY RELATIONSHIPS MAY FLUCTUATE

Although community relationships for an organization or business may not exactly parallel this neighborhood example, there are some similarities. Effective relationship building and maintenance with community stakeholders may also be variable and contextual. Many communities welcome the financial investment and opportunities of a new manufacturing plant but decry the increased traffic, noise, and waste produced at the plant. A corporation may seek locations that are quiet and relatively inexpensive, and then find transportation limitations and zoning restrictions a nuisance. As economic situations change, communities may find themselves faced with closing plant sites or empty "big-box" stores, even as businesses and corporations seek to adjust to the costs of modernization or environmental adaptation. Frequently, the basic premises for community relationships are somewhat contradictory in that they mix altruism and self-interest in many interwoven layers. Practicing good community citizenship through environmental consciousness, cultural support, and civic engagement helps develop and support a higher quality of life for an organization's employees and members, thereby making it easier to attract and retain quality employees. Such behavior may also generate goodwill that makes it possible for tax incentives, abatements, and zoning decisions that may support the most bottom line of all business motives. Clearly, community relations may also overlap other key areas of practitioner behavior, including management of employee relations, public affairs, consumer relations, and activist groups.

CHANGING DEFINITIONS OF COMMUNITY

Another challenge and opportunity for practitioners and executives may come in defining their organization's community—or communities. For one-site locations, this is simple. But consider the questions facing regional, national, or international organizations. The community may be the area around headquarters, or it may include all of the sites where there are major facilities. Community might also include all of the market areas from which employees, donors, or consumers are drawn. In a global economy, businesses and corporations may even be held publicly accountable for the community-based behaviors of their subcontractors or suppliers in areas far away from their headquarters, as well as for their own. Practitioners and executives must work together to define their communities and then to prioritize the publics within them.

RESULTS OF COMMUNITY RELATIONS

Why engage in community relationship building? Organizations and businesses that seek to be known as good neighbors may have different objectives. Some of those may include:

- Enhanced quality of life for employees and residents: Contributing to the cultural, recreational, and artistic life of a community may enhance an organization's ability to attract and retain high-quality employees. It may also foster positive relationships among all those who benefit from programming and mitigate future complaints about liabilities of being located in a given area, such as traffic, noise, and so on.
- Equipped and available labor force: Supporting local educational systems, from Pre K-12 through higher education, may further contribute to the employees' satisfaction as well as to the availability within the community of future employees

equipped for the workforce. Technical colleges and schools, for example, often closely work with industries and businesses to ensure that their curricula match the needs of the potential employers.
- Regulatory intervention: From the extensive tax breaks and incentives offered for building new facilities in a community to more commonplace requests for easing zoning or noise restrictions, businesses often need help from communities if they are to carry out their primary functions. These interventions may reflect the need for a mutually beneficial relationship. For example, plant sites may need traffic signals to be placed strategically or better highways built to accommodate shipping; governments may need cooperation from plant sites about shift changes to better regulate traffic flow around peak hours. Businesses that receive tax exemptions during a specific time period may need to offer public infrastructure support in other ways, such as using local vendors whenever possible so that funding is circulated throughout the community.
- Ethical obligation: Many organizations believe they have an affirmative duty to serve the communities in which they operate.

What benefits may communities receive from these public relations practices? Some of these may include:

- Increased resources for community activities: Community-based national organizations such as the United Way are often dependent on the cooperation of area businesses to help secure donations and volunteer leadership to support their network of social services. Employees who are encouraged by their businesses or organizations to volunteer also provide staffing and service help to agencies, schools, and cause organizations. Arts and cultural organizations may also find that businesses and corporations are a primary means of grant support, whether locally or through their foundations. Industrial and corporate facilities may be made available for civic meetings and celebrations or for public tours.
- Increased fiscal support: The financial contributions through taxes, payrolls, and purchases may be enormously important to local, or indeed regional, national, or international economies. Small businesses within a community may succeed or fail based on the "turnover" of such dollars in local commerce.
- Growth of related industries: Having a major manufacturer locate in one's community may sharply increase the likelihood of

attracting other similar large industries or even more industry-related small businesses, thereby increasing the economic health of the community. Improved transportation infrastructures such as highways and airports may result. Chambers of commerce within communities often point to this interlocking impact of industrial and business growth as they participate in recruitment efforts for individual and business relocation.

- Enhanced sense of local pride: Being known as the headquarters of a major company or organization or being known as a plant site for a national or international brand may offer communities "bragging rights" that instill pride and raise morale throughout a community. The combination of factors that contribute to an overall improvement in the quality of life for area residents manifests itself in this contagious enthusiasm, which in turn may lead to more growth and development.
- Heightened loyalty: Studies suggest that consumers and employees respond positively to organizations that seek to give back to their communities. Consumers' intentions to purchase goods or services may be strongly linked to their knowledge of the civic contributions of businesses; employee loyalty and pride may be similarly increased as they come to know about and perhaps participate in community service.

COMMUNICATING WITH COMMUNITY PUBLICS

Practitioners may use a variety of tools to send and receive messages from community publics. Local media may provide important tools. Face-to-face contacts, meetings, and special events may also be utilized in building relationships with key opinion leaders. It is important for organizations to publicly explain their views and positions and to create opportunities for members of publics to react and respond to them.

However, effective community relations practices demand more than just communication through word or image. Practicing corporate social responsibility—using the resources of an organization to promote ethically positive results for key stakeholder groups—may be the most effective public relations tool of all. Volunteering and donating are potent methods that demonstrate real commitment to enhancing and maintaining relationships.

Many national and international corporations and businesses now publish an annual corporate social responsibility report on their Web sites, which public relations practitioners may be asked to produce and update. Increasingly, corporations are including reports on the "triple bottom line" that offers goals, objectives, activities, and evaluation of action related to economic growth, social good, and environmental sustainability. These reports may include a variety of metrics used to show organizational commitment and activity in key areas, perhaps using short videos or photographs to illustrate how their contributions of money, time, and human capital are committed to community service. Graphics and news articles are often included. Printed reports or brochures may be ordered through these Web sites, and practitioners may be asked to produce those, as well news releases that detail the results of corporate social responsibility and triple bottom line initiatives.

Community relations may also include the practice of what some have called "strategic giving" whereby the good works of an organization or business directly tie into the branding of its products, goods, or services. Consider the book dealer who provides a free book voucher for every child who reaches the reading goal of his or her elementary grade level. Promoting reading? Yes. Stimulating traffic and building loyalty among families and potential customers at the same time? Yes.

Can businesses and organizations be good neighbors? Yes. When their behavior and communication supports the general well-being of their neighborhood, something that is defined by the organization in its dynamic 21st-century environment. The cases in this chapter will explore the neighborhood of community relationships, looking at how corporations and nonprofits are working together through philanthropy, direct action, and employee support. As you consider these cases, seek to identify the public relations problem or opportunity, the methods and tools used to resolve the situation, and how one might evaluate the success or failure of the public relations efforts. As you review the cases, ask yourself: In what ways do these groups define their communities? Who is their neighbor?

ADDITIONAL READINGS

Bhattacharya, C.B. (2011). *Leveraging corporate responsibility: The stakeholder route to maximizing business and social value.* Cambridge: Cambridge University Press.

Burke, Edmund M. (1999). *Corporate community relations: The principle of the neighbor of choice.* New York: Quorum.

Kim, S. (2011). Transferring effects of CSR strategy on consumer responses: The synergistic model of corporate communication strategy. *Journal of Public Relations Research, 23*(2), 218–241.

Sagawa, Shirley, Segal, Eli, & Kanter, Rosabeth Moss. (2000). *Common interest, common good: Creating value through business and social sector partnerships.* Boston: Harvard Business School Press.

Slaper, T.F., & Hall, T.J. (2011, Spring). The triple bottom line: What is it and how does it work. *Indiana Business Review, 86*(1), 4–8.

CASE 5: "MAKE IT RIGHT" IN NEW ORLEANS

Figure 3.1 Actor Brad Pitt visits the Make It Right Homes in the Lower 9th Ward in New Orleans on March 9, 2012. (AP Photo: Donald Traill.)

On TripAdvisor's Web site, the tour reviews of the Lower 9th Ward in New Orleans devastated by Hurricane Katrina in 2005 are in. Located down the Mississippi River, just below New Orleans, the Lower 9th Ward continues to be a contradiction and conundrum: having a visitor rating of 24 percent for "excellent" (as of 2014) and a mere 5 percent "terrible" rating. Five-star reviews label it as a "necessary" and "sobering view of New Orleans."

Long known for its large, poor African-American population, the Lower 9th Ward has been famous for its contributions to New Orleans culture. It has produced New Orleans legends like musician Fats Domino and NFL Hall of Famer and Pro-Football analyst Marshall Faulk. Its population's contribution to the labor force in the shipping industry in the 1970s was an important part of the transportation of materials all over the world.

Since the devastation of Hurricane Katrina that hit New Orleans and the Gulf Coast in 2005, other culturally rich neighborhoods like Treme and Lakeview have recovered by 60 to 75 percent. But the Lower 9th Ward has regained only 30 percent of its viable structures and population, even though all of the neighborhoods have received about the same amount of federal funding. While federal funding has been essential to the rebuilding efforts, private money and willing businesses seemed to have made a bigger difference to areas like Treme and Lakeview.

An Actor Takes Action

However, one nonprofit that stepped in early to rebuild the Lower 9th Ward was Make It Right, founded by actor Brad Pitt. The organization was Pitt's response to having visited the 9th Ward two years after Hurricane Katrina. The mission of the organization is to build affordable, safe, sustainable homes. He said he was shocked by the lack of progress in the historic, working class community. Pitt committed to building an aspirational community or "urban lab for design innovation" where 150 homes would be designed by famous architects to be the most sustainable and securely built houses in the world.

The Foundation offered a list of core beliefs on its Web site (http://makeitright.org/about/):

- Everyone has the right to live in a high-quality, healthy home that enhances the natural environment.
- Communities should be fully engaged in defining their own needs and have a leading role in designing appropriate ways to meet those needs.
- Design has the power to improve the quality of affordable housing and enhance occupants' living conditions; it also plays a key role in creating vibrant, sustainable communities.
- Innovation results in affordable building designs, methods and materials that drive new industry standards for green buildings.

As the face of Make It Right, Brad Pitt's high media profile meant there was a lot of attention for the nonprofit and the Lower 9th Ward in 2007 and beyond. Some of Hollywood's best-known personalities came to support the organization. Will Ferrell, David Spade, and Bill Clinton were just a few of the people who donated large sums of money and "adopted" the sustainable houses.

However, seven years later, only 100 houses have been built, and the Lower 9th Ward community has not been rebuilt to the extent that surrounding and equally devastated neighborhoods have. Nearly 10 years after the devastation, tourists can book one of many tours (and are encouraged to review them on TripAdvisor.com) along the streets of the 9th Ward to see the streets overgrown with vegetation and homes still bearing the "death marks" spray painted by first responders labeling structures as uninhabitable in 2005.

"Make It Right" Faces a Squall of Criticism

In March 2013, *The New Republic*, a magazine that covers "politics, culture and big ideas," published a piece criticizing Make It Right. Among the many criticisms, the one that seemed to resonate the most with other detractors was the fact that 150 houses weren't enough to meet the needs of the area. *The New Republic* article said the nonprofit could build more conventional houses with less green space for the money they were spending on the sustainable houses.

Tim Darden, executive director of Make It Right, countered this criticism on the organization's Web site, saying while that might be true, the houses Pitt's organization was building could withstand hurricane-force winds and rising water. Indeed, the "Make It Right" homes have survived hurricanes Isaac and Gustav since Katrina, sustaining only minor damage. Additionally, the organization was offering low-interest mortgages and financial counseling to the sustainable, secure homeowners, Darden said.

Another criticism leveled at the organization claimed the design of the homes was not traditional and therefore out of step with New Orleans culture. Darden's rebuttal referred detractors to the history of the New Orleans style housing in the Lower 9th Ward, which was post-WWII slab, ranch housing. Darden pointed out that such a style of houses were found across the South and were quite vulnerable to bad coastal weather.

The New Republic writer noted that the organization was opening the area to buyers who were not original Lower 9th Ward residents. In response, Darden said that was indeed true because they allowed 15 police officers, firefighters, emergency medical technicians (EMTs) and teachers who were Department of Housing and Urban Development (HUD)-eligible to buy homes, which he claimed was in response to requests from existing homeowners who "wanted to welcome new residents to their neighborhood."

In short, Darden called the criticisms celebrity bashing. He said Make It Right was open to criticism, seeking comments and suggestions through its Web site where detractors were free to have discussion and comment on articles through the "What we have learned" portal. However, he said the critical article was a "malignant distortion" and "smear tactic" that "negatively impacted people who have already suffered too much."

Sustainable Building

Others defended Make It Right's work, including Martin C. Pederson of *Metropolis*, an architecture and design magazine. He wrote:

> . . . it was aspirational from the start. It was never about building the most houses, the most expediently; never about rebuilding an entire neighborhood. FEMA and the Road Home were supposed to handle that. It was about building for returning residents 150 affordable LEED Platinum houses by some of the world's best architects. It was also about creating a model for sustainable development.

The Foundation has moved beyond its New Orleans beginnings to also support building in Newark, New Jersey, Kansas City, Missouri, and on the Fort Peck Reservation in Montana.

Questions for Reflection

1. What are the obligations of nonprofit organizations to the communities in which they operate?
2. What kinds of expectations should communities have from well-meaning philanthropies in the face of a crisis?
3. Would the organization be receiving the same kinds of criticisms if it weren't a charity run by an entertainment celebrity like Pitt?
4. How may nonprofits respond effectively to public criticisms?

Information for this case was drawn from the foundation Web site and from Darden, T. (March 18, 2013). Our response to *The New Republic*. Makingitright.org. http://makeitright.org/new-orleans/our-response-to-the-new-republic/; DePillis, L. (March 13, 2013). If you build it, they might not come: Brad Pitt's beautiful houses are a drag on New Orleans. *The New Republic*. http://www.newrepublic.com/; Jervis, R. (September 25, 2012). Lower 9th Ward passes test during Issac. USAToday.com. http://www.usatoday.com/story/news/nation/2012/09/25/lower-9th-ward-isaac/1591211/; http://makeitright.org/about/history/; *PBS Newshour* aired December 28, 2013. http://www.pbs.org/newshour/bb/nation-july-dec13-lower9th_12-28/; http://www.tripadvisor.com/Attraction_Review-g60864-d680803-Reviews-Lower_9th_Ward-New_Orleans_Louisiana.html; Vinnitskaya, I (April 8, 2013). The debate over Making It Right in the Lower Ninth Ward. ArchDaily. http://www.archdaily.com/?p=356483.

CASE 6: SHAQ-A-CLAUS SCORES FOR TOYS

'Twas right around Christmas, some 20 years ago
When along came a champion - seven feet, head to toe.
Eager to give, and to further a cause,
Kids in need would soon know him as Shaq-A-Claus . . .

(http://www.toysrus.com/shop/index.jsp?categoryId=10811020)

So begins the tale of "Shaq-a-Claus," the charitable persona used by NBA legend Shaquille O'Neal since 2009 to promote the Marines Toys for Tots campaign in partnership with Toys"R"Us stores. O'Neal, or Shaq, as thousands of sports and movie fans know him, had an outstanding career as a college and national basketball star. The NBA Rookie of the Year in 1993, he went on to garner three Most Valuable Player awards and four NBA championships while playing with teams in Orlando, Phoenix, Los Angeles, Miami, Cleveland, and Boston. Before being drafted by the NBA, O'Neal was honored as the 1991 NCAA Player of the Year at Louisiana State University and as an All-American twice. Since retiring from the NBA, O'Neal has recorded rap albums, appeared in children's television shows and feature films, and as a commentator for televised sports events.

Join Shaq, Give Back

The initial 2009 campaign used the theme, "Join Shaq, Give Back." To publicize the campaign that year, the Cleveland Cavaliers created a special "Shaq-a-Claus" bobblehead doll to give to 40 fans at a game in December 2009. Discussing the genesis of the campaign on the TNT network's "Inside the NBA" program, Shaq said he first became involved in shopping at Toys"R"Us to buy toys for needy children years ago after his mother told him of 500 children who were going to have no Christmas gifts. He, his son, and a couple of friends rented several large trucks and went shopping at Toys"R"Us to buy enough toys to fill the trucks. Such shopping became an annual event for the star and later led to the launch of the charitable campaign with the toy corporation and the U.S. Marine Corps Reserve Toys for Tots Program.

Shaq told *USA Today* in December 2009: "I used to get toys for 100 to 500 kids. Now, I can get them to hundreds of thousands."

Great Big Shaq-a-Claus Promotions

To promote the annual campaigns, in-store displays frequently show posters of the star wearing a Santa costume towering above a "Shaq-mas tree" shaped by a pyramid of toys. Various social media and Internet tools are used to promote donation of toys, through Facebook, O'Neal's Facebook, Twitter account and personal Web site, and a Toys for Tots microsite that offers the Great Big Shaq-A-Claus list of toys for various age groups that can be purchased for donation to the campaign (http://toysrus.com/ToysforTots). The campaign is also featured in the Toys"R"Us holiday sales circulars. O'Neal occasionally visits stores with local Marines when they go to purchase toys and when they distribute the gifts.

According to its Web site, the mission of the U.S. Marine Corps Reserve Toys for Tots Program is to "collect new, unwrapped toys during October, November and December each year, and distribute those toys as Christmas gifts to less fortunate children in the community in which the campaign is conducted." Similarly, the Toys"R"Us Web site explains that the corporation and its Children's Fund contributes millions of dollars annually to children's organizations and special needs organizations.

#NoWishTooBig

The 2013 campaign offered some additional opportunities for involvement. The #NoWishTooBig initiative encouraged children to draw a picture of a toy they thought should be added to the wish list and ask a parent to post it on to Facebook, Instagram, or Twitter with the hashtag #NoWishTooBig. For each drawing posted, Toys"R"Us agreed to donate the depicted toy to Toys for Tots, up to $1million worth of toys. According to a corporate release, about 700 children drew pictures of toys that were then posted online with the hashtag. Each child at the Humphries Elementary School in Atlanta, Georgia, participated in the initiative, and to say thank you, O'Neal delivered toys to those 400 in December 2013.

Another aspect of the 2013 campaign encouraged parents to "Wish It Forward" by paying off someone's layaway account. According to the corporate Web site, each time someone did so, $200 worth of toys was donated to the Marine Toys for Tots Foundation—$200 chosen because it's the typical amount of a layaway account. A corporate release in January 2014 noted that 597 accounts were paid off this way, and Toys"R"Us responded by donating $119,400 worth of toys to the Foundation. According to the Web site, "We continue to be inspired by many give-back stories of generous citizens who anonymously paid off another's layaway order just to make Christmas brighter for someone in their community."

The 2013 campaign was a success. The corporate release noted that more than 325,000 toys were donated. The tweet from O'Neal's @Shaq account on January 10, 2014, proclaimed, "Shaq-A-Claus and Toys'R'Us proved there's #NoWishTooBig . . . $3.9 MILLION raised for Toys for Tots in 2013!"

In the January 9, 2014, news release describing the campaign, O'Neal was quoted:

> I know firsthand that the gift of a toy on Christmas can change the life of a child. And, it is always my great pleasure to partner with Toys"R"Us and Toys for Tots to make the holiday season a bit brighter for millions of children in need. Shaq-A-Claus could never have granted so many wishes without the help of big-hearted Toys"R"Us customers and kids from across the country. Thank you to all who helped me show there's #NoWishTooBig!

Questions for Reflection

1. Identify and evaluate the efforts undertaken by Toys“R”Us to use the Toys for Tots campaign to establish a sense of community among its consumers. What is the strategic value of such an objective?
2. The coalition described in this case involves a nonprofit, a for-profit business, and a celebrity spokesperson. Can you identify other similar coalitions? What are the public relations pay-offs for each entity? What are the possible liabilities?
3. Describe some metrics Toys“R”Us might use to assess the success of these annual campaigns. How might these differ from the metrics used by Shaq O’Neal’s publicity team?

Information for this case was drawn from the Web site shaq.com and Bernstein, Margaret. (October 20, 2009). Cleveland Cavaliers center Shaquille O’Neal dons a Santa hat, leads Toys for Tots campaign. Cleveland Plain Dealer. http://blog.cleveland.com/metro/2009/10/shaq_dons_a_santa_hat_leads_to.html; Devine, Dan. (November 15, 2010). Shaq helps Toys for Tots, teases “Shaq-a-Claus” appearance. Yahoo! Sports. http://sports.yahoo.com/blogs/nba-dan-devine/shaq-helps-toys-tots-teases-shaq-claus-appearance—nba.html; Levere, J.L. (October 24, 2011). Shaq-a-Claus returns to Toys for Tots campaign. *The New York Times*. http://www.nytimes.com/2011/10-24/business/media/shaq-a-claus-returns-to-toys-for-tots-campaign-spotlight.html; O’Donnell, Jayne. (December 20, 2009). “Shaq-a-Claus’ scores with Toys for Tots at Toys R Us. *USA Today*. http://usatoday30.usatoday.com/money/economy/2009-12-20-sharing_N.htm; O’Hara, Adrienne & Hayes, Nicole. (January 14, 2014). Toys “R” US® raises $3.9 million to benefit the Marine Toys for Tots Foundation. Toys“R”Us News Release. http://www.toysrusinc.com/pressroom/releases/general/2014/toysrus-raises-3.9-million-to-benefit-the-marine-toys-for-tots/; U.S. Marine Corps Toys for Tots Program. http://www.toysfortots.org/about_toys_for_tots/toys_for_tots_program/default.aspx; Rayam, Lisa. (December 5, 2013). “Shaq-a-Claus” delivers presents to students at Atlanta school. Fox5News. http://www.myfoxatlanta.com/story/24149434/shaq-a-claus-delivers-presents-to-students-at-atlanta-school; Inside the NBA. (December 6, 2013). http://www.nba.com/video/channels/tnt_overtime/2013/12/06/20131205-inside-shaq-claus.nba/; Shaquille O’Neal Bobblehead Giveaway. (December 9, 2009). Cavs.Com, http://www.nba.com/cavaliers/news/shaq_bobblehead_091209.htm.

CASE 7: PEPSI REFRESHES LOCAL COMMUNITIES

What would happen if a major corporation chose to walk away from expensive Super Bowl advertising and instead chose to promote its brand by investing the $20 million in community philanthropy and social media engagement? What about a new playground in Corning, New York? Operation Gratitude that sent more than 100,000 care packages to members of the military in combat areas? Mandarin, Arabic, and Spanish classes in a Harlem, New York, elementary school? A new wind turbine on a high school campus in Iowa? A documentary, *Meet the Gulf*, about how the BP oil spill affected Gulf Coast fishermen? Donated prom outfits, iPod, and smartboards? Mentors? Music and dance classes? All these—and more.

"Refresh Everything"

In 2010 and 2011, PepsiCo Beverages worked with three online partners (GOOD, Global Giving, and Do Something) to solicit up to 1,000 community-improvement proposals during January and February that the public could then vote for online at www.refresheverything.com as part of the Pepsi Refresh Project. In a March 22, 2010, corporate release, PepsiCo Beverages Americas chief marketing officer (CMO) Jill Beraud explained: "The Pepsi Refresh Project was developed with the belief that great ideas can come from anyone, anywhere, anytime."

During the initial year, the proposals were solicited within six categories, Health, Education, Arts & Culture, Food & Shelter, The Planet, and Neighborhoods, and could be submitted by individuals, companies, organizations, or small groups. The ideas that got the most public votes received grants of $5,000, $25,000, $50,000, or $250,000. Following the Gulf oil spill in summer 2010, Pepsi added a "Do Good for the Gulf" competition, soliciting proposals for projects to help communities in the Gulf. In 2011, grants were capped at $50,000, and the categories were reduced to Arts and Music, Communities and Education.

The campaign was planned by Pepsi's ad agency, TBWA/Chiat/Day, building on the cola company's "Refresh Everything" initiative that began in 2009. Targeted publics for the campaign included female college and high school students and women from 18 to 54 years old. Social media strategy was directed by Weber Shandwick and Edelman, and media relations were directed by OMD. The Web site was designed by Huge, which received a "Best in Category" Interaction Award for the project.

Crowd-Sourced Support

Those who submitted proposals were encouraged to promote their ideas and solicit votes through social media. Of the more than 77 million votes cast in 2010, according to *The New York Times*, about one of five was through Facebook (Facebook.com/refresheverything), the others through phone apps. On Twitter, the campaign was promoted using the hashtag #PepsiRefresh. Some major league baseball teams submitted ideas for community-based projects and asked their fans to vote to support their ideas; with almost 2 million votes, the Minnesota Twins won a $200,000 grant to provide support for a youth softball wheelchair team. Similarly, some national football starts submitted ideas and solicited support from fans.

The campaign's impact was measured in several ways: social media activity; media coverage; brand image impact; sales and brand equity. The number of tweets and Facebook posts and "likes" were tracked. More than 140,000 tweets about the campaign or individual grant proposals were posted. Pepsi's Facebook "fans" increased from 225,000 to more than 1 million in the first year of the campaign, according to *Advertising Age*. More than 6.5 million individuals registered on the Web site in 2010, and by the end of the campaign, around 17 million unique visitors had come to the site, and 4.5 million individuals had voted in support of projects online.

Campaign Impact and Sales

Media stories were also tracked; the launch of the campaign was covered by *The New York Times*, *NBC* and *ABC*, *CNN* and *The Wall Street Journal*. A Pepsi representative told *Advertising Age* in 2012 that "consumers felt Pepsi was a brand that cared about the community" as a result of the campaign. However, sales of Pepsi drinks actually declined slightly during the first year of the campaign.

A planned expansion into Latin America, Europe, and Asia announced by the corporation in 2010 did not happen, and the campaign ended in March 2012. Pepsi ads were again seen in the 2011 Super Bowl.

Pepsi-Cola North America Beverages markets an assortment of beverage brands, including Pepsi, Mountain Dew, Sierra Mist, SoBe, IZZE, Naked Juice, Aquafina, AMP Energy, Propel, and Mug and is part of the PepsiCo food and beverage company, which also owns brands such as Frito-Lay, Quaker, Tropicana, and Gatorade. PepsiCo's corporate vision is to "put into action through programs and a focus on environmental stewardship, activities to benefit society, and a commitment to build shareholder value by making PepsiCo a truly sustainable company."

Questions for Reflection

1. Linking corporate philanthropic investment with crowdsourcing was an innovative strategy. What are the strengths and the challenges involved in such a strategy?

2. Evaluate the metrics used by Pepsi to determine the success of the Refresh campaign.
3. This public relations campaign did not result in increased sales of Pepsi beverage brands. Was it a successful campaign? Why or why not?

Information for this case was drawn from the corporate Web site at http://www.pepsico.com/ and from PepsiCo. (March 22, 2011). The Pepsi Refresh Project awards $1.3 million to support the public's favorite ideas to refresh the world. Release. http://www.pepsico.com/PressRelease/The-Pepsi-Refresh-Project-Awards-13-Million-to-Support-the-Publics-Favorite-Idea03222010.html; Pepsi Refresh Project. (May 31, 2011). Check out past Pepsi Refresh Project winners—and vote to fund the next inspiring ideas! Huffington Post. http://www.huffington-post.com/2011/05/25/check-out-past-pepsi-refr_n_867112.html; Pepsi Refresh Project—MLB.com: Sponsorship. Major League Baseball. http://mlb.mlb.com/sponsors/pepsi/refresh/y2010/; Preston, Jennifer. (January 30, 2011). Pepsi bets on local grants, not the Super Bowl. *The New York Times*. http://www.nytimes.com/2011/01/31/business/media/31pepsi.html; Schwartz, Ariel. (August 2, 2010). Pepsi Refresh Project's "Do Good for the Gulf" campaign takes off. Fast Company. http://www.fastcompany.com/1676942/pepsi-refresh-projects-do-good-gulf-campaign-takes; Zmuda, Natalie. (October 8, 2012). A teaching moment: Professors evaluate Pepsi Refresh Project. *Advertising Age*. http://adage.com/article/viewpoint/a-teaching-moment-professors-evaluate-pepsi-refresh-project/237629/; Zmuda, Natalie. (September 7, 2010). Pepsi expands Refresh Project. Social-media experiment becomes full-blown global marketing strategy. *Advertising Age*. http://adage.com/article/news/pepsi-expands-refresh-project/145773/.

CASE 8: OFFERING "1-888-995-HOPE" TO HOMEOWNERS

The sub-prime mortgage crisis that developed in 2007 did not surprise everyone. During the height of what some have called the "real estate bubble," home sales were booming and buyers were signing onto mortgages that put them at risk for too much debt. However, some began to recognize the risks as early as 2006, and a coalition of nonprofit organizations then worked together to develop a pilot public-education campaign to educate homeowners in an attempt to reduce home foreclosures in the metro Atlanta, Georgia, area.

Research and Planning

The organizations, Consumer Credit Counseling Service of Atlanta (CCCS), Fannie Mae Foundation, Homeownership Preservation Foundation, NeighborWorks America and the United Way, called on the Jackson Spalding agency to develop the campaign. Working with agency partners PRecise Communications and ignition, Inc., the creative team at Jackson Spalding began by reviewing research of the homeownership and economic conditions in the Atlanta metropolitan area. One study conducted in December 2005 indicated that about one-third of those who lose their homes through foreclosure had never contacted their mortgage companies. Georgia had one of the country's highest foreclosure rates in 2006, and the Atlanta area ranked second among the top 100 metropolitan areas. The research enabled the partners to target specific communities that were most at risk and in need of information.

The agency had to decide how to break through the complacency about risk and, indeed, excitement about opportunity that were present in the real estate market at that time. In 2008, account team member Victoria Lelash said that one of the most significant challenges faced in planning the campaign was "waving the red flag on foreclosures before most people really understood the crisis that was about to hit and the massive ripple effect it would have on the economy."

The goals of the campaign were simple:

- Publicize a trademarked telephone number, 1-888-995-HOPE hotline, to Georgia residents as the easy source of information for homeowners in mortgage difficulties or those who were facing foreclosure.
- Generate a minimum of 5,000 calls to the hotline.
- Convert 2,000 hotline calls into face-to-face counseling sessions through Local NeighborWorks organizations such as the Reynoldstown Revitalization Corporation, or into telephone counseling sessions with one of four counseling groups such as the Consumer Credit Counseling Service of Greater Atlanta.

Communication Tactics

Media relations and print and radio advertising therefore were critical to the information campaign. Direct mail was also implemented, with postcards mailed to more than 300,000 metro homes. The City of Atlanta helped support the direct-mail effort by including information on water bills that went to every resident. The tactics worked. More than 13 million media impressions resulted from the print, radio, television, and online coverage of the campaign.

Key partnerships helped generate coverage. On January 31, 2007, Atlanta Mayor Shirley Franklin and the chief executives of two major metro Atlanta counties formally endorsed the campaign. In a campaign release, Mayor Franklin stated: "Hope is not lost for homeowners in financial crisis. The city is committed to identifying ways to prevent foreclosure, and it begins with making sure homeowners know about the 888-995-HOPE hotline and options that can save their homes." U.S. Treasurer Anna Escobedo Cabral came to Atlanta in November to offer a speech about the ways homeowners could get help if they needed it. The speech was hosted by NeighborWorks America and CCCS of Greater Atlanta.

Nontraditional methods were also used. The businesses in targeted neighborhoods were canvassed by street teams with fliers; information about the impact foreclosures in the community would have locally was shared. Special events were held by community groups in salons to provide an informal setting for homeowners to ask questions and get information. Information, including posters and bookmarks, was sent to area churches for distribution.

Evaluation and Impact

Like the media tactics, these nontraditional tactics worked, too. Goals were exceeded within three months. By June, the hotline had received 8,205 calls, and 2,206 homeowners had participated in counseling sessions. By July 2008, more than 30,000 Atlantans had sought counseling from the CCCS of Greater Atlanta.

Questions for Reflection

1. This campaign relied on both traditional and nontraditional means of informing area residents. Critique the methods used. Can you identify others that may have been equally or more effective?
2. Discussing sensitive topics such as personal finance may be difficult for some members of the public. How did this coalition seek to ease such fears?
3. What are the advantages and disadvantages of a public/private partnership?
4. If you had been in the public relations department of a bank or other mortgage lender, how would you have reacted to this campaign?

Information drawn from this case came from Jackson Spalding Communications and from CCCS (July 17, 2008). 2008 housing counseling demand soars 184 percent at Consumer Credit Counseling Service of Atlanta. PR Newswire, www.prnewswire.com; CCCS. (January 31, 2007). Metro-Atlanta leaders announce HOPE for Atlanta residents in danger of foreclosure. PR Newswire US, www.prnewswire.com; States News Service. (November 27, 2007). U.S. Treasurer to Visit Atlanta to Offer Mortgage Financing Advice. Treasury Department.

PROFESSIONAL INSIGHT Should nonprofits be held to a higher standard of ethical communication?

Figure 3.2 James E. Moody, President, Georgia Builders Association

All communications professionals face marketplace challenges which require good ethical decision making. When the work environment is a nonprofit entity, the standard for ethics is even higher.

Nonprofits operate differently than for-profit corporations. There are no owners or shareholders. They are governed by boards whose authority is implicitly delegated by members or donors. They are chartered in the public interest and often benefit from tax advantages. Because of this, there is an expectation from the public, government, members, and/or donors that the work of the nonprofit and the communications emanating from the entity meet the highest ethical standards.

Alexander de Tocqueville noticed the seeds of the nonprofit movement in his treatise, *Democracy in America*. He talked about the uniquely American (at the time) concept of people coming together for the common good. Self-interest was less important than the needs of the community. Since then, our business law and tax codes have been written to encourage the development of nonprofits.

When most people think about nonprofits, they think about charities. Indeed, those are a significant segment of the nonprofit market. Generally these entities pay no income taxes. Contributions to these groups are tax-deductible for the donor. In exchange, the nonprofit conducts work that benefits society, whether it is medical research or helping wounded veterans assimilate back into civilian life.

Other nonprofits are designed to serve professions or trades. These associations are often referred to as special interests, often with a negative connotation. Still, they serve the common good by providing continuing education for technical professionals like doctors and engineers. They do research and set standards that serve the public need but for which the government does not have the expertise or resources to do itself. They also allow groups of citizens with common concerns to speak more effectively to the government. Despite the opportunity for corruption, in a representative democracy where the voice of the people matters, associations provide a valuable service in helping elected leaders understand what the people want and need. In exchange for serving the public in these ways, trade and professional associations generally are exempted from paying income tax.

Because nonprofits exist in the public interest, there is an expectation that their communication with various publics will be accurate and complete.

When a nonprofit provides information to the government, whether to members of Congress considering a new law or to a regulatory agency drafting new rules, there is an expectation that the information is accurate. Certainly those communications are designed to lead to an outcome favorable to the group, and there is nothing unethical about doing so. But there are often huge amounts of money at stake, and there is always pressure to cross the line. When that happens, the inherent trust that the public—and public officials—have in the nonprofit erodes quickly. It may also trigger an investigation by the Internal Revenue Service and jeopardize the favored tax status.

When a medical society publishes its scientific journal, there is an expectation that the research is conducted properly and that the information is trustworthy. When humans are involved, however, there is opportunity for failure. I faced such a situation when I managed public relations for a nonprofit medical association. There was a medical device issue in the courts. The outcome of the case hinged on the fact that the devices actually caused diseases. Many studies had been conducted, and the scientific papers were published in our peer-reviewed journal. I received a call one day from an Associated Press reporter asserting that our journal was biased because the editor had served as an expert witness for the medical device maker. If that were true, it would be a clear breach of the public trust.

The easiest course would have been to make a statement about the editor being well respected in his field and above reproach. It was a minor story that was a bit hard for the public to understand; it likely would have died rapidly without much damage.

Because we existed in the public interest, and the integrity of our journal was the cornerstone of our existence, we chose to look at the issue more carefully. The association found that while the editor did not make false statements, the fact that he served as a paid advocate broached the trust of the public and of our members. He could no longer serve as editor.

The investigation took several months, and by the end, the Associated Press reporter had long forgotten the story. But because we had an ethical imperative to do so, we provided the report the Associated Press knowing it would lead to a follow-up story that reminded people of our misdeeds. In the long run, it was the right thing to do, and we never wavered about doing it.

Nonprofits face ethical issues just like for-profit corporations, but they make decisions through a different lens because of the trust placed in them by the public and the government. While for-profit corporations may be forgiven for an ethical wink or nod here and there, nonprofits should be held to a higher standard.

Jim Moody is president of the Construction Suppliers Association, the trade association for suppliers of home-building products in Alabama, Georgia, Louisiana, and Mississippi. He previously served as executive director of the Georgia Society of Association Executives, the trade association for staff members of associations and other nonprofits in Georgia. He graduated cum laude with a bachelor's degree in communication from Berry College and earned the certified association executive designation from the American Society of Association Executives.

CHAPTER 4

Stakeholders

Consumers

Think about your last trip to a shopping mall or complex. You may have visited stores such as Abercrombie & Fitch, Urban Outfitters, or Victoria's Secret that have established brand strength for themselves. Inside other stores you may have sought certain brands of clothing or accessories—Nike, Levi's, Russell, Guess, or Fossil—and avoided others you don't like or don't recognize. You may have completed some purchases after extensive research and others on an impulse. Similar stories may be told of your latest car purchase or trip to a grocery store or discount store. When you visit your mailbox, you may find it crammed full of catalogs, and when you check your phone, it, too, may be crowded with promotional messages from retailers whom you've visited or purchased from online. As you visit social media sites, you may find advertisements popping up that reflect purchases—or searches for products—you've recently completed online.

THE CONTEMPORARY CONSUMER

Consumers—those who buy the products and goods or use the services businesses provide—are likely the most voluntary of all stakeholders. In the U.S. marketplace, consumers may be the most jaded of all stakeholders, as well, constantly provided with a variety of options, bombarded with messages and reminders of the merits, real or hyped, of the goods available. Conversely, sometimes they comprise the most loyal group of stakeholders—bound to certain brands by memories of in-home use from years ago or allied because of features and benefits derived from brands they enjoy. They are the ones who remember slogans and jingles better than their multiplication tables, and they are the ones who willingly become walking billboards for the logos and brands emblazoned on the hats, T-shirts, jackets, and bags they carry.

Consumer groups also reflect the rapid changes in national demography. Practitioners should remain knowledgeable about the growing racial and ethnic diversity of their key consumer publics and be able to strategize with management personnel about the most effective ways to reach these consumers by noting and researching changes in the age patterns or social-role patterns of consumer groups. Stereotypes about the needs of varying groups among consumers should be replaced with sound research into needs, desires, and capabilities of key publics.

Contemporary consumers are also protected by a variety of national, state, and local regulations promoting their safety, as well as a growing slate of civil torts that enable them to sue when they assert that a product, good, or service was delivered in a deceptive or injurious manner. Maintaining a Twitter feed, a Facebook page or a product-information app may become the full or partial responsibility of the public relations department, perhaps working in concert with customer service representatives. Well-publicized consumer-related crises of the past 20 years should remind practitioners of the need for extreme care during initial or reactive product-related communications. Practitioners must be aware of the need for clarity when communicating with various consumer groups and particularly conscious of the varied abilities of groups to understand technical or product-related communication.

KEY OBJECTIVES

Maintaining a relationship with a satisfied consumer is far easier than trying to rebuild a relationship that has been hurt by poor service, pricing disagreements, or product failure. Building and maintaining brand loyalty may be a central objective for the practice of consumer relations. Other key objectives may include:

- Providing clear and timely information about products, goods, or services so that consumers may make good decisions.
- Providing avenues for feedback so that consumer questions and complaints are handled in an efficient and cordial manner.
- Supporting the introduction of new products, goods, or services through coordinated media relations, advertising, and product publicity efforts.
- Celebrating successes of branded products or services through special events and other publicity efforts.
- Developing relationships with emerging consumer groups, such as those found in new cultural or ethnic communities, new age or gender demographic groups, and so on.

INTEGRATED MARKETING COMMUNICATION

Developing relationships with consumers is a multidimensional affair that often requires cooperation across departments or personnel within a business or corporation. The practice of integrated marketing communication may better describe how organizations can reach and hear from these stakeholders. For example, consider an American automaker that is introducing a new ecologically friendly model to its line. Certainly, the product should be introduced at the annual car shows for automotive beat journalists and critics to assess and comment. Vehicles should be made available for test drives by these same media opinion leaders. Releases about the new line and its features and benefits should be disseminated. An advertising campaign geared to begin with the actual release of the line would be essential. Yet even that may not be enough. What about brokering use of the car as the central vehicle in a major motion picture due for a Labor Day release, or using it as the grand prize in a national contest geared at high school and college students, or working with local distributors to link sales of the unit to a sales competition? The manufacturer may also use its national clout to offer buyers a zero-percentage car loan for purchases within its first month on the market. The public relations, advertising, and marketing efforts would all work together to target key consumers and to establish the new brand as one with a distinct image and personality attractive to those consumers. Practitioners increasingly must be effective at integrating marketing goals and objectives into their own plans for fostering consumer relationships.

This multiplicity of messages is even more necessary in a crowded media marketplace. Consumers receive messages about products, goods, and services from all forms of mass media: online persuasive messages may be found in obvious places, such as a constant stream of pop- up ads, and more subtle venues, such as chat rooms and national review services where browsers find open, frank, and the occasional staged discussions of the merits and drawbacks of particular brands and suppliers. Canny consumers have at their fingertips the ability to search for reviews of products, multiple price comparisons, and deep background on corporations and businesses. No longer are shoppers merely comparing prices between competing grocery ads in the Thursday newspaper. Among the plethora of tools available to practitioners seeking to disseminate information about products, goods, and services are direct mail, broadcast advertisements, print ads, Internet ads, product inserts, packaging, catalogs, brochures, branded content, YouTube channels, trade shows and exhibits, displays, outdoor ads, specialty products, product placements, spokespersons, logos, personal appearances, and media placements—and the list changes with each new technology. The merchandising move from "bricks to clicks" continues to expand, making it easy for consumers to compare product prices and user reviews. Certainly, the need for veracity and constancy in messages grows in this environment.

BUSINESS-TO-BUSINESS COMMUNICATION

Similarly, public relations may form the conduit for communication between businesses and industries. Vendor-to-vendor relationships, supplier-to-supplier relationships, and wholesaler-to-retailer relationships may all depend on the ability of public relations practitioners to identify needs or motivations and to supply the type of information and opportunity in a trustworthy manner that would establish a mutual ground for business exchange. From the production of clear catalogs, brochures, and Web sites to engaging exhibits and demonstrations at trade shows, the practitioner may need to facilitate communication between businesses hungry for profitable advantages.

As you consider these cases, seek to identify the public relations problem or opportunity, the methods and tools used to resolve the situation, and how one might evaluate the success or failure of the public relations efforts. Ask yourself questions such as: How have these corporations and businesses emphasized the importance of their consumer stakeholders? In what ways do these organizations communicate with their consumers and build opportunities for consumers to communicate with them? Could the communication patterns be improved? If so, how? How do these cases illustrate the importance of planning for crisis communication?

ADDITIONAL READINGS

Caywood, Clarke. (Ed.) (2011). *The handbook of strategic public relations and integrated marketing communication.* (2nd ed.) New York: McGraw-Hill.

Dilenschneider, Robert L. (2000). *The corporate communications bible.* New York: New Millennium Press.

Ries, Al, & Ries, Laura. (2002). *The fall of advertising and the rise of PR.* New York: HarperBusiness.

CASE 9: ENTREPRENEURSHIP WITH SOLE: TOMS SHOES SHOWS HEART THROUGH CAUSE-RELATED MARKETING

Marketing, public relations, and entrepreneurship collide on a regular basis these days as companies keep rediscovering what sells: Heart. The corporate name for heart is cause-related marketing (or CRM), which is a strategy designed to promote brand sales via company support of social causes.

Take TOMS shoes, for example.

Blake Mycoskie, the social entrepreneur and chief shoe giver at TOMS shoes, wants to eradicate elephantitis of the foot (podoconiosis). The disease is prevented simply by wearing shoes while walking on silica-rich soil, which most commonly occurs in Africa and South America. So, Mycoskie is selling $60 espradrilles and cordones to mostly Americans, promising that if they buy a pair of shoes, he will send an additional pair to someone in danger of contracting podoconiosis or at least to people around the world who can't readily afford shoes.

The corporate Web site for #IAMTOM, at http://www.toms.com/stories/we-are-en/iamtom, explains, "If you shop consciously, volunteer with an organization that is changing lives, take part in creating a sustainable future or help raise awareness of issues affecting lives across the globe – you are TOM."

By spring 2014, the company had given away more than 20 million pairs of shoes to children in more than 60 countries. TOMS shoes are constructed in factories in regions around the globe, from Haiti to Argentina to countries in Asia and Africa. The shoes are sold through the corporate Web site and in department stores and boutiques.

A "One-for-One" Company

Taking the corporate philosophy of "one-for-one" further, in 2011 TOMS shoes expanded its product line to include sunglasses. Each time a customer purchases one pair of sunglasses, it will beget one sight-saving medical treatment (medicine, medical procedure, or prescription glasses) for a person in need.

"From this day forward, TOMS will no longer just be a shoe company, it will be a one-for-one company," Mycoskie said at the launch event in Santa Monica, California.

This time TOMS partnered with Seva Foundation, which has led a global initiative to provide eye care and education in order to reduce visual impairment and blindness around the world for more than 30 years.

In 2014, Mycoskie is breaking into the coffee business. By buying coffee at one of his planned coffee bars or joining his coffee club, consumers will be providing one week of water for a community in five countries such as Honduras or Rwanda.

Another initiative links the sale of special TOMS shoes that offer an embroidered figure of a gorilla on the side of the shoe and a special patch with funding for wild animal preservation. The TOMS Animal Initiative, created by the founder's wife, Heather Mycoskie, works with the Virunga National Park in Rwanda to try to save endangered mountain gorillas and other species. Ms. Mycoskie explains on the Web site: "Combining my love for animals and my love for TOMS made perfect sense." Information about the One for One project is provided in an annual Giving Report available on the Web site.

Right Time for Word of Mouth

Mycoskie credits the right time in media and marketing history for the success of TOMS shoes (short for "tomorrow's shoes") as a word-of-mouth business that spends none of its "for-profit profits" on advertising.

Of course, it didn't hurt that for Mycoskie, the "right time in media and marketing history" also coincided with his own personal marketability, having competed in CBS' reality TV show "Amazing Race" where he and his sister were the youngest competitors and placed third in a competition against other teams in a global scavenger hunt of sorts.

Mycoskie's "right time in media and marketing history" has led to programs like the Pampers and United Nations Children's Fund (UNICEF) marketing campaign, which raised $15 million toward maternal and neonatal tetanus elimination. By appealing to the connection felt among mothers everywhere, the campaign resulted in consumers helping to buy 200 million vaccines for children in the world's poorest nations.

Cause-Related Marketing grew out of the 1990s marketing trend of relationship marketing, itself a natural progression of the Grunig two-way symmetrical model of public relations. Most definitions of cause-related marketing say it is the partnering of a for-profit business with a nonprofit organization for mutual benefit.

In the beginning, TOMS shoes did not fit this definition exactly. It was a simple business model created by Blake Mycoskie to capitalize on his fame to create a shoe that would appeal to the young, hip and globally minded. He would then sell that shoe without traditional marketing or advertising means—in other words, taking a more public relations approach—for enough money to make and distribute shoes to children in need on a global scale. Mycoskie believed if he told his story repeatedly to the right people, discussed the shoe and what buying it meant to him and needy children around the world, he would not have to buy any traditional advertising to market the shoe.

He was so committed to the mission that he tried to meet criticism head on. In a *Fast Company* magazine article, Mycoskie said:

> I've asked people, 'What could TOMS do better?' I've learned that the keys to poverty alleviation are education and jobs. And we now have the resources to put investments behind this. Maybe five years from now, we'll be able to say it's really good for business. But the motivator now is, how can we have more impact? At the end of the day, if we can create jobs and do one-for-one, that's the holy grail.

So, Mycoskie has planned to open factories in some of the countries in which he drops shoes, like Ethiopia and Argentina, by 2015.

TOMS' mission and passionate, effective marketing earns high praise from consumers and business partners alike. A partner and well-digging non-governmental organization (NGO) consultant, Lane Wood, credits Mycoskie with stretching business models beyond basic corporate social responsibility. In the *Fast Company* article, he said, "People have seen the success of TOMS and said, 'How do I get a piece of that?'"

Questions for Reflection

1. What's the difference between cause-related marketing and corporate social responsibility?
2. Do these programs make a difference when you decide how you spend your money? Why or why not?
3. Is this "creative and open-hearted" business model a lasting one? Why or why not?

Information for this article came from Chu, J. (July/August 2013) Toms sets out to sell a lifestyle, not just shoes. *Fast Company* magazine; Frazer, G. (October 2008) Used-clothing donations and apparel production in Africa. *The Economic Journal*, *118*, 532, 1765–1784; Mycoskie, B. (2012) *Start something that matters*. New York: Spiegal & Grau; Otto, I. (July 24, 2013) Toms shoes responds to critics, but it may not be enough. Globalvision.org. http://www.globalenvision.org/2013/07/23/toms-shoes-responds-critics-it-may-not-be-enough; Roberts, Daniel, (March 11, 2014) Can TOMS break into the coffee business? Fortune. http://fortune.com/2014/03/11/can-toms-break-into-the-coffee-business/.

CASE 10: WE'VE GOT REAL BEEF! TACO BELL COUNTERS LAWSUIT

"Thank you for suing us," the unusual headline on the Taco Bell advertisement read. "Here's the truth about our seasoned beef."

The ad went on to say that "Plain ground beef tastes boring," so some spices and flavors are added, totaling about 12 percent of the total content.

Taco Bell Counters Allegations about Quality

The class-action lawsuit had been filed on January 19 by a California consumer who charged that Taco Bell was engaging in false advertising by calling its product "beef" when the corporation's beef filling was actually less than 40 percent beef. The remainder was binders, preservatives, additives, and extenders. The plaintiff called for Taco Bell to stop advertising that the meat used in its products was beef.

The filing of the law suit generated a great deal of media coverage nationally in print, broadcast, and digital outlets.

In response, Taco Bell purchased ads in major national newspapers, including *The Wall Street Journal*, *The New York Times* and *USA Today*, and metro newspapers such as the *Boston Globe*, *Chicago Tribune*, *Los Angeles Times*, and the *San Diego Tribune*. The fast-food restaurant ran national television commercials, posted videos on YouTube (http://www.

youtube.com/watch?v=ah05FEWcJWM) and messages on Facebook and Twitter, and offered releases and video on its corporate Web site, spending an estimated $3 million to $4 million on the campaign. A list of all the ingredients in its seasoned beef was shared on the Web and in other messages (http://www.tacobell.com/nutrition/ingredientstatement).

A statement from President and Chief Concept Officer Greg Creed posted on the Taco Bell Web site on January 26 read:

> The lawsuit is bogus and filled with completely inaccurate facts. Our beef is 100% USDA inspected, just like the quality beef you would buy in a supermarket and prepare in your home . . . The lawyers got their facts wrong. We take this attack on our quality very seriously and plan to take legal action against them for making false statements about our products.

Creed quickly responded on television as well, appearing on ABC's "Good Morning America" where he was interviewed by anchor George Stephanopoulos.

Continuing the Defense

In April, the lawsuit was voluntarily dismissed by the plaintiff, with the law firm saying that the suit was no longer necessary because Taco Bell had disclosed the content of its products. The corporation reacted by posting a release on its Web site on April 19 with the headlines: "Law Firm Voluntarily Withdraws Class Action Lawsuit Against Taco Bell. Claims about Company's Food Quality and Advertising Were Wrong; Taco Bell Has Not Made Any Changes to Products Or Advertising Contrary to What Plaintiff's Lawyers Say." The release quoted CEO Creed: "This is a victory for truth over fiction and we're glad the lawyers voluntarily withdrew their case once they learned the truth."

But the corporation continued its public response, with a new print ad campaign in national newspapers, again including *The Wall Street Journal*, *The New York Times* and *USA Today*, and other regional papers, that proclaimed "Would it kill you to say you're sorry?" on a bold headline. The ad pointed out that the lawsuit was withdrawn without any change to the corporation's products or advertising and with no settlement or damages being paid.

"We hope the voluntary withdrawal of this lawsuit receives as much public attention as when it was filed," the ad read. It concluded: "As for the lawyers who brought this suit: You got it wrong, and you're probably feeling pretty bad right about now. But you know what always helps? Saying to everyone, 'I'm sorry.' C'mon, you can do it!"

In addition to the advertisements, President Creed was featured in a YouTube video talking about why the lawsuit was dropped. The video was promoted on the Taco Bell Web site and Facebook page. A campaign to reach Hispanic customers was also launched.

The CEO told Fox News in April 2011 that the publicity from the lawsuit may have led to flattened sales during the first quarter of the year.

Taco Bell and its franchise organizations operate almost 6,000 restaurants in the United States.

Questions for Reflection

1. Which stakeholders was Taco Bell trying to reach through its aggressive media counter-offensive?
2. What advantages and disadvantages might corporations face in using humor while countering public criticism or a crisis?
3. How effective do you think the campaign was? What are some metrics that might be used to gauge the usefulness of these tactics?
4. Why is it important for top management to be visible during a crisis?

Information for this case was drawn from the corporate Web site (www.http://www.tacobell.com/Company/) and Daitch, C. (February 4, 2011). Taco Bell uses humor, social media to dig itself out of beef scandal. *Advertising Age*. http://adage.com/ article/digitalnext/taco-bell-social-media-emerge-beef-scandal/148675/; Hutchison, Courtney, & Moisse, Katie. (January 28, 2011). Taco Bell fights "where's the beef" lawsuit. ABC News. http:abcnews.go.com/Health/Wellness-taco-bell-defends-beef-legal-action/print?id=1278 . . . ; Macedo, Diane. (April 26, 2011). Taco Bell still has beef with firm that dropped lawsuit. FoxNews.com. http://www.foxnews.com/us/2011/04/26/taco-bell-threatens-sue-law-firm-brought-beef-suit/; Stempel, Jonathan. (April 19, 2011). Taco Bell lawsuit dropped after dismissal by plaintiff. *The Christian Science Monitor*. www.csmonitor.com/Business/Latest-News-Wires/2011/0419/Taco-Bell-lawsuit-dropped . . . ; Stevens, Alyssa, & Belsie, Laurent. (January 26, 2011). Taco Bell meat? Beef, says firm. Filling, says suit. *The Christian Science Monitor*. www.csmonitor.com/Business/new-economy/2011-0126/Taco-Bell-meat-Beef-says- . . . ; Taco Bell. (April 19, 2011). News Release. Law firm voluntarily withdraws class action lawsuit. http://www.tacobell.com/Company/newsreleases/LAW_FIRM_VOLUNTARILY_WITHDRAWS_CLASS_ACTION_LAWSUIT_2011.

CASE 11: "COMING TOGETHER" TO FIGHT OBESITY

How many fun ways are there to burn off 140 calories? Many—at least according to a television commercial placed by Coca-Cola in January 2013 designed to remind drinkers of its regular sodas that they can fight obesity by "coming together" by engaging in activities such as dancing, walking, laughing, and playing sports. Another longer commercial was more serious in tone, offering more details on the ways in which the international corporation was trying to respond to concerns about increasing obesity through different product lines, calorie information, and activity promotion.

The commercials ran on a host of broadcast and cable entertainment and news and before the 2013 Super Bowl game; in addition, newspaper ads, press interviews, and special events were employed.

A "Serious, Complex Problem"

The statistics about increasing individual weights in the United States and around the world were alarming—one in three adults and about one in six children and teens considered to be not just overweight but medically obese, many also affected by related illness such as diabetes. New York City Mayor Michael Bloomberg sought to impose a cap on the size of soft drinks sold at regulated outlets in the city. After a United Nations report identified Mexico as the nation with the most overweight citizens, Mexican President Enrique Peña Nieto proposed enactment of a soda tax on sales of colas in his country where sodas are widely popular.

The multinational corporation's 2011/2012 Sustainability Report had identified the global problem of obesity as a "serious, complex problem." According to the report, "As the world becomes more concerned about the public health consequences of obesity, some researchers and health advocates have unfairly blamed the consumption of sugar-sweetened beverages as the cause."

The world's largest beverage company, Coca-Cola markets more than 500 brands in more than 200 countries. Its Web site says it is the world leader in sales of sparkling beverages, ready-to-drink juice and juice drinks, and ready-to-drink coffee. *Fortune* magazine recognized it as the sixth most admired company in 2014.

The Corporate Response

Coke said it planned to work with a variety of governmental and private groups to address obesity in six ways: "We use evidence-based science. We innovate. We provide hydration choices and educate consumers about them. We inform with transparency. We market responsibly. We promote active, healthy living."

Consumers would be offered more informed choices about its products and on encouraging healthy lifestyles by partnering with other groups to fulfill its 2008 pledge to sponsor "at least one physical activity program in every country we operate in by the end of 2015."

The "Coming Together" Campaign is Launched

In May 2013, the corporation announced a "Coming Together" campaign to focus attention on its anti-obesity commitments, which were noted on the campaign Web site as:

- Offer low- or no-calorie beverage options in every market. (According to its Web site, 19 of Coke's 20 top brands have a low- or no-calorie alternative or are low- or no-calorie beverages.)
- Provide transparent nutrition information, featuring calories on the front of all packages.
- Help get more people moving by supporting physical activity programs in every country where it has business.
- Market responsibly, including no advertising to children under the age of 12 anywhere in the world (which the corporation interprets to mean advertising in outlets that have more than 35 percent children in the audience.)

In a May 8, 2013, corporate release announcing the campaign, Muhtar Kent, Chairman and CEO, was quoted:

> Obesity is today's most challenging health issue, affecting nearly every family and community across the globe. It is a global societal problem which will take all of us working together and doing our part. We are committed to being part of the solution, working closely with partners from business, government and civil society. Today's announcement is another step forward on our journey, as we take action with scale and reach across every country and continent where we operate.

The campaign was kicked off in Atlanta, home of the headquarters of Coke Inc. Georgia Governor Nathan Deal and Atlanta Mayor Kasim Reed joined CEO Kent who announced that the Coca-Cola Foundation was donating $3.8 million to Georgia programs that would encourage physical activity and nutrition education. One program, Georgia SHAPE, targets children with activities before, after and during school, and helps support nutrition education efforts in Georgia schools.

Another initiative, Walk Georgia, from the University of Georgia's Cooperative Extension Service, challenged adults to exercise and then convert their activities into steps that could be tracked on a virtual state map. Seven other organizations or initiatives also received grants from the Foundation.

But the focus was not just on Atlanta. Initiatives and activities were funded and/or sponsored around the globe. These included, among others, Copa Coca-Cola, youth soccer tournaments held at local, state, and national levels that culminate in an international tournament each summer; working with the Boys & Girls Club of America to offer an after-school education and exercise program called Triple Play; Mission Olympic that involves almost half of the secondary schools in the Netherlands in sports competitions; Marxa Beret, a cross-country skiing marathon co-sponsored with Salomon; and Balanced Diet-Active Living, designed to educate students at 36 universities about diet, exercise, and nutrition.

Visitors to the attractive Web site (http://www.coca-colacompany.com/coming-together/) were encouraged to read health tips, watch videos, participate in polls, and learn about Coke's active-living initiatives around the globe. An October 22, 2013, release about the campaign noted: "The 'Coming Together' campaign reflects our belief that addressing obesity requires new ideas and the collective effort of all segments of society. It also provides another opportunity for engaging directly with our consumers."

Criticism of the Effort

The U.K. Advertising Standards Agency banned the "happy calories" commercial in July 2013, arguing that the commercial did not make it clear that one would have to engage in all the activities depicted to actually burn enough calories to balance consumption of a Coca-Cola.

Some bloggers criticized the Coke "Come Together" campaign as a calculated move to offset increased regulation of its products. Writing on the *Forbes* magazine Web site, Waters and Haar compared the Coke campaign to the 1954 newspaper ad campaign initiated by the Tobacco Research Institute titled "A Frank Statement to Cigarette Smokers" that asserted a belief that tobacco products were not harmful to anyone's health while accepting an interest in the health of its consumers as a basic business responsibility.

In another critique of the initiative, a columnist on the Huffington Post asked why there was not a more active response to the campaign from opponents of "Big Soda." The column pointed to the campaign developed by The Center for Science in the Public Interest that had produced an animated video titled "The Real Bears," drawing on the polar bear images often used by Coca-Cola in its marketing. In the video, a family of bears grows fat and the father develops diabetes before the family finally pours its soda bottles into the ocean. A companion Web site (therealbears.org) developed by the Center offers the video and a text response called "The Truth" that offers counterpoints to statements made by soft-drink executives.

Questions for Reflection

1. Evaluate the tactics and messages used in the "Coming Together" campaign. Are there other techniques you might suggest that could strengthen the communication of key messages?
2. What are the implications of this case for fostering mutually beneficial relationships with soft-drink consumers, and with other strategic stakeholders?
3. What advice would you offer the corporation as to how it should respond to criticism of the campaign?
4. Were the public relations actions taken by Coca-Cola reflective of a commitment to social responsibility or more of a defensive campaign in order to deflect increased government regulation or taxation of their products?

Information for this case was drawn from http://www.coca-colacompany.com/our-company/?WT.cl=1&WT.mm=top-left-menu3-about-red_en_US and CBS Interactive. (January 15, 2013). Coca-Cola ads to address obesity epidemic. http://www.cbsnews.com/news/coca-cola-ads-to-address-obesity-epidemic/; The Coca-Cola Company. (October 22, 2013). Inspiring the world to come together to help address obesity. Release. http://www.cocacolacompany.com/sustainability/inspiring-the-world-to-come-together-to-help-address-obesity; The Coca-Cola Company. (May 8, 2013). Shaping a healthier Georgia, one step at a time. Release. http://www.cocacolacompany.com/northamericacommunityconnections/shaping-a-healthier-georgia-one-step-at-a-time; Guthrie, A. (August 29, 2013). Health battle over soda flares in Mexico. *The Wall Street Journal.* http://online.wsj.com/news/articles/SB10001424127887323407104579037320321621280; Hall, Emma. (July 18, 2013). U.K. bans Coca-Cola ad for misleading exercise claims. *Advertising Age.* http://adage.com/article/global-news/u-k-bans-coca-cola-ad-misleading-exercise-claims/243138/; Huehnergarth, Nancy. (January 16, 2013). Coke's ad on obesity is brilliant—where's the well-funded national, anti-soda counter-marketing campaign? Huffington Post. http://www.huffingtonpost.com/ancy-huehnergarth/coke-obesite=ad_b_2487353.html; Waters, Rob, & Haar, William L. (May 21, 2013). Coca-Cola's "frank statement" a slick move to stave off regulation. Forbes.com. http://www.forbes.com/sites/robwaters/2013/05/21/coca-colas-frank-statement-a-slick-move-to-stave-off-regulation.htm.

CASE 12: HARRY POTTER'S WONDERFUL WORLD OF MARKETING RELATIONSHIPS

If the goal of good public relations is to build mutually beneficial relationships, then the multi-billion dollar Harry Potter franchise has built a perfect relationship with fans everywhere. Between the books, movies, and theme parks focused on bringing fans into the wonderful Wizarding World of Harry Potter, the creators and marketers have topped previous standards. The Harry Potter franchise may well be the point in which our culture's need for a narrative became synergistic with commerce. The plot of the books and movies exemplify the classic good versus evil storyline and was right for marketing to story-starved consumers.

The Magic of the Franchise Numbers

Even though the symbiosis of the release of books and movies and massive merchandising is ubiquitous now, Warner Bros. and J.K. Rowling set the standard. The seven books in the series have sold more than 450 million copies worldwide in 73 languages, and sales of the final volume, *Harry Potter and the Deathly Hallows*, sold 8.3 million copies in the United States during its first 24 hours on sale.

Warner Bros. and its parent company, Time Warner Inc., grossed an estimated $1.5 billion in revenue from worldwide box office receipts and DVD, television, and merchandising sales of *Harry Potter and the Sorcerer's Stone*, the first film in the series. In all, the box office take of all eight movies is upward of $7 billion, and each falls within the top 30 highest box office grossing movies of all time, the last one, *Harry Potter and the Deathly Hollows Pt. 2*, occupying the fourth highest spot (behind *Avatar, Titanic*, and *The Avengers*).

Even though the story of the young wizard and his friends is much loved, it doesn't necessarily carry $7 billion worth of movie revenue or make its author more wealthy than the Queen of England on its own. Merchandising and marketing of the stories certainly extended the love across generations and time.

The Magic of Books

As each book in the series was released, the book publisher and bookstore owners held special events and promotions to tout the new novels. For example, to celebrate the publication of the final Potter book, the U.S. publisher of the series, Scholastic, Inc., created a street celebration in New York City it called "Harry Potter Place," which opened one day before the book release. It featured a giant Muggle Board, a 20-foot high moving Whomping Willow, and various entertainments such as wand-making, fire-eaters, and magicians. A replica of the triple-decker bus from the Potter books, the Deathly Hallows Knight Bus, was parked for children; inside, children could film a 20-second video featuring their views about the books.

Scholastic also sponsored a sweepstakes that would give seven fans a prize of joining author J.K. Rowling in London for the midnight launch of the *Deathly Hallows* book. Earlier, Scholastic had spent more than $3 million to promote the June 2003 release of *Harry Potter and the Order of the Phoenix*. Readers could reserve copies of the book during the five months prior to its release. More than 1.3 million copies of the book were ordered through Amazon's websites; Barnes & Noble.com reported it sold 896,000 copies the first day, and the Barnes & Noble bookstores sold 286,000 copies in just 60 minutes. The book's release at 12:01 a.m. on June 21 was touted through parties, advertising, and promotions.

A countdown in New York's Times Square and a billboard on Sunset Strip announced the release. Walmart supercenters held special midnight events featuring cupcakes with Harry Potter themes. Many bookstores across the globe featured theme parties with employees dressed as characters.

A national billboard campaign supported the book's release. The Seattle Mariners, Baltimore Orioles, Oakland Athletics, and Houston Astros held "Harry Potter" days with costume contests and scoreboard promotions. Scholastic distributed more than 15,000 "event kits" to bookstores and other retailers that planned release parties. The kits included stickers, buttons, a trivia quiz, and suggestions for handling long lines of prospective buyers. Scholastic distributed 3 million bumper stickers, 50,000 window displays, 9,500 countertop cutouts, 24,000 stand-up posters with countdown clocks, and 400,000 buttons to promote the *Phoenix* release. Scholastic also held an essay contest with the top prize of a trip to London to hear J.K. Rowling read from the book and participate in an interview at the Royal Albert Hall.

Scholastic Inc. planned a first printing of 6.8 million copies, an all-time U.S. publishing record. When Scholastic released *Harry Potter and the Goblet of Fire* in July 2000, it became the fastest-selling book in history. Within 48 hours, 3 million copies were sold and Scholastic went back to press for an additional 3 million immediately.

Scholastic also used its Web site to promote the Potter books. Readers could use a pronunciation guide and find discussion guides for the five books. There was also a chat room for comments from student readers and a downloadable screensaver.

The Magic of the Movies

The film studio got involved in the Potter phenomenon early and inexpensively. Just before the first book, *Harry Potter and the Sorcerer's Stone*, became an international sensation, Warner Bros. reportedly paid Rowling $50,000 for film rights to the book. The following year, the studio paid an additional $500,000, this time to exercise its option to make a movie.

AOL Time Warner/Warner Bros. offered a variety of ways to promote the films and merchandise. AOL Moviefone offered advance ticket sales for *Harry Potter and the Chamber of Secrets* three weeks before its U.S. premiere. In addition, AOL 8.0's Sneak Peek Sweeps of *Harry Potter and the Chamber of Secrets* offered chances to win passes to preview screenings taking place across the country before the film's U.S. release. Entrants were also given the chance to win *Harry Potter and the Chamber of Secrets* gift packs, a $1,000 holiday shopping spree, or a year of AOL membership. More than 1 million advance tickets were sold.

Symbiotic relationships with other traditional media became ubiquitous when a two-minute promotion for *Harry Potter and the Chamber of Secrets* was aired on the WB network. It was the first time such a long clip was used to promote the movie. Additionally, editorial and marketing collided when *Entertainment Weekly* featured a cover story on the release of *Sorcerer's Stone*, and an advance review ran in *Time* containing a seven-page article with sidebars titled "The Real Magic of Harry Potter."

Warner Bros. developed a Web site (http://harrypotter.warnerbros.com) that featured information on the characters, cast, and crew of the films, Hogwarts-inspired games, merchandise, activities, music from the soundtrack, deleted scenes from the films, and a chat room. Reuters reported that in the weeks prior to the November 2001 release of *Harry Potter and the Sorcerer's Stone*, the Web site drew some 573,000 unique visitors, and more than 3.8 million unique visitors visited the site when the film opened. In November 2002, when the second movie was released, more than 3 million visitors again went to the site.

Magical Merchandising

EastWest Creative designed a four-week promotion to support the release of *The Sorcerer's Stone* video and DVD that involved a Web-based trivia competition. As players answered questions correctly, they were sent to one of 90 worldwide partner sites to search for the messenger owls. Those who found them earned rewards such as a screensaver or bookmark, and some 17,000 "instant pop-up" winners received posters, coloring books, postcard books, and T-shirts. Ten grand-prize winners were flown to London for the release of the *Harry Potter and the Chamber of Secrets* film, and one bonus winner got a walk-on role in the film. The game, launched in 12 countries and in seven languages, was promoted in the United States by print ads in AOL Time Warner's *People*, AOL banners, and on-air live "owl sightings" during national broadcasts of the Atlanta Braves games.

Coca-Cola invested an estimated $150 million to participate in the Potter film promotion in 43 countries. The investment included usage rights to advertising campaigns to contests. In October and November, Coca-Cola offered a "Catch the Golden Snitch and Win" promotion in which game cards were enclosed in multipacks of Coca-Cola Classic and caffeine-free Coca-Cola. Those who found the Golden Snitch card were then eligible to win a trip to London and receive $5 movie certificates. The 925 game winners were rewarded with visits to castles such as Herstmonceaux Castle, Great Fosters, and Windsor Castle in which Potter themes were developed through costuming and special events. The closing banquet in the Natural History Museum featured appetizers and drinks named after Potter characters or objects.

To avoid oversaturation, Warner Bros. offered licenses to fewer than 90 U.S. licensing partners, and only a few hundred products were released. But that left room for the development of Harry Potter party napkins, figurines, snow globes, stuffed animals, candy, bookends, lamps, candy, tattoos, wrapping paper, lunchboxes, picture frames, calendars, ornaments, sweatshirts, backpacks, key chains, CD wallets, stationery, and rubber stamps. Retailers such as Toys"R"Us and Kmart featured merchandise tied to *The Sorcerer's Stone* film, and sales were strong. Mattel Inc. was the master licensee for the games, puzzles, trading cards, and other items. Lego Systems Inc. offered a Hogwarts Express train and Hogwarts Castle kits. Electronic Arts offered video games and computer-based ancillaries. The release of the fifth book, *Harry Potter and the Order of the Phoenix*, brought with it new merchandise, such as a robe with fiber-optic lights, a magic wand, and fake forehead scars.

The promotions were apparently effective. The NPD Group, a firm that provided marketing information online, began offering a "Harry Potter Prophet" in March 2001, a series of seven reports to track popularity of the Harry Potter products and attitudes and behaviors of children and adults relating to the books and films. According to their first report based on a March 2001 survey, 95 percent of children and 90 percent of adults surveyed had heard of Harry Potter, more than half of the children had read at least one of the books, and of those who read at least one book, almost two-thirds of children planned to see the movies. The Prophet also reported that 40 percent of children and adults who had read at least one of the books had already purchased a Harry Potter-related product.

Enter the Wizarding World

Soon after all books had been read, the movies watched at least once and the lingo had been memorized, Disney and Universal Studios launched the Wizarding World of Harry Potter theme parks—Hogsmeade in 2010 and

Diagon Alley in 2014. In hard economic times, theme parks might expect to experience a downturn, but in 2010, Universal Studios (owned by NBC and in 2011 Comcast became a partner) saw a 30.2 percent bump in income thanks to the release of the last Harry Potter movie coinciding with the opening of the first park, The Wizarding World of Harry Potter, Hogsmeade. In the first quarter of 2011, The Universal's Islands of Adventure theme parks raked in $95 million despite a steep decline in ticket sales at Seaworld.

The weeks before Diagon Alley theme park opened in 2014, NBC featured a primetime special called "The Making of Diagon Alley." The hour-long program was hosted by Meredith Viera and included interviews with cast members and showed how many of the 3-D features in the attractions were created. Jimmy Fallon hosted "The Tonight Show" from Universal Orlando resort, and the "Today" show offered extended packages covering the opening of the theme park. Of course what would a theme park be if a visitor couldn't buy a wand or a sorting hat, which further extended the brand and promotion.

All told, the Harry Potter franchise was not simply a seven-episode serial about good versus evil, but a rags-to-riches story of the author herself, a tale of friendship, adventure, love, fear, and on and on. Its many plots are translated and dispersed via story platforms and merchandise. Overstating the part that consumers play in the Harry Potter story is likely impossible. Outside of Rowling's original story, the narrative is a public relations creation and a marketing darling about which it is hard for outsiders to be cynical because billions of customers are greatly satisfied. A genuine grassroots enthusiasm for the boy wizard that started a whole industry of fan fiction and college club quidditch teams can attest to the fact. Today's corporate storytellers can take a lesson. Even though marketing often consists of 140 characters and catchy half-sentence mission statements (e.g. Google's "To make the world's information universally accessible and usable"), the story is not only "a machine to think with," as literature scholar I.A. Richards extolled, "it as a machine to sell with."

Questions for Reflection

1. How may public relations practice supplement product promotion? What aspects of this case illustrate traditional public relations practice and which illustrate more integrated-communication efforts?
2. Should the techniques of product promotion be the same for products marketed to children as those marketed to adults?
3. What are the benefits gained by generating such widespread publicity for a product's release? Are there cautions as well?

4. Evaluate the strengths and weaknesses of the cross-merchandising efforts highlighted in this case.
5. What are the public relations challenges and opportunities when a highly successful series or product like the Potter novels comes to an end?

Information for this case was drawn from the Web site cited earlier and www.aoltw.com/companies/warner_bros_index.adp and www.scholastica.com. Other sources included A.C. Nielsen. (July 10, 2007). Harry Potter charms the entertainment industry. PR Newswire US, www.prenewswire.com; Blais, J. (June 5, 2003). Creating magic with marketing. *USA Today*, p. D2; Box Office History for Harry Potter. http://www.the-numbers.com/movies/franchise/Harry-Potter; Brady, D. (June 30, 2003). Harry Potter and—what else? *BusinessWeek*, pp. 79–80; Brown, S. (2005). *Wizard! Harry Potter's brand magic*. London: Cyan. Brown, S., and Patterson A. (June 2010). Selling stories: Harry Potter and the marketing plot. *Psychology & Marketing, 27(6)*, 541–556; Capell, K., et al. (August 9, 1999). Just wild about Harry Potter. *Business Week*, p. 54; D'Innocenzio, A. (October 29, 2001). Harry Potter merchandise is magical. AP Online; Fifty Highest Grossing movies of all time. http://www.imdb.com/list/ls000021718/; Germaion, D. (July 16, 2007). "Phoenix" works magic in debut. *Atlanta Journal-Constitution*, D1; Gibbs, N. (June 23, 2003). The real magic of Harry Potter. *Time*, pp. 61–67; (June 19, 2003). Harry Potter fever heats up as "Phoenix" readies to rise. *Agence France Presse*; Hein, K. (October 7, 2002). Coke puts players in the game to help unveil Potter's secrets. *Brandweek*, p. 6; Hobbs, L. (July 4, 2000). Greet Harry at a Potter party: Stores get mystical for latest book in series. *Palm Beach Post*, p. A1; Italie, H. (June 5, 2003). Publisher revs up promotion for new Harry Potter Book. Associated Press Worldstream; Katz, R. (December 9, 2002). Harry Potter fans get thrills at Coke incentive. *MeetingNews*, p. 11; Kirkpatrick, D.D. (June 16, 2003). Merchandisers try to harness Harry Potter's magic. *International Herald Tribune*; Leith, S. (February 1, 2002), Coke confident of "Potter" benefits. *Atlanta Journal-Constitution*, pp. C1, 8; Lyman, R. (December 30, 2002). A big fat increase at the box office. *The New York Times*, p. E1; Murphy, D. (June 21, 2003). Harry fans count down, raise a butterbeer. *Portland Press Herald*, p. A1; Mnyandu, E. (June 11, 2003). Harry Potter not magic enough for U.S. bookstores. *Reuters Entertainment*; Odell, P. (May 1, 2003). Bird watching. *Promo, 16*(6); Palmeri, C., et al. (December 3, 2001). Boffo at the box office, scarce on the shelves. *BusinessWeek*, p. 53; Pomerantz, D. (June 24, 2011). Harry Potter paying off for Comcast. Retired from http://www.

forbes.com/sites/dorothypomerantz/2011/06/24/harry-potter-paying-off-for-comcast; Reuters (September 11, 2002). "Harry" synergy/The WB plugs "Potter" movie. *Newsday*, p. A18; (March 28, 2001). NPD introduces new report to track Harry Potter phenomenon. Release. *Business Wire*; Richards, I.A. (1925) *Principles of literary criticism*. San Diego, CA: Harcourt Brace Jovanovich; Sanger, E. (July 10, 2000). Potter and the toymakers' tale. *Newsday*, p. 18; Scholastic Corp. (August 2, 2007). Scholastic announces record breaking sales of 11.5 million copies of Harry Potter and the Deathly Hallows in first ten days. PR Newswire. www.prnewswire.com; Scholastic Corp. (June 26, 2007). Scholastic to host "Harry Potter Place." PR Newswire US, www.prnewswire.com; Thorn, P. (February 11, 2001). Potter, Potter everywhere. *Denver Rocky Mountain News*, p. 1E; Thorn, P. (June 20, 2003). Get caught up on all things "Potter": The future. *Denver Rocky Mountain News*, p. D27; (November 1, 2001). Traffic skyrockets at studio's Harry Potter Web site. *The Toronto Star*.

CASE 13 WENDY'S RELIES ON REPUTATION TO COMBAT "FINGER" FRAUD

During dinner one evening at a Wendy's restaurant in San Jose, California, Las Vegas resident Anna Ayala claimed she bit into a partial finger that had been served in a bowl of chili. The fingertip was about one and one-half inches long. The woman told health authorities that when she found the finger in her mouth, she spit it out and began vomiting. After investigators arrived, they closed the restaurant that evening and took the remainder of the chili for analysis.

Wendy's employees were asked to show their hands to Department of Environmental Health employees after the March 22, 2005, incident, and all were whole, prompting an investigation into the source of the finger. No hand injuries were found among the suppliers of ingredients to Wendy's, either.

Wendy's conducted its own investigation. A health department inspection found no problems at the restaurant, and suppliers were ruled out as a source after analysis of the chili ingredients turned up no evidence of the finger. Employees completed a polygraph test.

Search for Finger Leads to Convictions

A search for the owner of the finger began, with Wendy's offering a $100,000 reward for information. A hotline was set up for use in offering information about its source. "The only thing we could think of is either somebody played a practical joke that went bad or it's going to be fraud," CEO Jack Schuessler told the Associated Press.

Following a tip, the finger was identified as the finger of one of the men who worked with Ayala's husband. The injured co-worker told him the couple had offered him $250,000 not to report the plot.

Ayala filed suit against Wendy's in April, but then withdrew the suit. On April 21, Ayala was arrested and charged with attempted grand theft. Police suspected she put the finger in the chili herself. The finger, the Santa Clara County coroner's office told the Associated Press, "was not consistent with an object that has been cooked in chili at 170 degrees for three hours."

In September, Ayala and her husband pleaded guilty to attempted grand theft and conspiracy to file a false insurance claim. She was sentenced to at least 9 years in prison, and her husband was sentenced to more than 12 years. They were ordered to pay about $170,000 in restitution for the wages lost by employees following the incident. In addition, the judge ordered them to pay almost $22 million to Wendy's International and the local owner of the restaurant; the corporations agreed not to seek the money if the couple never benefited from the hoax.

Wendy's later gave the $100,000 reward to two sources, one of whom was the employer of the man whose finger was used in the hoax. The second reward recipient was anonymous.

Reactions to the Story Vary

News of the supposed finger in the chili spread rapidly. Sales at Wendy's declined, leading to dozens of employee layoffs and a reduction in hours the restaurants were open. The Associated Press reported that the Wendy's lost $2.5 million in sales because of the incident, with the local restaurant losing almost $500,000. The 2005 annual report noted that the incident hurt sales "not only in the Western Region, but also throughout the entire U.S. for months afterward."

Early in the scheme, Ayala and her attorney appeared on "Good Morning America" and described the incident. She said, "Knowing that there was a human remain in my mouth, you know, something in my mouth, it's disgusting." Newspapers around the world recounted the story. Late-night talk show hosts joked about the incident.

Wendy's Relies on the Strength of Its Reputation

Wendy's sought help from the Ketchum agency. During the investigation of the incident, the nation's third largest burger chain did not alter its public communication strategy. No public apology was offered customers, and executives were not asked to go on television to defend the restaurant's reputation. National advertisements were not changed. The reputation of Ayala was not attacked. The chain did use daily crisis-management conference calls with eight executives and attorneys to discuss the incident. The results of its internal investigation that cleared its employees and processes were announced only in a brief statement.

However, once Ayala was arrested, the tactics changed. Within one day, Wendy's executives were involved in more than 2,000 national newscasts. Denny Lynch, Wendy's senior vice president for communication, appeared on the *CBS Saturday Early Show* on April 23. He was asked how the restaurant was planning to persuade customers to return. He said it would be the company's reputation that would draw customers:

> A company's reputation is built on the things that it does every day; the food that it serves, the way it treats its customers, its employees in the communities that it is in. And we are hoping that America remembers the Wendy's of a month ago, the Wendy's that is open for business and welcomes them. That is, the strength of our company is our reputation.

To help draw consumers back in, Wendy's sponsored a national Customer Appreciation Free Junior Frosty Giveaway and served 18 million customers over the three-day period.

The campaign won an honorable mention in crisis communication from *PRWeek* magazine in 2006. At the time of the crisis, Wendy's International, Inc. was the third largest burger chain in the world, with more than 6,300 Wendy's Old Fashioned Hamburgers restaurants in North America and more than 300 international Wendy's restaurants.

Questions for Reflection

1. Evaluate the communication strategies used by Wendy's during this crisis. What are the advantages and disadvantages of using a restrained approach during bad publicity?
2. Identify the priority stakeholders involved in this case. How did Wendy's seek to protect the interests of those stakeholders during this crisis?
3. Humor such as that used during the late-evening talk shows can be a difficult communication to combat. What tactics might Wendy's or other corporations facing these crises do to counter the effect of the negative jokes?

4. As suspicions of fraud emerged, Wendy's refrained from attacks on the perpetrators. Why?

Information for this case was drawn from the corporate Web site at www.wendys-invest.com/main/cp.php and the *2005 Annual Report to Shareholders* at www.wendys-invest.com.fin/annual/2005/wend05ar.pdf; Chadwick, A., & Burbank, L. (January 19, 2006). Wendy's still smarting from finger-in-chili hoax. *Day to Day*, National Public Radio; (September 20, 2005). Chili finger tipster has beef with Wendy's. Associated Press; Curtis, K. (January 18, 2006). Nev. Pair sentenced in chili finger case. Associated Press Online; Curtis, K. (April 23, 2005). Wendy's hopes customers will return after woman who claimed she found a finger in his chili was arrested. Associated Press Worldstream; Curtis, K. (April 22, 2005). Woman who claimed she found a finger in bowl of Wendy's chili arrested, police call it a hoax. Associated Press; Drew, J. (May 20, 2005). Wendy's CEO had to endure the finger-in-the-chili jokes, bide his time. Associated Press; (March 8, 2006). Honorable Mention-Ketchum and Wendy's: Wendy's sticks to values to weather chili incident. *PRWeek*, p. 33; McPherson, K. (January 19, 2006). Near maximum sentences in Wendy's finger case. *San Jose Mercury News*; Norton, J.M. (April 21, 2005). Wendy's closes internal investigation, finds no link between finger in chili and its operations. Associated Press Worldstream; (April 7, 2005). Police search home of Nevada woman who claimed to find a finger in her chili. Associated Press; Reed, D. (March 22, 2005). Woman finds human finger in Wendy's chili. *San Jose Mercury News*; Ritter, K. (April 8, 2005). Woman claiming finger in chili sues often. Associated Press Online; Sandoval, G. (May 13, 2005). Fingertip traced to man who lost finger in accident. Associated Press State & Local Wire; Skoloff, B. (March 24, 2005). Search continues for origin of finger found in Wendy's chili. Associated Press; (September 27, 2005). Two to share $100,000 reward from Wendy's finger case. Associated Press Worldstream; Smith, T. (April 23, 2005). Denny Lynch of Wendy's and Sheriff Rob Davis of the San Jose Police Department discuss the woman who claimed to have found a finger in her bowl of Wendy's chili. *The Saturday Early Show*, CBS: Smith, T., & Bowen, J. (May 14, 2005). Police say they found the man who lost the finger said to be found in a bowl of Wendy's chili. *The Saturday Early Show*, CBS.

CASE 14: CARNIVAL CRUISE LINES SAILS THROUGH ROUGH WATERS

Figure 4.1 The luxury cruise ship *Costa Concordia* leans on its starboard side after running aground on the tiny Tuscan island of Giglio, Italy, in 2012. (AP Photo: Gregorio Borgia.)

When one cruise ship experiences a crisis, travelers might call it an isolated incident, but still set sail. When more than one cruise ship experiences a crisis, the whole industry may have to start bailing water. When Carnival Cruise Lines and its subsidiaries experienced a series of crises, one of which resulted in 32 fatalities, the industry also had to weather the storms.

The Year of "Accidents"

In 2012 and 2013, two major crises occurred onboard Carnival-owned ships. The first and most severe was the incident involving the *Costa Concordia*, a ship owned by a subsidiary of Carnival. In January 2012, the *Costa Concordia* set sail for a Mediterranean trip with 3,206 passengers and 1,023 crew aboard. Shortly after the ship set sail, the crew guided it out of the deep water to 150 meters off the Tuscan shore of Giglio to show the boat to the local residents. While passengers enjoyed a meal in the dining room, the ship ran aground on an outcropping of rocks beneath the water's surface, which ripped a series of holes into the hull, flooding the engine rooms and causing the ship to lose power.

Frightened passengers called the Italian Coast Guard, which contacted the captain to investigate the trouble. Without power, the wind and current caused the ship to list more than 30 degrees and eventually come to rest on the rocky sea floor. An hour and 10 minutes after the ship ran aground, the captain ordered the passengers to abandon ship. Less than half an hour later, while many passengers and crew still clung to the sides of the upturned ship, Captain Schettino left his post and went ashore. Thirty-two passengers and crew died, and one passenger was never found.

Unfortunately, another accident was soon to follow. In February 2013, the Carnival Ship *Triumph* set sail from Galveston, Texas, with 4,000 passengers and crew members aboard for a four-day tour. Halfway into their trip, passengers were stranded aboard what has been referred to in social media and mass media accounts as the "poop cruise" or the "cruise from hell" after a fire caused the ship to lose power. For five days the ship drifted without air conditioning and largely without lights, water, food, and working toilets.

The overflowing toilets became the complaint most highlighted in the media. Passengers noted it did not take long for toilets to fill on the first day without power. After toilets were no longer usable, crew provided biohazard bags for passengers to fill. However, the biohazard bags quickly piled up, repulsing passengers. The heat, the smell, and the full bags within the cabins and halls of the cruise ship drove passengers to the deck where strangers lined up mattresses in the shade and slept, ate and passed the time communally while they waited for the ship to be towed to port in Mobile, Alabama. Boats were sent to provide food and other supplies to the ship.

Travel industry insiders referred to the reports and plans posted by Carnival to rescue passengers from the hobbled ships as direct and transparent responses. As they examined all of their options, Carnival reported they were unable to disembark passengers in Mexico because nearly 900 travelers were without passports. Some 100 buses and 1,500 hotel rooms and charter flights were scheduled for guests when they did eventually disembark. Meanwhile, Carnival Cruise Lines updated their Web site and social media pages to notify *Triumph* guests, family members of guests on the cruise, as well as future Carnival guests of the progress in rescuing the passengers on the crippled ship.

Community Responses

For the *Costa Concordia* incident, ire focused primarily on the captain, who was later charged with manslaughter and abandoning ship. However, stunned and confused passengers all agreed the everyday Italians on shore were more than helpful and hospitable after the accident. Regular people motored out in their boats and rescued some passengers. The whole town appeared at the shoreline with towels, clothes and food, according to cruise guests. On the small island, passengers were welcomed into homes and given beds, meals, and phones.

As for the *Triumph* cruise, images of passengers in robes, holding up "S.O.S." signs, pictures of biohazard-bag-lined hallways and explanations of makeshift tents on decks were uploaded to social media sites and photographed from hovering helicopters. Panicked passengers called ashore to media describing dire circumstances. Finally, the news media, late-night talk show hosts, and friends of friends of passengers flooded the airways with anecdotes, jokes, and uninformed and implausible solutions. Lawsuits, some seeking a monthly pay-off of $5,000 for life for passengers, were filed.

The Aftermath

The Concordia disaster became more than a year-long story of keeping the stuck and sunken ship from emptying tons of fuel into the Mediterranean and raising and removing it from the otherwise pristine view of a major vacation destination. While the parent company of the ship initially said it would pay for the captain's legal fees, the first charges of manslaughter released them from the obligation and they backed away from the captain. Four crew members and one member of the ship's operating company accepted plea bargains, and the captain faced trial in 2014 on charges of manslaughter and abandoning the ship.

Carnival offered *Costa Concordia* passengers who were not injured during the incident $14,500 and free counseling for having to suffer the disaster, costing the Carnival Cruise Lines' subsidiary $45 million. The figure was agreed upon through negotiations between the company and an Italian travel-consumer group, Astoi Confindustria, and other parties from Spain, France, and Germany. However, not many passengers were willing to accept the offer. According to the Huffington Post and Cruise World, hundreds of *Costa Concordia* passengers and many businesses on the island where the capsized cruise ship ran aground sought millions of dollars in damages through lawsuits filed against the Miami-based Carnival Corp. The lawsuits filed in both federal and state courts say the ship's corporate parent operated the vessel and is ultimately responsible for any safety violations, negligence, or recklessness that may have led to financial and emotional hardships stated in the lawsuit.

Once the *Triumph* was towed to port and the passengers and employees disembarked, lawsuits, competitive cruise lines, and regulators set about assessing the damage to passengers and the industry alike. Carnival offered passengers a full refund of all expenses for the trip including on board purchases and transportation costs, plus $500 and discounts on a future cruise up to the amount of the *Triumph* cruise.

In the Wake of the Crisis

In the wake of all that transpired, the cruise industry was on high alert. After the *Concordia*, some reported cruise ship prices dropped by

12 percent. Of course the cruise industry denied any negative effect on the industry as a whole. However, *Time* magazine and *The New York Times* reported that during the high booking season after the *Concordia* sank, sales rates were flat and ticket prices fell, not just in the Mediterranean, but in the Caribbean and other destinations as well.

After the *Triumph* incident, the cruise industry again denied any negative impact. Insiders claimed travelers understood that the problems with the *Triumph* were an "outlier." They also pointed out that Carnival handled the situation well by acknowledging mistakes and compensating injured parties.

Some disagreed. A Harris Interactive Poll released in March 2013 showed "the majority of Americans agree that air travel is *much more reliable* than taking cruises (57 percent) and half agree that air travel is *much safer* than taking cruises (50 percent)." The poll also showed the "purchase intent" of travelers was low across the board. In other words, not only were Americans not intending to purchase tickets on Carnival cruise ships—there was a 13 percent drop in purchase intent numbers from the year before—but seven other cruise ships tested showed no growth in purchase intent. In fact, 53 percent of respondents said they "somewhat agree" or "strongly agree" with the statement, "I am less likely to take a cruise now than I was a year ago."

By May 2013, the Cruise Line Industry Association (CLIA) provided a "Passenger Bill of Rights." Although the bill was being proposed to the international cruise community, the American cruise line CEOs, who were members of the organization, had already instituted it.

Questions for Reflection

1. How might the Carnival Cruise Lines strengthen consumer confidence? What message themes would you recommend?
2. Who should institute the "Passenger Bill of Rights" for the cruise industry? Federal government? The travel trade industry? Companies themselves? Explain your answer.
3. What effect does a "Bill of Rights" have on passengers? How would an organization like CLIA "enforce" a bill of rights?
4. What are the ethical implications of cruise industry spokespeople denying any negative impact on the industry as a whole after the two disasters?
5. How do consumer lawsuits affect the practice of public relations for a company?

Information drawn from Brady, P. (January 17, 2014) 8 cruise trends to watch in 2014. Conde Nast Traveler. http://www.cntraveler.com/daily-traveler/2014/01/cruise-ship-trends-2014; Campos-Flores, A.

(2013) Carnival Cruise mishap creates public-relations mess. *The Wall Street Journal*; Carnival deserves praise for disaster relief. (February 17, 2013) *The Vancouver Province* (British Columbia). www.lexisnexis.com/hottopics/lnacademic; Choppy waters ahead for Carnival and Other leading cruise brands (March 4, 2014). http://www.harrisinteractive.com/NewsRoom/HarrisPolls/tabid/447/ctl/ReadCustom%20Default/mid/1508/Articleld/1161/Default.aspx; Cruise industry adopts "Passenger Bill of Rights" (May 22, 2013). http://www.cruising.org/news/press_releases/2013/05/cruise-industry-adopts-passenger-bill-rights; Knight, J. & Lane, M. (2007). Carnival Corporation. In *Encyclopedia of major marketing campaigns*, Volume 2. Detroit, MI: Gale, pp. 293–296. Nadeau, B.L. (January 27, 2012) Why survivors aren't buying Costa Concordia's compensation offer. http://www.thedailybeast.com/articles/2012/01/27/why-survivors-aren-t-buying-costa-concordia-s-compensation-offer.html; Pianigiana, Gala. (February 27, 2014). Costa Concordia captain returns to ship as trial examines generators. *The New York Times*. http://www.nytimes.com/2014/02/28/world/europe/costa-concordia-captain-returns-to-ship-as-trial-examines-generators.html?_r=0.

PROFESSIONAL INSIGHT Are social media really social?

Figure 4.2 Paul Bernardini, Senior Associate, Eastwick Communications, San Francisco.

Call me old school, but no, social media isn't social. To be social or to socialize means having one-on-one conversations and contributing to the rumble of small talk at gatherings. It demands to be physically present. Speaking *out loud*, understanding body language, learning how to listen, respond, retain, and relate are the constructs of socializing and foundational skills that deserve time and attention.

However, it's not lost on me that social media is redefining the term "social" and the lens through which corporate America views it. The number of followers or connections that reporters, job prospects, or companies have is becoming primary criteria in earning clout. Social media has built a world where Twitter dominates the news cycle, LinkedIn can build careers and Facebook does the impossible by interlinking the world.

It's a big deal.

The goal with any social media campaign is to gain followers that are influential and turn influencers into advocates—an influencer being someone who is recognized in a specific industry with a well-established voice. For tech, folks like Robert Scoble and Mary Meeker are considered influencers, Robert for his connections in the industry and astounding social following (as of July 2014 Robert had 406K followers on Twitter and more than 5 million followers on Google+), and Mary for her annual Internet trends report which, for the investor community, is a coveted source for future investments. Social channels give the opportunity to interact directly with these influencers and help nurture relationships to make advocates.

It's the job of public relations practitioners to educate clients on the importance of this. Social media is *not* a numbers game. It will always be preferred to have 10 highly influential advocates versus 1,000 everyday followers. It's about quality over quantity, and to earn mindshare from an advocate takes time, patience, and nurturing.

Beyond building advocates, it's also about being a part of a conversation. Every company has a choice: be a part of the conversation (supplement its point-of-view, message, and thought leadership), or don't. Having a well-oiled social media presence establishes the rapport needed to earn credibility with the unforgiving Internet. A good example is in 2014, Malaysia Airlines had two major crises back-to-back within a six-month time frame. First, on March 8, 2014, flight MH370 vanished over the Gulf of Thailand causing one of the most expensive multinational search and rescue mandates in history. Then, on July 17, 2014, just as flight MH370 was fading from the headlines, flight MH17 was shot out of the sky in Eastern Ukraine. Two flights lost, representing 525 lives from more than 15 nations, over a five-month period and all from one airline. For the media, the need to talk about Malaysia Airlines was insatiable. For Malaysia Airlines, social media was the primary outlet for them to reach audiences and reach them immediately. It was vital that they had an already established presence on social channels well before the incidents. The airline had a pre-built audience to speak with during the crises. Malaysia Airlines tweeted condolences, offered refunds for any passenger wanting to cancel future flights, gave updates for affected families and loved ones and translated the posts into different languages. Their situation needed a global effort for global news and social media provided the vehicle for their voice.

Consider these core things when interacting on social channels. For one, it's not about revenue—it's about relationships. Be mindful of the audience you're trying to reach. Who are they? What do they care about? How can you contribute to the conversation? Then identify the top 10 influencers in your industry and devise a plan to listen, respond, and relate to them.

Paul Bernardini is a PR professional working in Silicon Valley, representing a variety of companies in the public and private sector, as well as regional and global markets. He has represented clients in fields including clean-tech, enterprise storage, Hollywood-tech, mobile, transportation, consumer-tech, digital marketing and digital media. Before technology, Mr. Bernardini also represented country artists in Nashville, Tennessee. He is a graduate of Middle Tennessee State University.

CHAPTER 5

Stakeholders

Media

Since the explosion of digital and social media, media relations has become a multi-lane highway where the rules of the road are observed as courtesies rather than enforceable regulations. In one direction, journalists ask practitioners for help in gathering information for news stories or verifying details. In another, practitioners distribute news announcements to the media or ask journalists to consider story ideas for publication. But short-cuts to publication are also available as practitioners blog, post, and tweet content directly to key publics.

This traffic generally moves smoothly at high speed, though collisions occur when drivers don't know the rules or don't care to follow them. For practitioners, the rules include conventions like the use of Associated Press style in news releases, courtesies like returning phone calls and updating posts promptly, and an absolute rejection of falsehoods and deception.

MEDIA SERVE AS INTERVENING PUBLICS

Although digital tools have made it somewhat easier to reach directly to the consumers, regulators, government officials, activists, and others whose opinions and actions will affect the practitioner's organization, traditional media relations continues to be a key practice. The gatekeepers who work in broadcasting and publishing represent an intervening public, often controlling the flow and presentation of information to readers, listeners, and viewers, or these gatekeepers may also magnify the impact of digital content through third-party endorsements or publicity.

PURPOSES OF MEDIA RELATIONS

Reaching target publics through news media exposure is a common practice in public relations for at least six reasons:

- Efficiency: Mass media, such as Web sites, daily newspapers, radio and television, reach individuals by the hundreds of thousands or even millions with unsurpassed speed.

- Credibility: Individuals often believe that information in reputable media, such as *The New York Times* or CBS TV's "60 Minutes," is more trustworthy than the same information presented by an organization.
- Targeting: Individuals who read or watch certain kinds of media or programming may have predictable interests or habits, enabling the practitioner to tailor messages with greater precision and mutual benefit.
- Agenda setting: Media attention often determines which topics come up in general conversation, and a practitioner may want to get people talking about a specific subject.
- Economy: Messages that appear in the news media involve comparatively low costs for the practitioner's organization.
- Time shifting: Print, broadcasting, and digital media allow individuals to pick their own best time and place to digest information.

SELF-INTERESTS OF THE MEDIA

Reporters and editors care little about the reasons that lead practitioners to favor news media for distributing information. Instead, journalists focus on satisfying their audiences' needs for news and their preferences in entertainment. If public relations materials help a news organization do its job well, journalists are happy to use them. Materials that contain no news or useful information are tossed.

In developing strategies and key messages to reach the ultimate target public, practitioners usually give painstaking thought to the target's self-interest and to circumstances that will make it easy for a target public to follow through with whatever action is desired. Yet, practitioners often neglect the self-interests of the intervening public—the editors and reporters—as well as the mission of a news organization.

At a personal level, journalists want many of the same things practitioners want: good income, increasing responsibility, stability with a respected employer. In journalism, these rewards depend on gaining the respect of peers, career advancement, challenging assignments, and recognition.

Reporters rate themselves and others according to the importance of assignments they handle, the number and quality of the stories they get published or broadcast, and the prominence given their stories in the news product (front page, above the fold, top of the newscast, and so on).

TIME PRESSURES IN MEDIA RELATIONS

To do their jobs well on a daily basis, most reporters must focus on choosing a story idea or chasing one down, gathering information efficiently, finding a strong news peg, and writing a vivid and compelling account. They must do it quickly, never falling behind the competition and beating it if possible, and they must meet the deadline of their publication or newscast. Before handing in a news story, a reporter needs time to check it to make sure that it's fair, accurate, and reasonably complete.

Considering these time pressures, no one should be surprised that journalists prefer to deal with a practitioner who has earned their trust by providing information that's never misleading, earned their appreciation by providing it quickly, and earned their respect by packaging it in formats that are easy to digest and use. Accommodating the self-interests of intervening publics serves the self-interest of the practitioner's organization.

DIGITAL MEDIA RELATIONS

The Internet gives a media relations practitioner a number of tools to use in helping reporters do their jobs faster and better. Almost all organizations—big and small—maintain Web sites used as electronic newsrooms. Because it's available around the clock and throughout the week, reporters can get details they need whenever they want them.

An electronic newsroom usually contains recent news releases and archives of old ones. An elementary online newsroom also should list the names, phone numbers, and e-mail addresses of the media relations staff. Better Web sites contain much more. The newsroom page should offer links to:

- Fact sheets.
- Organizational history.
- Executive biographies.
- High-resolution photos of leaders, products, and operations.
- Short videos of events or speeches.
- Reproducible charts and graphs.
- Annual and quarterly reports.
- Electronic news kits.
- Executive speeches.
- Significant dates in the organization's past.
- A calendar of major upcoming events.

Some sites also include audio files for radio actualities, PowerPoint presentations, and spreadsheets for financial information.

UP TO DATE AND EASY TO USE

To protect reporters from using out-of-date information, media relations sites need regular attention from practitioners to keep facts, figures, and faces current. Items like biographies and fact sheets should indicate when their most recent update occurred, reassuring journalists that the information is fresh.

Because these pages for the news media should load quickly into an Internet browser, they should look spare, clean and uncomplicated, placing a premium on ease of navigation. A search function can make a Web site easier to use, but it's not a substitute for careful planning in creating and positioning hypertext navigation links.

The newsroom pages should avoid files that load slowly or that are difficult or slow to print through office printers. Some portable-document-format (PDF) files preserve the appearance of the original paper document; it may be helpful to offer links so users can download computer programs needed to access such files.

The Internet also gives media relations practitioners the opportunity to maintain relationships with reporters through e-mail or texts, but it's a mixed blessing. Because e-mail has been abused by marketing spammers and lazy public relations practitioners, reporters may not bother to read your e-mail unless they know you, trust you, and sense news potential in the subject line of your message. The purpose of the subject line is similar to that of a headline: to get attention and convey the essence of a message.

Research reported by PWRchives in 2012 indicated that 86 percent of reporters said they preferred to receive pitches by e-mail; those that included links to backgrounders, bios, and other Web information resources were highly valued. Reporters say that they're unlikely to open an e-mail with attachments because it carries the risk of a computer virus infection.

NO SUBSTITUTE FOR HUMAN CONTACT

Despite the efficiency offered by the Internet, reporters and practitioners point out that it's no substitute for a trusting relationship. Web sites make facts and figures easily accessible, but tracking down non-routine details still requires human contact. To make stories come alive, journalists need to quote what people—not documents—say, and media relations managers set up the interviews that add depth and humanity to news. Reporters and practitioners need each other.

Bobbie Battista, former host of CNN's *Talk Back* cable program and now a media relations consultant, offered this advice: "Establish a relationship with one reporter at each station or publication. Over time, if you always are honest and straight, rapport will become trust."

The cases in this chapter illustrate the many ways in which organizations interact with media stakeholders, using the controlled media of advertising and publicity materials, focusing on the type of coverage desired, and responding to investigative reporting and documentaries, which may prove uncomfortable and negative. As you probe the cases, seek to identify the public relations problem or opportunity, the methods and tools used to resolve the situation, and how one might evaluate the success or failure of the public relations efforts.

Ask yourself these questions: What news values were demonstrated in the stories carried by media outlets? What news values were promoted by the public relations practitioners here? What has been the impact of the shift toward digital, individual media, and what further impacts might be anticipated? What would the practitioners in these cases have wanted their media counterparts to do, or to do differently, and how might they have promoted those alternatives?

ADDITIONAL READINGS

Henderson, David. (2006). *Making news: A straight-shooting guide to media relations*. Bloomington, IN: iUniverse.

Howard, Carol M., & Mathews, Wilma K. (2012). *On deadline: Managing media relations*. (5th ed.) Long Grove, IL: Waveland Press.

Jones, Clarence. (2001). *Winning with the news media*. Tampa, FL: Video Consultants, Inc.

Kent, Michael L., & Taylor, Maureen. (2003, Spring). Maximizing media relations: A Web site checklist. *Public Relations Quarterly, 48(1)*, 14–18.

Wade, John. (1992). *Dealing effectively with the media*. Menlo Park, CA: Crisp Publications.

Wright, Donald K. (2001). *The magic communication machine: Examining the Internet's impact on public relations, journalism, and the public*. Gainesville, FL: Institute for Public Relations.

CASE 15: MEDIA INTEREST IN TRANSPLANT DRAMA EVOKES ANXIETY IN HEALTH CARE PROFESSIONALS

Written by Larry F. Lamb

Figure 5.1 During the 2002 holidays, Jesica Santillan posed with her mother, sister and brother for a family photo. (Photo by Mack Mahoney.)

Figure 5.2 The Discovery Channel ran a 13-part documentary series on the lives of the patients and caregivers at Duke University Hospital.

Jesica Santillan spent most of her childhood in Arroyo Hondo, a sun-baked Mexican village of 400 people surrounded by fields of sugarcane. Located halfway between the Jalisco state capital of Guadalajara and Puerto Vallarta on the Pacific Coast, the village has one paved road and little else in community resources. Arroyo Hondo families have a hard life. Many depend on work in cane fields or the local sugar mill, and individuals often earn less than $10 for a 12-hour day.

Jesica's mother, Magdalena, learned early that her daughter suffered from restrictive cardiomyopathy, a condition involving heart muscle stiffness that also affects breathing. No cure for the disease exists, and about 70 percent of those who develop it die within five years of the onset of symptoms. In most cases, the only satisfactory solution is a heart transplant.

The Santillan family could not arrange transplant surgery for Jesica in Mexico. Desperate and determined, they took their 13-year-old daughter to the United States illegally in 1999 and made their way to North Carolina, where relatives were living. The family moved into a mobile home in a rural county northeast of Raleigh and began investigating what they would have to do to get Jesica's life-threatening condition corrected. Knowing medical care for Jesica would be far beyond their means (some estimates put the figure at a half-million dollars), the family solicited donations from friends and neighbors, while churches and civic groups put containers in local shops to collect contributions.

Now Near Duke

The Santillans' new Carolina home was only an hour's drive from the Durham campus of Duke University Medical Center, one of the preeminent health care organizations in the United States. Year after year, *U.S. News & World Report* had ranked Duke among the nation's top hospitals. Separately, Duke specialities such as heart, pulmonary, and pediatrics also earned high rankings on the *U.S. News* lists. The Discovery Channel ran a documentary series, called "Hospital," on the lives of patients and caregivers at Duke Hospital, and *Time* magazine published a cover story on a day in the life of Duke. CBS TV's "60 Minutes" program profiled a Duke oncologist in 2002.

By most accounts, the institution's public relations efforts were highly successful. The medical center is proud of its reputation—justifiably so. Describing its approach to medicine, Duke says that:

> patients can count on receiving high-quality healthcare that is delivered with empathy and compassion. The medical leadership that has earned Duke such renown is the result of an innovative approach that stresses multidisciplinary collaboration and a close "bench-to-bedside" relationship between clinical care and research that gives our patients access to the very latest treatments.

For Jesica, her family, and friends in North Carolina and Arroyo Hondo, Duke Hospital represented her best chance at life. They were full of hope.

Mack Mahoney Aids Santillan Family

One of Jesica's new friends was Mack Mahoney, a Carolina homebuilder who'd seen her story in a local newspaper. Inspired by her struggle for survival, he organized efforts to raise funds for a transplant operation. Fluent in Spanish, Mr. Mahoney also assisted Jesica's family, whose conversational English was limited, in their discussions with the health care professionals at Duke. Subsequently, he received medical power of attorney to participate in the Santillans' health care decisions.

As Jesica's case attracted the attention of major news outlets in Raleigh and Durham, Mr. Mahoney persuaded one of North Carolina's U.S. senators to help shield the family from deportation while they waited for organs that would be suitable for transplant. The operation, surgeons had decided, would require a set of lungs as well as a heart.

Finding compatible organs for a heart-lung transplant is a long shot. To match an organ donor and recipient, health agencies consider their physical size, blood type, the expected time in transit for the organs, and the recipient's position on the national waiting list. At any time, the national list of individuals awaiting this combination may include 200 names, but the number of heart-lung transplant operations performed in the United States in a single year might not exceed 30.

The United Network for Organ Sharing administers the nation's organ procurement and transplantation network, collecting and sharing information on organ need and availability. The network includes regional organizations that enlist donors and monitor availability.

Transplant Surgery Scheduled

On Friday, February 7, 2003, a Duke surgeon learned from the network that a heart and lungs were available from the New England Organ Bank. He reserved them for Jesica, now 17, who was expected to live only six more months with her own heart. A Duke surgical team flew to Boston to remove the organs and hurry them back to Durham. (Heart and lungs ordinarily must be implanted no more than eight hours after removal.)

Meanwhile, Jesica's surgeon timed his procedures so that he would complete the removal of her organs at about the same time that the donor's heart and lungs arrived at Duke. The coordination itself was successful, but routine tests performed near the end of the surgery disclosed a tragic error. Although the transplant network and Duke both had procedures to ensure blood group compatibility between donor and recipient even before surgery could be scheduled, the safeguards had failed somehow.

The donor's blood group was A, and Jesica's was O. People with blood group O, the most common group in the U.S. population, are universal donors; they can give blood to other groups. However, people in blood group O can safely receive blood or organs only from people in group O.

The operating team finished its work, and the surgeon went immediately to Jesica's parents to tell them of the mistake and its implications. Her body's immune response would attack the incompatible organs as it would an infection, and her only hope of survival would be a second heart-lung transplant using organs from a group O donor. Duke notified the United Network for Organ Sharing that Jesica urgently needed another set of organs.

Media Kept in the Dark

Meanwhile, the family, physicians, and hospital's public relations staff agreed privately that, until more was known about what went wrong, the media would be given only basic reports on her condition. The organ mismatch would remain confidential as the search for a new donor was pressed.

In the days immediately after the operation, the director of the medical center's news office told reporters: "She is rejecting the organs that were transplanted into her." Nothing was said about the error.

Hour by hour, the Santillans and Mr. Mahoney grew more fearful that the girl would die before the transplant network could find a donor in blood group O, and they apparently came to believe that a directed donation—where the family of a dying patient would choose Jesica to receive the organs—was the quickest and best solution. To reach as many potential donor families as possible, a broad public appeal in the media would be needed.

While impatience was agitating those closest to Jesica, Duke's reticence stirred suspicion in news reporters from Raleigh and Durham. Five days after the surgery, some reporters heard privately from Mack Mahoney that the transplanted organs came from a donor with a different blood type, but the media held back those details, apparently unable to verify them.

The director of the medical center's news office told the media: "It's far too early to have definitive answers regarding this case. Any comments now would be speculative. Nevertheless, this patient's sequence of care is under careful review."

News of Error Breaks

Then, Mr. Mahoney openly discussed the organ mismatch on Friday, February 14, after waiting a week for Duke to get results using the transplant network. The first media report of the error appeared the same day. A day later, Duke dodged the truth when reporters asked if the family's version of events was true. The associate director of the medical center's news office told reporters:

> Duke Hospital is continuing a careful review of the sequence of care that she received. That's the only information I have for you. This is all I can say. At this point, our priority is to help Jesica and her family through this difficult situation. We hope a suitable donor can be found.

While Duke remained tight-lipped, the family's account of the surgery gained the attention of national news organizations and received heavy coverage in North Carolina. Late on Monday, February 17—10 days after the surgery—Duke acknowledged the mismatch in a public statement given to the media and posted on the medical center's Web site under the headline "Duke University Hospital Implements Additional Transplantation Safeguards." Quoting the hospital chief executive officer, the statement said, "This was a tragic error, and we accept responsibility for our part."

The New England Organ Bank said its records showed Duke was told the donor's blood group at several points in the procurement process, and the information also accompanied the organs on the trip to Durham. Duke did not dispute the statement.

On Tuesday, the organ mismatch story got coverage throughout the day on CNN Headline News and Fox News Channel, as well as on cable's news/talk programs. *The New York Times* was preparing a front-page article for the following day. The Associated Press, Reuters, BBC, and other worldwide news organizations carried reports.

A Second Donor is Found

Despite the long odds against finding a compatible set of organs for a second operation, the transplant network told Duke near midnight Wednesday that a donor had been identified. Surgery began at 6 a.m. Thursday and finished at 10:15 a.m. At first, Jesica appeared to tolerate the second operation well, but the initial outlook dimmed quickly. She was pronounced dead on Saturday, February 22.

Seventeen days after Jesica's death, the CEO of the Duke University Health System sent a memo to the health care staff offering his perspective on the tragic error and suggesting what the institution might learn from the following events and the attention they received in the media. The CEO, a physician named Ralph Snyderman who also served as Duke's chancellor for health affairs, said the case involved three central issues:

- Medical questions about mistakes and how to prevent them.
- Ethical questions about transplants and end-of-life decisions.
- Communications questions about a patient's privacy rights, needs of the patient's family, and the public's right to know.

"Some have asked, why didn't Duke announce the blood-typing mistake immediately after the first transplant and launch a public appeal for compatible organs?" he wrote on March 11. "One reason is that Jesica's family initially asked us not to. Another reason is that it would not have been appropriate for us to initiate publicity. The organ procurement system used by all hospitals was designed to allocate organs on a fair and equitable basis while considering the degree of need."

A "60 Minutes" Interview

As Duke employees were digesting the memo, Dr. Snyderman and Jesica's surgeon, Dr. James Jaggers, were sitting for videotaped interviews with CBS TV's "60 Minutes." In a segment that aired March 16, the two physicians and others at Duke recounted the fateful steps that led to the failed transplant.

When journalists in Durham and Raleigh learned that "60 Minutes" was interviewing Duke's top medical officer, some suggested that the medical center was continuing to stiff-arm them. Durham's *Herald-Sun* noted that Dr. Snyderman "still hasn't responded to repeated requests by *The Herald-Sun* for an on-the-record interview about the tragedy," but the CEO and Jesica's surgeon "have granted interviews to CBS '60 Minutes' reporter Ed Bradley."

On the day after the "60 Minutes" broadcast, the medical center's Web site offered this explanation for Duke's decision to welcome the CBS crew:

> Because of the widespread publicity regarding this patient, Duke University Hospital felt it important to address some of the complex issues in a nationwide forum. We agreed to participate in a "60 Minutes" story because they offered to address this event in a fair and comprehensive manner.

Acknowledging Mistakes

Dr. Snyderman wrote a reflective op-ed column, published under the headline "Owning Up to Mistakes in Medicine," that appeared April 26, 2003, in the *News & Observer* of Raleigh.

"In order to prevent mistakes, one needs a culture of safety and an openness to identify risks freely," he wrote. "If mistakes or near misses occur, healthcare workers must own up to them promptly and honestly so they can be addressed and corrected. But doing this is extremely difficult because the current environment for litigation encourages professionals to do otherwise."

He mentioned, approvingly, proposed federal legislation that would create a system for voluntary, confidential, nonpunitive error reporting to encourage analysis of mistakes and improvement of patient safety. "We believe that disclosure of errors in an atmosphere that focuses on solutions, not blame, will make healthcare safer for everyone," he wrote.

Questions for Reflection

1. What's meant by a "bench-to-bedside" relationship?
2. What reasons might explain Duke University Hospital's initial decision to provide the news media with reports only on Jesica's condition?
3. The Santillan family and friends decided to pursue a broad public appeal for a second set of organs for transplant. What strategy and tactics would you have recommended?

4. Duke's chancellor for health affairs said the case involved questions concerning a patient's privacy rights, needs of the patient's family, and the public's right to know. How would you rank or balance these three?

Information for this case was drawn from the following: the Duke University Medical Center Web sites at http://news.mc.duke.edu/mediakits/detail.php?id=6498 and http://www.dukehealth.org/news/default.asp; Avery, S., & Martinez, A. (February 25, 2003). Duke caught in PR quagmire. *The News & Observer*, p. A1; Cheng, V. (February 19, 2003). Duke's image takes a blow. *The News & Observer*, p. A9; Draper, M. (February 13, 2003). Girl's miracle fleeting. *The News & Observer*, p. A1; (May 30, 2003). Duke's amazing PR coup continues. *The Herald-Sun*, p. B1; Eisley, M. (February 16, 2003). Mistake alleged in blood match. *The News & Observer*, p. B1; Fass, A. (June 9, 2003). Duking it out. *Forbes*, p. 134; Grady, D. (February 19, 2003). Donor mix-up leaves girl, 17, fighting for life. *The New York Times*, p. A1; Kirkpatrick, C. (June 18, 2003). Duke Hospital admits to botching transplant. *The Herald-Sun*, p. A1; Snyderman, R. (April 26, 2003). Owning up to mistakes in medicine. *The News & Observer*, p. A19; Weissert, W. (March 7, 2003). Mexican village was ready, but Jesica's funeral not to be. *The Herald-Sun*, p. A10.

CASE 16: GENERAL MILLS RETREATS FROM LEGAL CHANGE

"Dear #GeneralMills, I reserve the right to sue anyone including you. Maybe you missed it in my fine print so here it is on Twitter."

Terms Change without Notice

On April 22, 2014, this tweet summed up the consumer reaction to a change in General Mills' legal terms that had indicated that anyone who downloaded coupons on its Web site, entered a sweepstakes or a contest, subscribed to digital newsletters or "joined" one of its online social media pages forfeited their right to sue the company. Instead, these consumers would be consenting to what the terms called "binding arbitration" or informal negotiations. The change in legal terms occurred with little notice or consumer notification.

The New York Times reported that the change in terms was linked to a suit brought against the corporation in California about the claim that its Nature Valley products were "natural" while they contained genetically engineered and processed ingredients. But General Mills was not the only corporation that had enacted such legal rules. Corporations ranging from telecommunications to pest control have done so since the 2011 U.S. Supreme Court ruling in *AT&T Mobility* v. *Concepcion* that found such agreements legal.

General Mills reports on its Web site that its mission is to "make lives *healthier, easier and richer.* General Mills is Nourishing Lives" (www.generalmills.com). Its wide range of brands and products, from Pillsbury to Yoplait to Häagen-Dazs, generated $17.8 billion of sales in fiscal 2013 in more than 100 countries. Consumers are encouraged to interact with the General Mills community through Facebook, Twitter, YouTube, LinkedIn, and a corporate blog.

General Mills Changes Direction

After media outlets publicized the change in legal terms, consumers reacted with a barrage of angry tweets and posts. Within a few days, the corporation announced it would reverse the policy—a move the April 20, 2014, *New York Times* called a "stunning about-face." "We've listened-and we're changing our legal terms back to what they were," read an April 19 tweet from @GeneralMills.

The Taste of General Mills blog carried a longer post from Kirstie Foster, director of external communications for General Mills that admitted the corporation had been surprised by the strong reaction to the change.

> Those terms—and our intentions—were widely misread, causing concern among consumers. So we've listened—and we're changing them back to what they were before . . . We stipulate for all purposes that our recent Legal Terms have been terminated, that the arbitration provisions are void, and that they are not, and never have been, of any legal effect.

The post ended with an apology. "We're sorry we even started down this path. And we do hope you'll accept our apology. We also hope that you'll continue to download product coupons, talk to us on social media, or look for recipes on our websites."

Questions for Reflection

1. This case illustrates the growing power of social media and the continuing power of traditional media to affect public opinion. Identify ways in which corporations can use this power to their advantage.
2. How actively should corporations monitor social media and traditional media coverage? What advice would you offer a corporation that is being criticized in social media?

3. Corporate apologies occur in many different circumstances. How effective was the General Mills apology in this situation?
4. What are the legal and ethical implications of joining a community on a corporate social media site?

Information for this case was drawn from the corporate Web site at http://generalmills.com, and Foster, Kirstie. (April 19, 2014). Blog. http://www.blog.generalmills.com/2014/04/weve-listened-and-were-changing-our-legal-terms-back-to-what-they-were/; Griswold, Allison. (April 18, 2014). Why people are freaking out over General Mills' new legal policy. *Slate*. http://www.slate.com/blogs/moneybox/2014/04/18/general_mills_new_legal_policy_suddenly_customers_are_reading_the_fine_print.html; Kim, Susanna. (April 17, 2014). Do companies void your right to sue after you "like" them on Facebook? ABC News. http://abcnews.go.com/Business/companies-voiding-sue-facebook/story?id=23363842; Public Citizen. (April 17, 2014). Forced arbitration rogues gallery. http://www.ctizen.org/forced-arbitration-rogues-gallery; Strom, Stephanie. (April 17, 2014). When "liking" a brand online voids the right to sue. *The New York Times*, B1; Thompson, Derek. (April 2014). General Mills: If you clip this coupon, you can't sue us! *The Atlantic*. http://www.theatlantic.com/business/archive/2014/04/general-mills-facebook-sue/360826.

CASE 17: A NEW POPE ADOPTS A NEW COMMUNICATION STYLE

The director of the papal press office is a 71-year-old priest who was appointed to the office by Pope Benedict XVI in 2006. Father Federico Lombardi's job during Pope Benedict's tenure was often to clarify what the Pope meant. For instance, in July 2010, the Pope, while discussing how the priest sexual abuse cases should be dealt with, referred to other "more grave crimes" including "attempted sacred ordination of women," which prompted criticism of his language.

In a 2013 *New Yorker* article, Father Lombardi described his job under Pope Benedict as one where he was always telling people, "No, this is not the right way!" as he was called upon to always correct people's behavior.

"The people thought I always had a negative message for them," he said.

When the 115 Cardinals elected Jorge Mario Bergolio as the 266th pontiff in 2013, he said his job changed.

"I am very happy that, with [Pope] Francis, the situation has changed. Now I am at the service of a message . . . of love and mercy," Father Lombardi said.

Even the press corps has noticed the difference. One journalist reported Father Lombardi had a nervous cough when he spoke with them about Pope Benedict, but since Pope Francis began speaking for the church, the cough seems to have disappeared.

The "People's Pope"

Dubbed "the People's Pope," by *Time*, Pope Francis has a career record as a doctrinal conservative. The Pope is, after all, a son of the church. Church doctrine is not his to rewrite, so the same "rules" under Pope Benedict still reign under Pope Francis. So why is Father Lombardi's job as a public relations specialist so different?

On NBC's "Meet the Press" Cardinal Timothy Dolan of New York said: "A Pope . . . can't make doctrinal changes. He can make a lot of changes in the way, the style, the manner in which it's presented."

Pope Francis' style has been noted in stark contrast to Pope Benedict's. Where Pope Benedict, as was the tradition of popes, wore red satin shoes made by Prada, Pope Francis chose his old plain, brown walking shoes. While Pope Benedict's cross is made of gold, Pope Francis wears one of iron. Of course, style goes beyond papal vestments. Pope Francis has opted to live in a two-room apartment that used to be reserved for visiting clergy and lay people, shunning the apostolic palace where most popes have lived during their tenure in the office. He has opted for a Ford Focus as his car, instead of the more traditional papal Mercedes. The "Pope mobile," a small car where the pope can be seen in a bulletproof box as he waves to people en route to engagements, has been dismantled. The car was designed after an assassination attempt was made on Pope John Paul II in 1981. Pope Francis has called it a "sardine can" that keeps him separated from people.

Then there was the time he paid his own hotel bill.

Shaping a New Public Image

From child sex abuse scandals to misappropriation of money at the Vatican bank, the Roman Catholic Church had a lot of media capital to gain. The simple pictures of the Pope paying his hotel bill and then hopping on the bus, forgoing a limousine ride, his white skullcap on his head in a sea of red cardinal birettas on the bus just hours after he was named Pope was a picturesque start to building that capital. The world has seen pictures of the Pope washing the feet of female convicts. They have seen him touching and kissing malformed heads and letting children play with his cap.

There is also his name. Most new popes choose a name of a previous pope, but Cardinal Bergoglio chose St. Francis of Assisi as his namesake, a saint known for protecting the powerless—the poor and animals.

It's not only Pope Francis' vestments, photo opportunities, or name but also his language choices for papal messages that suggest a style change that have made Father Lombardi's job tensions dissipate. Instead of moralizing about cultural topics, the Pope responded "Who am I to judge?" when a reporter asked about the status of gay priests in the church during a press conference on a flight from Brazil to Rome in July 2013. While church policy may not change, the message of acceptance or inclusiveness counters the culture wars that Pope Benedict's "non-negotiable imperatives" may have stirred.

The response to the "people's pope" hasn't been just from 1.2 billion Catholics. *Time* magazine named him its "Person of the Year" in 2013. In a 2014 Gallup poll, 76 percent of American adults reported that they viewed him favorably. Even 73 percent of those with no religious identity said they viewed him favorably.

Questions for Reflection

1. What can corporate clients learn from Pope Francis about connecting with stakeholders?
2. What are some of the essential public relations principles Pope Francis seems to be enacting?
3. What is the right balance of style and substance?

Information drawn from Carroll, J. (December 12, 2013). Who am I to judge? *The New Yorker*, p. 80; Catholic Online (June 9, 2013). Dramatically different! Check out all the differences between the dress styles of Popes Benedict and Francis. http://www.catholic.org/news/hf/faith/story.php?id=51286; Chua-Eoan, H., & Dias, E. (December 11, 2013). Pope Francis, the people's pope. *Time*. http://poy.time.com/2013/12/11/person-of-the-year-pope-francis-the-peoples-pope/?iid=poy-main-lead; Goodwin, D. (July 15, 2014). Vatican vanguard: What the Pope can teach us about public relations. PRSA.org. http://www.prsa.org/Intelligence/TheStrategist/Articles/view/10710/1096/Vatican_Vanguard_What_the_Pope_Can_Teach_Us_About#.U9MX3YBdWAQ; Hunt, M. (July 15, 2010). Vatican equates women's ordination with priest pedophilia. http://religiondispatches.org/vatican-equates-womens-ordination-with-priest-pedophilia/; Newport, F. (March 26, 2014). Americans see Pope in favorable light. http://www.gallup.com/poll/168098/americans-pope-favorable-light.aspx; Smith-Spark, L. (June 14, 2014). Francis ditches bullet proof Popemobile, says "at my age I don't have much to lose." http://www.cnn.com/2014/06/14/world/europe/pope-francis-interview-popemobile/;

Squires, N. (May 29, 2013). Pope Francis shunned papal apartments to live "normal life." *The Telegraph Herald.* http://www.telegraph.co.uk/news/worldnews/the-pope/10086876/Pope-Francis-shunned-official-papal-apartments-to-live-normal-life.html.

CASE 18 : LANCE ARMSTRONG APOLOGIZES

In a 2001 Nike Ad, Lance Armstrong's voice narrates footage of the athlete first sitting before reporters and a doctor getting ready to get his blood tested before a race, then a series of clips of him training and ends with blood being drawn. He says:

> This is my body and I can do whatever I want to it. I can push it, and study it, tweak it, listen to it. Everybody wants to know what I'm on. What am I on? I'm on my bike, busting my ass six hours a day. What are you on?

But nine years later, Armstrong would appear on a television talk show to talk about some of the other choices he made—choices that would eventually cost him some of his medals, his endorsements, and, at least partially, his public image as a hero.

The Race to Win

Armstrong began his professional career after finishing 14th in the men's road race during the Olympics in Barcelona, Spain, in 1992. The following year, he earned a million dollar bonus for winning all three legs of the Thrift Drug series as well as an international title at the 1993 World Road Championship in Oslo, Norway. And, in his first appearance in the Tour de France, he won stage eight.

Perhaps Armstrong's most defining year came in 1996 when he started the year as the top ranked cyclist in the world and then won two more international competitions before competing in the Olympics in Atlanta. However, by October, Armstrong was diagnosed with testicular cancer, which had spread to his lungs and abdomen. He endured brain surgery to remove lesions from his brain and suffered through chemotherapy treatments.

After the cancer went into remission the following year, Armstrong restarted his training and created his foundation, which came to be known as "Livestrong" (http://www.livestrong.org/). The foundation would advocate for cancer patients and medical research.

Armstrong began winning races again, and in 1999, he became the second American ever to win the Tour de France. Then he did what seemed to be the impossible: he kept winning it. In all, he won seven times, but by the sixth win, which is the one that made him the most accomplished racer in the history of the sport, allegations of doping began widely circulating with the publication of Pierre Ballester's and David Walsh's book *L.A. Confidential*. The book, only published in French, included an interview with the masseuse for the U.S. team, and thus Armstrong's, Emma O'Reilly, who said she believed she delivered doping materials. (Walsh would go on to publish two more books on the subject.)

Armstrong retired in 2006 after being cleared of doping charges by sport officials. However, in 2008, he came out of retirement and finished third in the Tour de France in 2009, but doping charges resurfaced. The charges came to a head in 2010 when Floyd Landis, the 2006 winner of the Tour de France, was immediately stripped of his win after testing positive for performance-enhancing drugs. Floyd admitted to widespread drugging and accused Armstrong, specifically.

In 2011, Armstrong retired again, but then other teammates and witnesses admitted to doping, and all included Armstrong in their accusations. A federal investigation followed, but in 2012, federal prosecutors dropped their investigation without bringing charges. But the U.S. Anti-Doping Agency (USADA) did charge Armstrong with doping and trafficking performance-enhancing drugs. Armstrong decided to give up the fight and accepted the USADA's sanctions, which stripped him of his seven Tour de France medals and imposed a lifetime ban from the sport.

However, the medals were not the only things Armstrong lost. He eventually stepped down from the Livestrong Foundation in an effort to save it. He lost his long-time sponsor and partner in the wildly popular "Livestrong" armbands, Nike. Other sponsors such as Anheuser-Busch, Oakley and Trek, among others, quickly defected.

The "Oprah" Appearance and Apology

In January 2013, Armstrong appeared on "Oprah," the highly watched talked show hosted by Oprah Winfrey, in a two-part, 90-minute interview detailing a laundry list of "what he was on." From drugs to lying about drugs, bullying others to lie about drugs, and an indictment of the sport culture that perpetuates a drug culture, Armstrong pulled back the curtain on a career that was the opposite of what millions of "Livestrong" bracelet wearers believed to be true.

"This is too late," Armstrong said late in the interview with Oprah Winfrey. "It's too late for probably most people, and that's my fault."

The interview opened with a series of questions from Winfrey:

Winfrey: Yes or no. Did you ever take banned substances to enhance your cycling performance?

Armstrong:	Yes.
Winfrey:	Yes or no. Was one of those banned substances EPO?
Armstrong:	Yes.
Winfrey:	Yes or no. Did you ever blood dope or use blood transfusions to enhance your cycling performance?
Armstrong:	Yes.
Winfrey:	Did you ever use any other banned substances like testosterone, cortisone or Human Growth Hormone?
Armstrong:	Yes.
Winfrey:	Yes or no. In all seven of your Tour de France victories, did you ever take banned substances or blood dope?
Armstrong:	Yes.

During the next hour, Armstrong called himself callous and controlling and a person who must win at all costs. His matter-of-fact demeanor in absolutely not defending his behavior was disconcerting for many.

Apology Accepted—or Not?

The made-for-TV apology was received in a flurry of emotions from fellow athletes, sponsors, Livestrong employees and volunteers, sports fans, and cancer patients. Some public reactions suggested relief at hearing him actually admit to allegations that had followed him since the mid-1990s. Author David Walsh tweeted, "First reaction is Oprah began the interview brilliantly with her series of 'yes or no' questions. It felt good to hear him admit to doping."

Certainly, an apology is an important tool in the public relations toolbox. According to Executive Communication Coach and Crisis Expert Virgil Scudder, an effective apology has four parts: It has to be timely; it should be specific and sincere; it should explain the reason for the apology and a pledge to do better, and it should provide a plan for remedial action to those harmed.

However, the Twitter comments as posted during the airing of the show trended more negative as the interview went on. At one point, when Armstrong said he couldn't remember that he had sued the masseuse O'Reilly, the executive producer and head writer for "The Late Show with David Letterman" tweeted, "I mean seriously, how are you expected to remember all of the people you've sued?" Serena Williams tweeted, "Wow, Watching @Oprah interview. Just WOW."

After the apology, there was widespread public debate on whether or not Armstrong and the Livestrong Foundation could rise from the ashes. Scudder said: "His body language during the interview was bad and, in my view, telling. He was low on energy and emotion—resembling a school child who admitted to cheating on a test. Armstrong didn't say why he cheated."

USA sports writer Christine Brennan agreed. In an article after the interview aired, titled "If possible, Armstrong less likeable after Oprah," Brennan said by admitting his story for more than a decade was the opposite of what the world believed, Armstrong could not expect people to accept what he says now as the truth. She called into question his credibility, demeanor, sincerity, and memory.

The official statement from the Livestrong Foundation, reported by the Associated Press on January 18, 2013, said:

> We at the LIVESTRONG Foundation are disappointed by the news that Lance Armstrong misled people during and after his cycling career, including us. Earlier this week, Lance apologized to our staff and we accepted his apology in order to move on and chart a strong, independent course. We look forward to devoting our full energy to our mission of helping people not only fight and survive cancer, but also thrive in life after cancer.

Questions for Reflection

1. Did the seven-time Tour de France winner apologize appropriately enough to be able to rebuild his reputation? Explain.
2. How does Armstrong compare to other famous apologizers such as Michael Vick, Mark McGuire, or Tiger Woods? What about Bill Clinton?
3. How did the media help or hurt Armstrong's reputation?
4. If it is an American cultural habit to give media celebrities second chances, will Armstrong's reputation make a comeback? Why or why not?

Information for this case was drawn from Ballester, P., & Walsh D. (2004). *L.A. confidential.* Lyon: La Martinière; Brennan, Christine. (January 16, 2013). Life of Armstrong over as he knows it. *USA Today*; Colbert, A. (January 18, 2013). Lance Armstrong Nike Ad: "What am I on?" http://mashable.com/2013/01/18/lancearmstrong-nike-ad-what-am-i-on/; Hampson, R. (January 18, 2013). Can you forgive Lance Armstrong? http://www.usatoday.com/story/news/nation/2013/01/17/forgive-lance-armstrong-redemption/1843073/; MSN News (January 16, 2013). A timeline of doping denials by Lance Armstrong. http://news.msn.com/pop-culture/a-timeline-of-doping-denials-by-lance-armstrong; Rapp, T. (January 14, 2013). Timeline of Lance Armstrong's career and eventual downfall. http://bleacherreport.com/articles/1484496-timeline-of-lance-armstrongs-career-and-eventual-downfall; Schrotenboer, B. (October 23, 2012). After years of denials, Armstrong's strategy collapses. *USA Today.*

http://www.usatoday.com/story/sports/cycling/2014/04/09/lance-armstrong-named-names-written-answers-doping/7532825/; Schrotenboer, B. (January 18, 2013). Lance Armstrong to Oprah: Story was "one big fat lie." *USA Today.* http://www.usatoday.com/story/sports/cycling/2013/01/17/lance-armstrong-oprah-winfreycon-fession/1843641/; Scudder, V. (April 9, 2014). A sorry state: Learning from Lance Armstrong. PRSA.org. http://www.prsa.org/Intelligence/TheStrategist/Articles/view/10152/1076/A_Sorry_State_Learning_from_ Lance_Armstrong#.U-F-PoBdWAR.

PROFESSIONAL INSIGHT Do traditional news and news media matter?

Figure 5.3 Brian Brodrick, Jackson Spalding Public Relations

Sometimes a question that seems rather simple is not. Do traditional news and news media matter? The obvious answer is this: Not as much as they used to. But the fact that we ask implies a need to examine the matter more deeply.

First of all, does news matter? Absolutely. News, I would argue, matters more than ever. In an increasingly connected and global society, news—critical, unbiased information of vital importance to a given audience—is a currency *du jour* for civic, thought and business leaders, and those who aspire to positions of leadership. Whether it is news about an event in a small community, a critical detail in a corporate earnings announcement, or news of vital import for international politics, information—and who acts on it first—is a vital unit of exchange in the marketplace of ideas.

One reason for the increased value of news is the speed with which it moves. The connection between information and action has been compressed. In fact, a mathematical argument could be made that (quality of news) + (speed of delivery of news) = (potential impact of news). Old news is just that, and the most well-crafted piece of journalism, delivered after the facts have been shared by others, is devalued by half or more.

This discussion of quality and speed leads us naturally to the second part of our seven word query: Do news media matter?

Only the most ardent newsman or press operator will argue that the model that sustained the "news business" from the 1960s through the late 1990s is not dead. This era, which saw the rise of television and reasonably stable revenues across the industry, began a steady decline in the late 1990s. Unless you have been under a rock (or a printing press), you will not be surprised that this decline is offset by the rise of online communications.

Since the mid-2000s, the speed with which news and information moved accelerated rapidly with the widespread acceptance of social media. News is no longer held and controlled by a few. For many, it is distilled and distributed on a one-to-one basis, often in 140 word or even 140 character bits. Even those who have not adapted to social media still rely on screens more than paper for their information. Vital news breaks on Twitter, is emotionally wrought on Facebook, is analyzed by bloggers, and the media are just one of the above.

Today, news media often still win on the quality side of the equation, but many sacrifice the speed necessary to compete. Even when they try to adjust, they resemble aging athletes, slowed by weighty staffs, reactions dulled by legacy systems and processes, their nose for the scoop obscured by internal politics, and the advantage of objectivity destroyed by reporters trying to compete with bloggers.

Many reporters and a few outlets have found the right balance and stand ready to compete in tomorrow's world where the best information, delivered with speed, clarity, and creativity wins.

But the greater challenge for tomorrow's PR professional is to scan the field, and understand that this business no longer depends on the media. But it does depend on news and information. At its most fundamental level, public relations is back to its original definition: relating to the public and sharing information effectively with key publics.

You must find and generate content to share and you must find a way to package and deliver it to the largest possible relevant audience. The channels are vastly different and more numerous than they were just five years ago. Media are just one of many channels. Audiences are highly fragmented. Attention spans are limited. But the opportunities are infinite.

For professionals seeking compelling ways to help their organizations, clients, and customers communicate effectively, inside or outside their organizations, there is not a better time to enter this industry, and this book by Richardson and Hinton will help you understand how to best identify, inform, and impact the publics that are vital to the success of any practitioner of "public relations."

Brian Brodrick is a partner with Jackson Spalding, Georgia's largest independent marketing communications firm. A 1997 graduate of Berry College, Brian is an experienced crisis counselor who also has specialties in public affairs, land use, education, and health care communications. He is also an elected official in Watkinsville, Georgia.

CHAPTER 6

Stakeholders

Investors

One of the hottest investment stories of the decade involved Facebook's plan for an initial public offering (IPO) of common stock. Created in 2004 by Harvard sophomore Mark Zuckerberg, Facebook had quickly become the world's largest social network. It seemed that almost everyone, from investment bankers to high schoolers, "liked" the company. The story of its creation and the legal squabbles that resulted were recounted in a film, *The Social Network*, that won three Oscars and the 2010 Golden Globe award for Best Motion Picture Drama. Yet its public stock launch on May 18, 2012, though "breathlessly hyped," according to CNNMoney, was complicated by Nasdaq technical issues and questions about financial disclosures. Its initial valuation was set at what *The Wall St. Journal* called then the biggest ever for an American company.

The "friends" of Facebook knew that it was innovative and engaging, but extensive information about its performance as a business—its operating and financial results—was hard to obtain. As a privately owned company, Facebook was not obligated to share the details with anyone. It did not publish an annual report and did not release news about quarterly earnings, generated by selling advertising space. Despite this, however, more than 80 million shares of the company were sold in the first 30 seconds of trading. Amid proposed lawsuits from those concerned about the timing of financial disclosures, the price of the shares varied dramatically during the days that followed but settled at around $42 a share.[1]

INVESTMENT BANKING ADVISORS

Generally, companies had used investment bankers, such as Morgan Stanley or Goldman Sachs, for help in issuing new securities, including IPOs of common stocks. The 2008 whirl of mergers, bankruptcies, and bailouts thinned the ranks of these investment advisors and changed the nature of their structures, but public companies will continue to need assistance from surviving advisors who offer expertise in:

- Setting the price at which new stocks will start trading.
- Lining up likely investors in advance.
- Using networks of stockbrokers to market the new securities once they are available.

Investment advisors also help companies prepare the documents they are required to file with the Securities and Exchange Commission (SEC) in advance of an IPO. For weeks before a public offering of stock and for weeks afterward, companies face SEC restrictions on what they may say publicly about their operations, their outlook, or their results. This interval is called the quiet period, and its purpose is to restrain exuberant promotion of stocks. It applies to all newly registered securities, not just IPOs. Companies generally avoid publicity during the quiet period and use their Web sites to fully disclose relevant information in dispassionate terms. In investor relations, the quiet period is a sensitive time. Fearful of risking SEC sanctions, practitioners often avoid public statements altogether because the SEC has provided little guidance. The same restraint applies to other functions in public relations, such as media relations and employee communication.

QUIET PERIOD NOT DEFINED

According to the SEC:

> The federal securities laws do not define the term "quiet period," which is also referred to as the "waiting period." However, historically, a quiet period extended from the time a company files a registration statement with the SEC until SEC staff declared the registration statement "effective." During that period, the federal securities laws limited what information a company and related parties can release to the public.

Despite the restrictions, the SEC encouraged companies to continue making normal corporate announcements in the ordinary course of business during the quiet period. In 2005, the rules were relaxed somewhat, recognizing the role of Internet communications and the general value of sharing, rather than restricting, information.

When the quiet period is over, companies are free to provide investors and potential investors with as much information as they might need to make a sound decision on whether to buy, sell, or hold securities. Additionally, the commission watches companies closely to ensure that investor information does not frame the facts to emphasize the good news and obscure the bad news. Regulations also govern the minimum amount of information that companies must disclose.

ROLE OF THE SEC

The mission of the SEC is simple: "to protect investors, maintain fair, orderly, and efficient markets, and facilitate capital formation." It seeks to accomplish that mission, according to the SEC, in this manner:

> The laws and rules that govern the securities industry in the United States derive from a simple and straightforward concept: all investors, whether large institutions or private individuals, should have access to certain basic facts about an investment prior to buying it, and so long as they hold it. To achieve this, the SEC requires public companies to disclose meaningful financial and other information to the public. This provides a common pool of knowledge for all investors to use to judge for themselves whether to buy, sell, or hold a particular security. Only through the steady flow of timely, comprehensive, and accurate information can people make sound investment decisions.
>
> (http://www.sec.gov/about/whatwedo.shtml#.VHImCIvF-Ck)

The commission enforces rules to prevent an inequitable distribution of information that might benefit large or well-connected investors at the expense of smaller investors or those who are less sophisticated. The fair disclosure rule, known as Regulation FD, aims to give everyone an equal chance to gain from stock market opportunities and avoid losses in market declines. According to the SEC:

> Regulation FD provides that when an issuer discloses material non-public information to certain individuals or entities—generally, securities market professionals, such as stock analysts, or holders of the issuer's securities who may well trade on the basis of the information—the issuer must make public disclosure of that information. In this way, the new rule aims to promote the full and fair disclosure.

INDIVIDUAL AND INSTITUTIONAL INVESTORS

A little more than half of U.S. adults reported to Gallup that they owned stock equities in 2013, down from the high of almost the more than 62 percent who reported owning stocks in 2007 before the recession. Many individuals and families have built up investment portfolios in stocks and mutual funds through 401(k) plans offered by employers. Usually, an employer contributes a certain amount for each dollar that an employee puts into the plan. Some companies offer employee stock ownership programs, using a system similar to a 401(k) plan, that enable employees to buy stock in the employer at a discount.

Investor relations professionals agree that companies now must do a better job of informing individual investors about business plans, performance, and prospects. Many practitioners have been accustomed to focusing their communications efforts on institutional investors. Compared with individual investors, institutional investors are small in number but huge in the volume of shares they own and trade. Institutional investors include pension funds, such as CalPERS (California Public Employees' Retirement System); mutual funds, such as the Vanguard Group; insurance companies, such as Prudential; and similar large financial organizations. A report issued by The Conference Board in 2010 said that institutional investors owned more than 73 percent of the shares of the 1,000 largest U.S. corporations, and Towers Watson reported that U.S. pensions funds that manage workers' retirement savings owned $18.9 trillion in assets in 2014. For example, CalPERs alone owned almost $290.5 billion on April 30, 2014.

COMMUNICATING WITH SHAREHOLDERS

Managing investor relations is a multifaceted undertaking. The National Investor Relations Institute (NIRI) describes the practice as:

> a strategic management responsibility that integrates finance, communication, marketing and securities law compliance to enable the most effective two-way communication between a company, the financial community, and other constituencies, which ultimately contributes to a company's securities achieving fair valuation.

Effective practitioners must have a thorough understanding of finance and market principles and practices and be able to communicate often intricate data and information in ways that do not violate legal and ethical guidelines. Investor information is often global in scope, so practitioners may be communicating with publics and adhering to legal mandates in many nations. Confidentiality and diligent attention to conflict of interest must be maintained.

Increasingly, communication with individual and institutional investors requires strong writing skills and relies on well-designed corporate Web sites, social media, and videoconferencing, along with the traditional quarterly and annual reports, news releases, conference calls, speeches, and annual meetings.

As you approach these cases, explore these questions: what motivates individuals and investment groups to invest capital in these corporations? What information do investor stakeholders want and need from businesses, and what are the most effective ways for such information to be provided? How can corporations maintain credible relationships with key investors, even during times of crisis or transition? What ethical principles should underlie investor communication?

NOTE

1. For more information, see Raice, S., Das, A., & Letzing, J. (May 17, 2012). Facebook prices IPO at record level. *The Wall Street Journal.* http://online.wsj.com/news/articles/SB10001424052702303448404577409923406193162; and Pepitone, J. (May 23, 2012). Facebook IPO: What the %$#! happened? CNN Money. http://money.cnn.com/2012/05/23/technology/facebook-ipo-what-went-wrong/.

ADDITIONAL READINGS

Bragg, Stephen M. (2010). *Running an effective investor relations department.* Hoboken, NJ: John Wiley & Sons.

Droms, William G. and Wright, Jay O. (2010). *Finance and accounting for non-financial managers.* New York: Basic Books.

Guimard, Anne. (2013). *Investor relations: Principles and International best practices in financial communications.* New York: Palgrave MacMillan.

CASE 19: A HABIT OF ACTIVISM

Sister Patricia Daly, a member of the Sisters of St. Dominic of Caldwell, New Jersey, is in the habit of using the power of stock ownership to lobby U.S. corporations. She and her colleagues at the Tri-State Coalition for Responsible Investment characterize an emerging and powerful type of investor who seeks to affect corporate actions through investor resolutions and shareholder voting.

A "Visionary Leader"

Sister Daly was awarded the 2014 Ceres-Trillium Joan Bavaria Award in recognition of her leadership in pressuring Fortune 500 companies to reduce greenhouse gas emissions. According to the release about the award, while presenting the award, William Clay Ford Jr. of the Ford Motor Company observed: "Sr. Pat was an important catalyst in Ford's own sustainability journey. She is a visionary leader identifying issues of social and environmental concern."

Sister Daly committed to the convent right after graduating from college in 1976. She taught at a Catholic high school in New Jersey but soon became interested in corporate management practices.

She told the *Chicago Tribune* that a labor dispute at J.P. Stevens & Co. textile mills, the story eventually portrayed in the film *Norma Rae*, drew her to her first stockholder activities. The nuns in her convent owned some Stevens shares in their retirement portfolio, which entitled them to attend the shareholder annual meetings. At these meetings, Daly says she met others who were interested in pressuring the companies in which they owned stock to address critical social issues. She became her order's representative on the Tri-State Coalition for Responsible Investment; she later also worked with the Christian Brothers Investment services.

Daly explained to *The New York Times* that she did not select the investments for the convent's retirement accounts, but that she was responsible for noting those who could be encouraged to improve. Describing her work, she said: "The Dominicans are an order of preachers. I do it in boardrooms, and those kind of inner arenas. It's not always public preaching. But preaching is really the mission."

Interfaith Center for Corporate Responsibility

As her interest and energies began to focus more and more on responsible investing, she became executive director of the Tri-State Coalition for Responsible Investment and, later, its representative on the Interfaith Center for Corporate Responsibility (ICCR), a group of almost 300 faith-based institutional investors with a portfolio of more than $100 billion in value. The ICCR uses the power of that portfolio to gain the attention of corporations through involvement in shareholder meetings, resolutions, and lobbying.

"I use the term 'engaged shareholder,'" Daly told the November 2011 *U.S. Catholic*. "I'm a very reasonable person in the midst of these companies. The ICCR and Tri-State CRI communities are voices of reason."

The ICCR states on its Web site that it "is a coalition of faith and values-driven organizations who view the management of their investments as a powerful catalyst for social change." Its mission? "Through the lens of faith, ICCR builds a more just and sustainable world by integrating social values into corporate and investor actions." It identifies issues ranging from the environment to water and food to financial services to corporate governance as areas of ICCR involvement. The organization publishes a Social Sustainability Resource Guide that is available free on its Web site.

Activist Shareholders Increase

Such shareholder involvement is becoming more common. According to Section 14a-8 of the Securities Exchange Act of 1934, those who own at least $2,000 worth of stock or 1 percent of a corporation's stock can submit a shareholder resolution. The resolution should address decisions or actions outside the ordinary business of the company and should have what the SEC calls "material impact" on the company. More than 400 proxy resolutions addressing sustainability were filed in 2013.

However, proxy resolutions are usually not binding on the corporate board of directors, so their influence may not be direct. But they may make it possible for dissident shareholders to express their views through the language chosen for the resolutions. Their introduction may also present opportunities for proponents to make argumentative presentations to the board of directors who attend shareholder meetings.

For example, in May 2011, Nora Nash, a Sister of St. Francis of Philadelphia, introduced a resolution drafted by several religious orders and other groups at the annual meeting of Goldman Sachs. The resolution called for the bank's executives to reconsider the compensation plan for its top leaders and to report the findings to all shareholders. The bank had just offered some $70 billion in bonuses to its executives, while it was laying off other employees and paying more than a billion dollars in fines to the SEC and in related legal fees. According to U.S. Catholic.org, 4.1 percent of shareholders voted in favor of the resolution.

From 2006 to 2012, resolutions presented by religious investors comprised 42 percent of all proxy resolutions, according to the Center for Legal Policy at the Manhattan Institute, with resolutions from Catholic orders of nuns offering 16 to 19 each year. In 2013, 25 percent of the resolutions came from religious investors.

Not all activist investors have religious or social-justice motivations. Some, like legendary investor Carl Icahn, are eager for increased profitability or for different leadership. Yet a consistent number of investors, in formal groups or through dedicated money-management accounts, want their faith or ethical commitments to determine how they invest.

Describing her personal approach, Sister Daly told the June 12, 2005, *Chicago Tribune*: "I don't use the God card. I'm not saying I'm speaking for Jesus here. But if people see the Dominicans and the Jesuits on a shareholder resolution, they're going to say, 'These are people with some credibility.'"

General Electric's Reaction

Such involvement from the religiously motivated shareholders has not always been welcomed. In one example, the *Chicago Tribune* reproduced part of an exchange originally published in *Harper's* between Sister Daly and then General Electric (GE) CEO Jack Welch during the 1998 GE shareholders' meeting. For years, Sister Daly and her colleagues had lobbied for GE to clean up the polychlorinated biphenyl (PCB) contamination it had caused in the Hudson River and other plant locations.

According to the *Tribune*'s recounting, Daly compared GE's denials of the harms caused by PCB to those of the CEOs of tobacco companies who had testified that cigarettes were not harmful.

Mr. Welch replied: "That is an outrageous comparison . . . "

Daly: "Mr. Welch, I am sorry, but we need to have the independent scientific community decide this, not the GE scientific community."

Welch replied: "Twenty-seven studies, twenty-one of them independent, have concluded there is no correlation. . . . You have to stop this conversation. You owe it to God to be on the side of truth here."

Yet in 2006, after 10 years of shareholder resolutions introduced by the Tri-State Coalition, GE did disclose the $800 million it had spent on PCB-related matters from 1990–2005 cleaning up three sites, some $122 million spent on public relations and lobbying, $2.1 million on governmental relations, and $86.6 million in legal costs. An ICCR release quoted New York Attorney General Elliot Spitzer: "I applaud Sister Pat Daly and the Tri-State Coalition for Responsible Investment for their efforts to obtain full disclosure from GE."

Other Results

Some other examples of Sister Daly's and her group's successes:

- In December 2006, a group of auto industry companies including Ford, General Motors, Johnson Controls, DaimlerChrysler, Exel, Honda North America, and Yazaki announced they would collaborate to improve the working conditions for those employed by their suppliers. ICCR had promoted this for more than five years.
- In May 2008, Ford announced that it would become the first U.S. auto company to reduce by at least 30 percent the greenhouse gas emissions from its vehicle fleet. The Sisters of St. Dominic and 14 other members of the Interfaith Center had filed the shareholder resolution. In a May 27, 2008, ICCR release, Sister Daly said: "Ford has set the bar at a high level for the auto industry. It has done the hard work of scenario planning and developing models to insure future profitability and reduced emissions." She called on General Motors to follow suit. Her group and other supporters filed a similar resolution to be considered by shareholders at the 2008 General Motors annual meeting.

During a May 2, 2006, presentation on environmental stewardship for the Center for American Progress, Sister Daly acknowledged that many within corporations share her group's priorities and concerns:

> Some of the work over the years—I think it appears that some of the faith communities have attempted to demonize some of the corporations. I think especially on this issue, and in many others, once we actually get in the door, it's truly an honor to work with people who come at these concerns, not just for the business health of that company, but [who]are really driven by many, many other values and are committed to working within the corporation to bring about a really new day—that this company will be responsible and will contribute to sustainability as we look to the future.

And Sister Daly, her coalition and many others will continue to press for that type of investor–management partnership.

Questions for Reflection

1. Why would corporations encourage all shareholders to be actively involved? Why might they discourage such involvement?
2. What communication tools and practices would help activist shareholders be effective? How might they attract media coverage?
3. Evaluate the practice of the coalitions described in this case. What advantages and risks are present when an individual or group joins with others of similar interests?
4. Do shareholders bear ethical or moral responsibility for the actions of corporations in which they own stock?

Information for this case was drawn from the following: the Web sites of the Tri-State Coalition for Responsible Investment at www.tricri.org and The Interfaith Center on Corporate Responsibility at www.incr.com; The Center for American Progress (May 2, 2006). Climate and culture: religious perspectives on environmental stewardship. http://www.americanprogress.org/events/2006/05/02/16402/climate-culture/; Copeland, James. R. (2014). *2014 Proxy Season Midterm Report.* Proxy Monitor 2 Center for Legal Policy of the Manhattan Institute. http://www.proxymonitor.org/Forms/pmr_08.aspx; Copeland, James R., Feyman, Yevgeniy, & O'Keefe, Margaret. (November 2012). *Proxy Monitor 2012.* Center for Legal Policy of the Manhattan Institute. http://www.proxymonitor.org.pdf/pmr_04.pdf; Dougherty, G. (June 12, 2005). Face of faith-based investors a nun CEOs are recognizing. *Chicago Tribune*, Business p. 1; Hannum, Kristen. (December 2011). Sister Pat battles the board: How women religious are protecting consumers. *U.S. Catholic,* 76, 12, 18–22; ICCR (May 28, 2008). After Ford takes historic step, GM faces shareholder vote next week seeking a comparable plan for a major cut in greenhouse gas emissions.

Release. www.iccr.org/news/press_releases/2008/pr_gm05.27.08.htm; ICCR (December 4, 2006). Faith-based investors applaud the automotive industry's collaborative project to advance workplace human rights. Release. PR Newswire. www.prnewswire.com; Investrend (January 11, 2006). Religious shareholders force GE to disclose millions spent to delay PCB cleanups. M2 Financial Wire. www.m2.com; Jarvis, Brooke. (October 14, 2013). Shareholder activism is becoming an increasingly common form of encouraging companies to adopt environmentally friendly practices, and it's yielding real results. Ensia Online. http://ensia.com/features/putting-stock-in-sustainability/; McDermott, S. (April 30, 2014). ICCR and Tri-CRI proudly honor Sr. Patrick Daly, 2014 winner of the Ceres-Trillium Joan Bavaria Award. ICCR release. http://www.iccr.org/iccr-and-tri-cri-proudly-honor-sr-patricia-daly-2014-winner-ceres-trillium-joan-bavaria-award; McGregor, J. (June 11, 2007). Activist investors get more respect. *Business Week*. www.businesweek.com; Slater, D. (August 12, 2007). Resolved: public corporations shall take us seriously. *The New York Times*. www.nytimes.com; Wray, R. (February 5, 2007). God and mammon on her side. *The Guardian*. www.guardian.co.uk/business.

CASE 20: APPLE CEO CHALLENGES CLIMATE CHANGE OPPONENTS TO DIVEST STOCK

Figure 6.1 Apple CEO Tim Cook speaks in San Jose, California, during an October 2012 event announcing the upcoming release of new products. (AP Photo: Marcio Jose Sanchez.)

"We lost one of the most influential thinkers, creators and entrepreneurs of all time," said News Corp. CEO Rupert Murdoch, reacting to the death of the Apple CEO. "Steve Jobs was simply the greatest CEO of his generation. While I am deeply saddened by his passing, I am reminded of the stunning impact he had in revolutionizing the way people consume media and entertainment." Time Warner Chief Jeff Bewkes said Jobs would be remembered for a thousand years.

Cook Replaces Apple's Iconic CEO

If tributes reflect impact, Steve Jobs certainly made an impression on culture. But for Apple investors, new CEO Tim Cook's impact could be equally or more important. The son of a shipyard worker in Mobile, Alabama, industrial engineer turned tech executive Tim Cook landed on *Time* magazine's 2012 "Most Influential People" list less than a year after his permanent appointment as CEO of Apple, Inc. Former U.S. Vice President Al Gore penned the article that appeared in *Time*. The two men have a deep concern for climate change in common.

Former Apple CEO Steve Jobs handpicked Cook as his stand-in amid three illness-related hiatuses. When Cook rose to the CEO position as Jobs' permanent replacement, investors supported him as a well-known commodity. In fact, the stock hit an all-time high in 2012 with the release of the iPhone 5. However, since that release, shareholders seem to have got bored with their new leader. Cook didn't have a hook—no famous black turtleneck, no famous "one more thing" transition before lowering the boom on the "wow" factor of a new product release. That's no small factor when other tech companies like Google and Samsung have tapped into lower priced and comparable devices.

But while Cook may lack the famed stage presence of Jobs, he cut his teeth as the senior vice president of operations in the company and was key to millions in profits due to his innovations in operations management. Cook also differs in other important ways. He is willing to concede the spotlight. Senior Vice President of Software Engineering Craig Ferderighl has emerged as an effusive speaker who is at the very least as engaging as Jobs, if not a more self-effacing, humorous, and softer product introducer.

A "Better" Earth Day

Cook's strong suit seems to be in the business end of Apple, Inc. He is reportedly well liked by employees, as he possesses a "Southern Cool" about him. And, while Jobs was once reported as saying charity is a waste of time, Cook has a heart for causes, particularly issues of sustainability. Cook proved it with a 2014 Earth Day video release titled "Better." In the video, a voice-over by Cook describes Apple's goal as making the world better than the company found it. The script for the video says:

> Better. It is a powerful word. And a powerful idea. It makes us look at the world and want more than anything to change it for the better. To innovate. Improve. To reinvent. To make it better. It is in our DNA. And better can't be better if it doesn't consider everything. Our products. Our values. An even stronger commitment to the environment of the future. To use greener materials. Less packaging. To do everything we can to keep our products out of landfills. Changes that will benefit people as well as the planet. To us, better is a force of nature. It drives us to build things we never imagined. New data centers powered by the sun and wind. A new manufacturing facility that runs on 100% clean energy. And new product designs that make use of recycled materials. All ways to reduce our impact on the environment. We have a long way to go. And a lot to learn. But now more than ever we will work to leave the world better than we found it and make the tools that will inspire others to do the same.

Shortly after the video appeared on Apple's homepage, Greenpeace International, a non-governmental environmental organization, issued a news release praising Cook and Apple for its ambitious sustainable goals. The release said:

> Cook's ambition deserves extra attention though. Under his tenure as CEO, Apple has been the most aggressive and innovative of any company that's set a 100% goal, and according to Clicking Clean, is the only company currently achieving it, having tapped wind energy in California and Oregon, solar energy in North Carolina and Nevada, and sustainable micro-hydropower in Oregon.

Some Shareholders Cool to Climate Change Concerns

Greenpeace's efforts to help promote Cook's sustainable program were in response to a highly publicized feud that broke out at a March 2014 shareholders meeting. The incident occurred when an investor group, National Center for Public Policy Research (NCPPR), asked Cook in the meeting "to refrain from putting money in green energy projects that were not profitable." The reportedly mild-mannered Cook became visibly angry, according to witnesses.

Technology writer Brian Chaffin said it was the only time he had ever seen Cook angry. He also said the usually levelheaded Cook spoke in rapid-fire sentences. He challenged the investor group, saying if they wanted him only to do things for a return on the investment, they should dump their Apple stock. He added he thought people and the environment were more important than pure profit, saying, "When we work on making our devices accessible to the blind, I don't consider bloody return on investment."

NCPPR proposed that Apple should report the complete costs of the sustainable programs in which it invested and be more transparent about its participation in "certain trade associations and business organizations promoting the amorphous concept of environmental sustainability." The majority of the shareholders voted against the proposal, with only 2.95 percent of shareholders voting in favor of it.

Balancing Profitability with Responsibility

Some contemporary business models, like Apple's, call for efficient supply chain management and a "customer ecosystem" that breed consumer loyalty, meaning they will pay a premium for a product that comes with that ecosystem. The business model supports long-term profitability even if it results in some sacrifices in short-term profitability. More traditional management models extol short-term profitability. Balancing the tensions among the concerns of investors poses a challenge for management, even at corporations with brands and profits as strong as Apple's.

Perhaps reflecting this reality, an investor once asked Cook's well known and sometimes over-confident predecessor what kept him up at night.

"Shareholder meetings," Jobs replied.

Questions for Reflection

1. How do companies build trust differently with investors than they do with consumers?
2. How do you think Tim Cook's publicized rant played with consumers?
3. Why was NCPPR's proposal so soundly defeated?
4. Is there ever a good time for corporate officials to be angry publicly? If so, why and when?
5. Was the "Better" video's audience meant to be investors or consumers? Why?

Information drawn from Apple investors back management as growth falters. (March 1, 2014). National Post's Financial Post and FP Investing (Canada), retrieved from http://www.financialpost.com/index.html; "Better" (April 21, 2014). Apple YouTube channel; Bloomberg News (August 26, 2011). A mixed bag when CEOs step down; Apple investors nervous about a Job-less future. Windsor Star (Ontario). Retrieved from www.lexisnexis.com/hottopics/lnacademic; Denning, S. (March 7, 2014). Why Tim Cook doesn't care about "the Bloody ROI." www.forbes.com; Ellatheriou-Smith, L. (March 3, 2014). Dear climate-change deniers, please don't buy shares in Apple, says green chief Cook. *The Independent* (London). Retrieved from www.lexisnexis.com/hottopics/

lnacademic; Goldsmith, J. (October 7, 2011) Tributes reflect impact. Daily Variety. Retrieved from www.lexisnexis.com/hottopics/lnacademic; Gore, A (April 8, 2012). The world's 100 most influential people 2012: Tim Cook, CEO. http://content.time.com/time/specials/packages/article/0,28804,2111975_2111976_2112101,00.html; Greenpeace International press release (April 27, 2014). Washington: Apple's Tim Cook sets the bar for corporate climate leadership. Plus Media Solutions. Retrieved from www.lexisnexis.com/hottopics/lnacademic; Santoriano, A., & Burrows, P. (October 9, 2011). New boss has big shoes to fill at Apple. *The Calgary Herald*, retrieved from www.lexisnexis.com/hottopics/lnacademic.

CASE 21: HEWLETT-PACKARD'S BOARD OF DIRECTORS SEEKS TO CORRECT GOVERNANCE PROBLEMS

Hewlett-Packard (HP), the world's largest technology company, offers printing, personal computing, software, services, and IT infrastructure to its clients, seeking, according to its corporate profile, to create "seamless, secure, context-aware experiences for a connected world." But internal governance has been less than seamless in recent years as internal scandals and rapid turnovers in executive leadership have caused the corporation and its board of directors to face media scrutiny and investor questions about its direction and leadership.

HP Investigates Press Leaks

Leaks from HP's board of directors' meetings led to a 2006 investigation of the private phone records of board members, two employees—including its corporate spokesman—and nine journalists, including at least one reporter from *The New York Times*, three from *CNET*, two at *The Wall Street Journal*, and three at *Business Week*. The investigation also resulted in the resignation of two members of the board of directors and its chair.

The HP investigation was prompted when an article posted on CNET, a technology news Web site, offered information about a HP board meeting that could only have come from someone at the meeting. The Associated Press said the offensive information was the quote, "By the time the lectures were done at 10 p.m., we were pooped and went to bed," describing a meeting of HP directors at a spa in California.

HP had experienced some difficult issues that had garnered a great deal of media scrutiny. In 2002, a merger with Compaq Computer had involved eight months of contentious shareholder debate, and the 2005 resignation of Chairman and CEO Carly Fiorina, who acknowledged differences with the board had influenced her decision, suggested continuing problems.

Perhaps that is why the chair of the HP board, Patricia C. Dunn, then ordered an investigation. She hired an outside firm to look into where the leaks were coming from—and to whom the information was being leaked. The firm she hired employed outside investigators who apparently engaged in a practice known as "pretexting" to get access to private phone records as part of the search.

"Pretexting" occurs when someone finds personal information online or by other means and then uses it to pretend to be the person in order to access other personal accounts. For example, someone might use Social Security numbers to access phone or bank records. It is against federal law to "pretext" in order to obtain financial information, and the Federal Trade Commission (FTC) and the Justice Department say it is illegal to use "pretexting" to obtain phone records.

The investigation pointed to board member George A. Keyworth II, who was the longest-serving board member. Results of the investigation were revealed at a board meeting; Keyworth was then asked to resign and would not. Another board member, Thomas J. Perkins, did resign immediately because he objected to the way the investigation had been conducted and his fellow board members had been treated.

Perkins then conducted his own investigation with AT&T, which confirmed that his phone records had been disclosed to a third party who had used the last four digits of his Social Security number in January. Perkins then requested that the FTC, Federal Communication Commission (FCC), and Justice Department investigate the surveillance of the directors. He insisted the corporation reveal to the SEC that he had resigned in disagreement, which is required by law, which eventually led to the public disclosure of the investigation and its methods.

Keyworth resigned from the board in September.

The Investigation is Investigated

On September 6, HP did disclose to the SEC that it had hired an outside consultant who had used "pretexting" as part of the probe and that the California attorney general was investigating the techniques used.

On September 12, *Business Week* reported, HP issued a statement explaining that it did believe that director Keyworth's discussions with the CNET reporter had been intended to further HP's interests, as Keyworth had maintained. Keyworth had apparently often been asked by the public relations staff to meet with reporters on behalf of the corporation.

The next day, responding to the controversy, board chair Dunn sent a message to all of HP's employees. According to Associated Press reports, she told them: "I extend my sincere apologies to those individuals who have been affected. What happened here is contrary to HP's values and business practices. And for that I will always be deeply sorry."

The House Energy and Commerce Committee held hearings about the matter in September 2007. The 10 witnesses from HP who were asked to appear didn't testify, citing a Fifth Amendment right against self-incrimination. According to the *Philadelphia Inquirer*, the committee did release documents that indicated the investigation cost HP about $325,000, with more than $51,000 used to have personal phone records checked. Background checks on HP's media-relations department cost $6,435.

Media Respond to the Investigation

The New York Times responded to news of the investigation in a statement from attorney David McCraw. In the September 8, 2006, edition of the paper, he stated:

> We are deeply concerned by reports that the rights of one of our reporters were violated. . . . We expect as an initial step that H.P. will make a prompt and full disclosure of what took place in regards to our reporter.

In the same *Times* story, CNET spokesperson Susan Cain stated, "These actions not only violated the privacy rights of our employee, but also the rights of all reporters to protect their confidential sources."

Corporate spokesperson Michael Moeller told *The New York Times*, "H.P. is dismayed that the phone records of journalists were accessed without their knowledge."

At a news conference held September 22, CEO Mark Hurd said, "I extend my sincerest apologies to those journalists who were investigated and to everyone who was impacted."

Consequences of the Investigation

Dunn resigned as chair of the board of directors and was replaced by CEO Hurd.

Felony indictments were filed in October 2006 by California's attorney general against Dunn, a former senior lawyer at HP, and three consultant investigators who had worked on the case for HP. Four charges were included: identity theft; unauthorized access to computer data; using of false or fraudulent pretenses to obtain confidential information from a public utility; and conspiracy to commit each of these. The charges against Dunn were dismissed in March 2007, and the judge in the case ruled that charges against the others would be dismissed if they completed community service and made any restitution required by September 12.

A civil suit filed by the state was settled, and HP paid $14.5 million in fines and agreed to other changes in practice.

In February 2008, *The New York Times* and three *Business Week* journalists agreed to a financial settlement with HP. Terms were not disclosed. *The New York Times* donated money from the settlement to several journalism groups, including the Center for Investigative Reporting and the Investigative Journalism Program at the University of California, Berkeley.

Turnover Continues

Then in August 2010, CEO Mark Hurd resigned, according to a corporate release, because of violations of the corporate Standard of Business Conduct uncovered during an investigation "surrounding a claim of sexual harassment against Hurd and HP by a former contractor to HP" in which no violation of the harassment policy was found. In the release, Hurd said:

> As the investigation progressed, I realized there were instances in which I did not live up to the standards and principles of trust, respect and integrity that I have espoused at HP and which have guided me throughout my career. After a number of discussions with members of the board, I will move aside and the board will search for new leadership. This is a painful decision for me to make after five years at HP, but I believe it would be difficult for me to continue as an effective leader at HP and I believe this is the only decision the board and I could make at this time.

Léo Apotheker was then hired to run the corporation, but his tenure was brief. *The New York Times* reported that he had been hired without actually being interviewed by many members of the board.

A New CEO Takes Over

In September 2011, Meg Whitman was hired as the president and CEO. Whitman had joined the HP board of directors earlier in the year. Before losing the 2010 election as the Republican candidate to become the California governor, she had served as CEO at eBay. Before that, Whitman had been an executive at Hasbro, FTD Inc., the Stride Rite Corp., Disney, and Bain & Co.

After taking over the corporation, Whitman led the company through restructuring and development. In a statement on the corporate Web site (http://www8.hp.com/us/en/hp-information/index.html), Whitman said: "We are in a multi-year journey to turn HP around, and we have put in place a plan to restore HP to growth. We know where we need to go, and we're making progress."

In April 2013, the board chair stepped down and an interim chair, Ralph Whitworth, was elected. Whitman was named chair of the board of directors in July 2014 after Whitworth resigned due to health concerns. In the news release announcing the appointment, Gary Reiner, the chair of the board's nominating, governance, and social responsibility committee, said, "Meg has been an outstanding leader since coming to HP, and we believe that as chairman she can most effectively drive the turnaround and continue to build value for our shareholders." Writing in the July 17, 2014, *Wall Street Journal*, Lauren Pollock concluded, "Indeed, the company has stayed out of the headlines as she has attempted to remake it as a software and services powerhouse, while paying down debts racked up by her predecessor."

Questions for Reflection

1. Actions taken by the HP board of directors have received a great deal of media attention, much of it negative. What advice would you have offered public relations strategists at HP about how to counter the media scrutiny? What advice would you have offered the investor relations strategists?
2. Relationships between directors and corporate executives should ideally be based on mutual trust and respect. How does the combined role of Whitman as CEO and board chair affect the communication and trust among these groups at HP? What advice would you offer Whitman in how to strengthen these aspects?
3. This case illustrates the sometimes contentious relationships between reporters and the businesses they cover. How should HP seek to repair relationships with the media in the aftermath of this incident?
4. HP also chose to investigate two of its public relations employees to see if they were the source of the leaks. What impact do you think such an investigation might have on internal relations at the corporation?
5. Media leaks can become problematic for corporations and other organizations. To what length should businesses go to uncover leaks within their organizations? What legal and ethical tactics and strategies might be taken within organizations to prevent such leaks from occurring?

Information for this case was drawn from Anders, George. (May 22, 2013). Meg Whitman jolts HP as its reluctant savior. *Forbes*. http://www.forbes.com/sites/georgeanders/2013/05/22/meg-whitman-jolts-hp-as-its-reluctant-savior/; Associated Press. (September 6, 2006). Hewlett-Packard says California attorney general investigating board leak probe. Associated Press Worldstream; Darlin, D. (October 5, 2006). Ex-head of HP is charged in spying case. *International Herald Tribune*, 1; Darlin, D. (September 8, 2006). Hewlett-Packard spied on writers in leaks. *The New York Times.* www.nytimes.com; Darlin, D. (September 7, 2006). Leak, inquiry and resignation rick a boardroom. *The New York Times.* www.nytimes.com; Guglielmo, C. (October 4, 2006). HP paid $325,000 to spy on its directors. *The Philadelphia Inquirer*, C3; Hardy, Quentin. (April 4, 2013). H.P. chairman steps down as 2 resign from board. *The New York Times.* http://www.nytimes.com/2013/04/05/technology/hewlett-packard-chairman-steps-down.html?_r=0h; Hardy, Quentin. (July 18, 2014). Now it's really Meg Whitman's H.P. *The New York Times.* p. B2; HP. (July 17, 2014). HP announces changes to its board of directors. http://www8.hp.com/us/en/hp-news/press-release.html?id=1736941#.U_GhAfldWAU; HP. (August 6, 2010). HP CEO Mark Hurd resigns; CFO Cathie Lesjak appointed interim CEO; HP announces preliminary results and raises full-year outlook. Release. http://h30261.www3.hp.com/phoenix.zhtml?c=71087&p=irolnewsArticle&id=1457795&jumpid=reg_r1002_usen_c-001_title_r0001; Kaplan, D.A. (October 15, 2007). HP may face civil charges. *Newsweek.* www.newswe ek.com/id/45239/; Kaplan, D.A. (August 21, 2007). Intrigue in high places. *Newsweek.* www.newsweek.com/id/37886/; Kaplan, D.A. (August 21, 2007). A playbook for the HP hearings. *Newsweek.* www.newsweek.com/id/37880/; Konrad, R. (September 6, 2006). HP probing directors' phone records to investigate leaky source. Associated Press Financial Wire; LaMonica, M. (February 9, 2005). Fiorina steps down at HP. CNET News. news.cnet.com; Lawton, C., Searcey, D., & Young, S. (September 7, 2006). H-P faces probe over handling of board leaks. *The Wall Street Journal*, A1, A18; Pollock, Lauren. (July 17, 2014). HP's Whitman to add chairman's title. *The Wall Street Journal.* http://online.wsj.com/articles/h-ps-whitman-to-add-chairman-title-1405628514; Richtel, M. (February 14, 2008). Hewlett-Packard settles spying case. *The New York Times.* www.nytimes.com; Robertson, J. (September 22, 2006). CEO expected to address leak probe as HP stock falters. Associated Press Worldstream; Robertson, J. (September 22, 2006). HP chair resigns amid fallout from boardroom leak probe, succeeded by CEO Hurd. Associated Press Worldstream; Steward, James B. (September 21, 2011). Voting to hire a chief without meeting him. *The New York Times.* http://www.nytimes.com/2011/09/22/business/voting-to-hire-a-chief-without-meeting-him.html?_r=0; Sandovel, G. (October 9, 2006). Dunn, Fiorina lash out at HP board. CNET News. news.cnet.com; Woellert, L. (September 25, 2006). HP's most trustworthy man; e-mails obtained by Business Week show that George Keyworth was considered a key part of Hewlett-Packard's media relations team. Business Week Online. www.businessweek.com/technology/content/sep2006/tc20060926_264939.htm

CASE 22: PHONY NEWS RELEASE LEADS TO ARREST

Original Case Written by Larry F. Lamb

The evening shift at Internet Wire in Los Angeles gave routine handling to a request from Porter and Smith PR for distribution of an Emulex Corporation news release. The e-mail message from Ross Porter, with release attached, asked for distribution the following day, Friday, August 25, 2000, at 9:30 a.m. EDT.

Porter's e-mail message used jargon, such as "please bill me as the first release out of the 10 pack," that was familiar to Internet Wire staffers and led them to accept its authenticity. Accordingly, they prepared the release for transmission to the thousands of news organizations and financial analysts reached by Internet Wire.

False Content Affects Values

Although the distribution request itself appeared routine, the content of the news release was anything but. It announced that:

- Emulex was revising downward the earnings figures issued earlier in the month.
- The SEC was investigating the company's accounting practices.
- Paul Folino, the Emulex CEO, was leaving.

As predetermined, Internet Wire dispatched the release as stock markets in New York City were opening Friday, and it was soon picked up and passed along by reputable financial news outlets such as Bloomberg News and the CNBC television channel. The price of Emulex common shares, which had closed the previous day at $113.06 on the Nasdaq Stock Market, began slipping, slowly at first and then with gathering speed after Bloomberg published its first headline at 10:13 a.m. EDT. Soon, the news was mentioned on CNBC, Dow Jones News Service, the CBS Marketwatch Web site, and others.

Back at Emulex headquarters in Costa Mesa, California, executives had begun arriving for work about 7 a.m. PDT and were stunned by the plunging share price. The company's recent financial results had been exceptional, and its outlook was promising. Emulex described itself in 2000 as "the world's largest supplier of fibre channel host adapters," devices used by equipment makers such as HP and IBM in networking applications. In an earnings news release issued August 3, Emulex had trumpeted record levels of revenues and earnings for the company's most recent quarter and reported revenues of $140 million and net income of $33 million for fiscal year 2000, which ended July 2. Emulex CEO Paul Folino indicated that Emulex was well positioned to benefit from growth.

Trading Halted

Like others at the company, Mr. Folino was shocked to hear about the stock's nosedive when he walked into his office shortly after 7 a.m. Friday and began trying to figure out what could account for it. He soon heard about the news release on Internet Wire and realized that the company was the victim of a cruel hoax. Promptly, he asked authorities at Nasdaq to halt trading in Emulex and protect investors from further effects of the fraud.

In the 16 minutes before Nasdaq suspended Emulex trades at 10:29 a.m. EDT, the price of a common share had plunged to a bottom of $43. Investors who sold shares that morning lost almost $110 million and had little hope of recovering it.

Once trading was suspended, Mr. Folino and others went to work on a news release explaining what had happened and refuting the claims contained in the false release. The rebuttal circulated widely across the Internet and financial news wires, and Nasdaq reopened trading at 1:30 p.m. EDT. By the end of the day, the stock had climbed to $105.75 a share.

Although the stock snapped back quickly, questions lingered about the performance of financial news organizations and their rush to publish without independent verification. At Bloomberg News, an editor said that standard practice calls for a reporter to check with a company before writing a story, but the protocol was skipped in this instance. A Dow Jones News Service editor said that his organization trusts the verification process of electronic-release distribution services, such as Business Wire and PR Newswire, and had received assurances that Internet Wire used a similar procedure.

From the moment the fraud was discovered, Emulex management had wondered who the culprit was and why he or she had done it. Authorities quickly determined that Ross Porter, author of the e-mail that conveyed the false release to Internet Wire, was fictitious, as was the Porter and Smith PR firm. They suspected that someone with inside knowledge of Internet Wire had concocted the hoax to drive down the price of Emulex shares. A drop in price could benefit an investor who had sold Emulex short.

Short Sellers Expect Bad News to Be Good

In investing, most people expect to benefit when good news causes a company's stock price to rise. However, some investors—short sellers—benefit when bad news causes a stock to drop in price. Here's how: a short seller anticipates, presumably for good reasons, that the price of a certain stock is too high and will fall below current levels. Using a brokerage firm's services, he or she *borrows* shares from a stockowner and sells them to other investors at the current price. The short seller expects to purchase shares after the price has fallen, replace the borrowed shares, and pocket the difference between the current and future (presumably lower) price.

The practice involves the risk of losing money—potentially a lot of money—if the share price goes up instead of down and the short seller must purchase pricier shares to replace the ones that he or she borrowed and sold.

Investigators Get a Lead

To solve the Emulex mystery, law enforcement authorities began looking for someone who knew Internet Wire's operating procedures and also had been involved in trading Emulex shares. They asked if any employees had recently quit the public relations wire service and were told that Mark Simeon Jakob, a 23-year-old man from El Segundo, California, had left on good terms about a week earlier. From separate sources, they learned that Mr. Jakob had been involved in short selling 3,000 Emulex shares on August 17 and 18, expecting the price to drop below $81 a share.

Mr. Jakob had studied during the summer at El Camino College in Torrance, a two-year institution not far from his home. Soon after classes ended, he quit his Internet Wire job and went on vacation, registering Wednesday, August 23, at the Luxor Resort & Casino in Las Vegas for a three-day stay.

The Luxor is a gambling palace that envelops guests in opulence and fantasy. A 10-story sphinx, taller than Egypt's original, towers above the entrance. The hotel is a 350-foot-high pyramid encased in glass the color of onyx, and the casino floor covers almost three acres.

While Mr. Jakob was enjoying what the hotel described as "accommodations and amenities worthy of Queen Nefertiti herself," Emulex began trading above $100 per share, far more than the $81 price that prevailed when Mr. Jakob borrowed 3,000 shares. On Thursday, the young man's brokerage firm issued a $20,000 margin call, requiring him to place that amount of cash into his account to partially cover the increased value of the shares he had borrowed and sold but had not yet replaced. With Emulex trading above $113 per share, Mr. Jakob faced a potential loss of $97,000 on his short sale if the stock did not come down.

After receiving the margin call, he flew back to Los Angeles and drove to the Library Media Technology Center at El Camino College, though he was no longer a student there. He used the library's computers to draft the fake Emulex news release and open a Yahoo! e-mail account under the name of the fictitious Porter and Smith PR agency. As Ross Porter, he sent the damaging release to Internet Wire, climbed into his car, and drove back to Las Vegas.

Timing is Everything

At Internet Wire, the staff accepted "Porter's" apparent authority and assumed the release had been verified. Using normal procedures, they readied it for distribution.

Internet Wire had been incorporated in 1999, evolving from a similar service started five years earlier. It has emphasized its pricing advantage in competing with the established giants of the electronic-release distribution business, PR Newswire and Business Wire. All three services offer publicly held companies a convenient and dependable mechanism for providing timely and fair disclosure of important news, as required by the SEC.

When a company plans to announce news that might affect an investor's decision on buying or selling its stock, it often provides the release to a service such as Internet Wire a few hours in advance, with instructions to distribute it when notified or, alternatively, at a specific time. Companies often prefer to issue major news outside regular trading hours of the major stock exchanges to give investors time to digest it before acting, sending it either after the market closes for the day or well before it opens in the morning. The Nasdaq Stock Market and New York Stock Exchange, for example, both are open from 9:30 a.m. to 4 p.m. on weekdays.

On Friday morning after the fake Emulex release went out, Mr. Jakob checked financial news sites on the Internet and saw that his plot was succeeding. His release had been used by major news services like CNBC, and the price of Emulex stock was slipping. Using his online brokerage account, he covered his short sales by purchasing 3,000 shares at about $62 per share to replace those he borrowed when the price was around $81. Far from facing a $97,000 loss, he made a profit of about $54,000.

When the price continued downward, Mr. Jakob purchased another 3,500 shares of Emulex for an average near $52, expecting the price would climb again when the hoax was discovered—as it did. He sold these additional shares on Monday at a profit exceeding $186,000.

An Arrest is Made

An investigation by the FBI, SEC, and U.S. Attorney's office identified Mr. Jakob in a matter of days, and he was arrested on Thursday, August 31. He pleaded guilty four months later to two counts of securities fraud and one count of wire fraud and was sentenced in August 2001 to 44 months in federal prison.

The day before Mr. Jakob's arrest, *The New York Times* scolded Internet Wire, the financial news media, Emulex, and the Nasdaq in an editorial headlined "Caveat Investors":

> Internet Wire has called the perpetrator a "very sophisticated criminal." But in truth, the low-cost service and several reputable media organizations dropped the ball; this criminal could have been thwarted with a single phone call. Emulex and the Nasdaq can also be faulted for not reacting more quickly to events. Surely in this day and age investors should not lose billions to fraud simply because California is in a different time zone.

In 2003, Internet Wire changed its name to Market Wire.

A Later Twitter Hoax Shocks the Market

A tweet supposedly issued by the Associated Press just after 1 p.m. in the afternoon on April 23, 2013, reported that there had been two explosions in the White House, injuring President Barack Obama. Within seconds of the report, the Dow Jones average dropped 145 points. The Associated Press quickly sent out messages disavowing the hacked tweet, and the market soon recovered from the sell-off. *The Wall Street Journal* reported that the faked Associated Press tweet was apparently sent by a group of Syrian hackers. The SEC investigated the incident.

Questions for Reflection

1. Internet Wire faced the challenge of restoring customer trust in its distribution services. What steps would you recommend to rebuild confidence?
2. Though Emulex was an innocent victim of this fraud, were there any precautions that the company might have adopted to prevent or minimize this situation?
3. The Dow Jones News Service said that it has relied on the verification procedures of distribution companies like PR Newswire and Internet Wire to confirm the authenticity of new releases. Do you agree that news organizations have no obligation to check further? How much responsibility do news organizations have to protect themselves from hackers?

Information for this case was drawn from the Emulex Web site at http://www.emulex.com/corp/index.html, and Market Wire Web site at http://www.marketwire.com/mw/corp_co_overview; (August 30, 2000). Caveat investors. *The New York Times*, p. A22; (August 8, 2001). Defendant in Emulex hoax sentenced. U.S. SEC news release; (September 11, 2000). Emulex's swift IR limits bogus release damage. *Investor Relations Business*, p. 1; Ewing, T., Rose, M., Rundle, R., & Fields, G. (September 1, 2000). E-mail trail leads to Emulex hoax suspect, *The Wall Street Journal*, p. C1; Ewing, T., Waldman, P., & Rose, M. (August 28, 2000). Bogus report sends Emulex on a wild ride.

The Wall Street Journal, p. C1; Gentile, G. (September 1, 2000). Portrait of a criminal. The Associated Press; Glassman, J. (August 30, 2000). Stock hoax should affirm faith in markets. *The Wall Street Journal*, p. A26; Lauricella, Tom, Stewart, C.S., & Ovide, S. (April 23, 2013). Twitter hoax sparks swift stock swoon. *The Wall Street Journal*. http://online.wsj.com/news/articles/SB100014241278873237356045784412016051934 8. (August 1, 2001). Hoaxer is sentenced to 44 months in jail in Emulex Corp. case. *The Wall Street Journal*, p. A4; Maynard, M. (September 9, 2008). A mistaken news report hurts United. *The New York Times*, C1. Mrozek, T. (August 6, 2001). Man who perpetrated $110 million fraud against Emulex stockholders sentenced to nearly four years in prison. U.S. Department of Justice news release; (August 31, 2000). Stock hoax suspect had motive. Wired News http://www.wired.com.

CASE 23: BASF'S FORMULA FOR EFFECTIVE INVESTOR COMMUNICATION

BASF, the world's leading chemical company, with 112,000 employees and 376 production sites worldwide, has also established itself as an international leader in investor relations. The German corporation's program has received numerous awards: ranked as the best in the industry in 2014 by Institutional Investor Europe and also by winning the 2014 Europe Grand Prix for best overall investor relations—large cap from *IR Magazine*. The investor relations Web site has similarly been recognized for excellence, earning a first rank from Net-Fed in 2013.

IR Team Mixes Innovation and Strength

Success in investor relations at BASF is not just measured by awards, however. In a 2011 interview with *IR Magazine* after winning the magazine's Grand Prix award for the second year in a row, Magdalena Moll, senior vice president for investment relations, pointed to the fundamentals of effective investor relations (IR) practice (available at http://www.businessinsider.com/investor-relations-basf-does-it-right-video-2011-7). First, she said, provide information in a way that makes it as easy to understand as possible. Second, seek to increase transparency. Third, provide investors with ongoing access to top management. Last, look at new technologies and strategize how to use them in the future.

Success comes when investors are attracted to the BASF story. Moll said the annual target goals are established for each IR employee in terms of how often they meet with key investors and how successful they are in helping them see that BASF is an attractive investment.

The IR staff meets each workday at 9 a.m. to discuss key information and activities for the day. A mentoring system pairs newer hires with more established employees. Staff members know the investor base well enough so that if one staff member is traveling, someone else can work with the client as needed. Moll says, "You must be very consistent in implementing what you promise."

Digital Tools Offer Potent Information

The investor relations Web platform offers a plethora of information: fact sheets, reports, stock charts, shareholder meeting information, reports, interviews printed in other media, information about products, news releases, information about the 2020 strategic "roadmap," and handouts from presentations offered at meetings. Sustainability reports are provided. A calendar highlights opportunities for investors to hear from or meet with top management.

Detailed financial data are available through the Web site. Investors can review financial statements, balance sheets, equity and cash flow analyses, and a 10-year financial summary. Tables and charts offer visual representations of corporate value. Most of the financial charts are downloadable as Excel files.

A special section of the Web site is devoted to creditor relations, as BASF also offers the opportunity for investment in bonds. The corporation explains, "BASF is a reliable and valued partner in financial markets. Thereby, cultivating the relationships with our key debt capital investors is an inherent part of our financing strategy."

Investor communication also occurs through an information-packed IR Mobile app and through social media accounts on Twitter, Facebook, LinkedIn, YouTube, and Google+. Shareholders also receive a quarterly electronic magazine and newsletter.

Meetings Allow for Stakeholder Interactions

Beyond the information provided through its Web site, the department helps plan and execute special events. The annual shareholder meeting provides an opportunity for the corporation to offer detailed financial and strategic reports. Invitations to the meeting, legally required financial reports, details of upcoming ballot motions, and keynote speeches must be prepared. Following the meeting, much of the information is made available through the IR Web site.

Other events are also planned and executed. For example, an Investor Day Chemicals was held in London in May 2014. Kurt Boch, the CEO of BASF SE, delivered a keynote that was shared through a webcast, and then he and a member of the board of directors participated in a Q & A session. During the afternoon, investors could attend breakout sessions with presidents of various chemical units. Transcripts and handouts from the day were then made available on the IR Web site.

Questions for Reflection

1. How much knowledge of sound business practices is required for the effective practice of investor relations by public relations professionals?
2. Working in a multinational firm can pose special challenges for practitioners, particularly in financial relations. Identify the key stakeholders BASF must interact with in order to develop mutually beneficial relationships across geographic boundaries.
3. Evaluate the strategies for effective investor relations offered by Ms. Moll. In what ways do they demonstrate best practice?
4. Apart from tracking investors' purchase of shares in a corporation, what other metrics might be used to assess whether an IR program is effective?

Information from this case is drawn from the BASF Web site (http://www.basf.com/group/investor-relations_en/index) and Steward, Neil. (July 13, 2011). Investor relations: BASF does it right. *Business Insider*. http://www.businessinsider.com/investor-relations-basf-does-it-right-video-2011-7#ixzz37v8bNhqX.

PROFESSIONAL INSIGHT How have media changes affected financial communications?

Figure 6.1 Susan Shaffer Guess, Senior Vice President of Marketing, Paducah Bank

Leading the public relations efforts for an organization in the 21st century is significantly different than even as little as a decade ago. The advent of social media and 24-hour news cycles creates a public forum that is both productive and challenging at the same time. The ability to reach your audience at a moment's notice provides for expeditious access to the public. However, the ability for the public to openly compliment *or* criticize your organization without accountability can be a daunting experience. Those of us in public relations must be adept at all times to address the myriad media options that face us on a daily basis.

The responsibility for managing a company's public relations persona is one that touches on virtually every aspect of the business. In the case of financial PR, the position that I hold, it ranges from internal communications with the staff to communications with our board of directors to building a positive relationship with our customers and target market to our reputation in the community at large. In the current global environment, our small town bank can even find itself involved in national and international efforts.

Public relations in the financial services industry is one with serious considerations. People take nothing more seriously than the bank they choose to partner with to build their future and manage their family's financial security. We understand the trust our customers place in us and therefore understand the importance of crafting and disseminating messages that show that we are safe, secure, and respected by our customers, regulators, and our community.

With the introduction of social media, businesses of every type can bring their own personality to those new channels of communications. Our bank chooses to use these media as a way to communicate with customers and our posts have very little to do with products and services. We don't find our followers wanting to learn about a checking account or searching for an article about a home loan when they visit our social media avenues.

They want to know who we are as a company. They want to know if we really care about them and their community. You certainly have to demonstrate competency, but you first have to show you care. And they want you to be fun! Walking into a bank can be a bit intimidating to many, and so breaking down that barrier is important.

We were an early adopter of Facebook and have been recognized as a leader among banks on a national basis. We stand out because we are talking about topics that truly connect the people inside the bank with the people outside in our community.

For example, these are a few of the topics that we have addressed recently.

- Chili fund-raiser dinners for a school custodian who was injured in a tornado.
- Photos of our staff handing out free ice cream from our WOW! Wagon ice cream truck.
- Receptions for local college students home for the summer.
- A project where our staff stuffed food backpacks for at-risk students.
- Fun items like giveaways for hamburgers on National Cheeseburger Day or a gift certificate to the local iHop on National Pancake Day.
- Dog and cat photo contests.
- A bank snowman contest when students were out of school for a snow day.
- A bank-themed Easter egg contest.

The ideas are endless and have very little to do with banking, but have everything to do with bringing us a bit closer together as human beings.

Social media, for our bank, is important, but it is an extension to our other modes of communication and allows us to share stories over and over again. It is important to tie your public relations efforts to all aspects of your marketing efforts and the brand of your company.

Having worked in the field for more than 25 years now, I have learned that every day is a new adventure, that I have so much still to learn, and that there is nowhere I would rather be than a part of the public relations profession.

Susan Guess is the senior vice president of marketing for Paducah Bank. She earned a bachelor of science degree in public relations from Murray State University and a master of public administration from the University of Louisville. She serves on the Murray State University Board of Regents. She and her daughter, Morgan, founded the Guess Anti-Bullying Foundation after Morgan was bullied. She is only the second person to chair the Paducah Area Chamber of Commerce Board twice. The governor awarded her the Kentucky Volunteer Service Award for chairing the Heath High School Memorial Garden after the 1997 school shooting. She also won a national community service award from HUD after starting Girl Scout troops in Paducah's low-income housing neighborhoods.

CHAPTER 7

Stakeholders

Members and Volunteers

Of all stakeholder relationships, those that nonprofit organizations have with members or volunteers may be at the same time the most tenuous and the most necessary. Stakeholders who enter into a relationship with a nonprofit group, whether it is an alumni association, a professional group, or a social service agency, usually have some need or goal that motivates their joining, donating, serving, or attending. Yet that need or goal is usually self-directed, meaning that if it is not satisfied or supported, the individual will find another source for satisfaction or motivation. Similarly, most, if not all, membership- or volunteer-based organizations have needs or goals as well. To address their missions, most often the need is financial, with the organization heavily dependent on donations to maintain activities or services. The need may also be for staffing, where, in essence, the volunteers are functioning as quasi-employees of the organization. Such great pressures may tempt organizations to exploit donors, volunteers, or clients or to forgo truthful disclosure when puffery or evasion may bring quicker returns.

MUTUAL TRUST, NEEDS, AND INTERESTS

The relationships between such organizations and their stakeholders are best maintained when they are founded on mutual trust, built and maintained through meeting mutually recognized needs and interests. Organizations with a clear sense of their mission and an articulation of how the stakeholders are aligned with that mission are the most likely to succeed in building those types of relationships. However, no matter how lofty the expressed mission and purpose statement of an organization may be, the most pertinent factor in determining an ongoing relationship is found in satisfying the donor's, volunteer's, or member's multiple motivations, as well as the overall objectives of the group. For example, donors may be highly sympathetic to the mission an organization has to offer, say, support services for cancer patients in their area. An altruistic desire to help those in need may drive donors to offer financial support.

Yet, donors may also be highly motivated by the need to obtain documentation of their giving so they may use it to reduce income tax liabilities, or they may be motivated by the desire to gain recognition for their donations as when a building or center is named in their honor. Such multiple motivations are to be expected—and indeed encouraged. Individuals are far more likely to continue a costly relationship such as this when they are given multiple incentives or rewards. The public relations pay-off for "catching someone doing good" may also serve as incentive for recruiting others to awareness or activity.

Practitioners may face the challenge of balancing their interactions with members or volunteers who have offered different levels of support to the organization. On a practical note, practitioners will need to develop ways of expressing appreciation for large and small levels of support so that neither group feels slighted, while also maintaining ways for both groups to offer input and feedback. Organizations also are dependent on increased involvement. Donors who may have offered initial small gifts or pledges, for example, may later become major donors or may become active volunteers. Volunteers may become so committed to the service or mission of the organization that they invest not only their time and talents, but also their financial resources. Individuals who find their own involvement to be rewarding will also become great ambassadors for the involvement of their friends or associates. Everyone in such an organization will benefit if the expressed and unexpressed motivations of donors, members, and volunteers are recognized, acknowledged, and authenticated by leadership within the organization.

COMMUNICATING WITH VOLUNTEERS AND MEMBERS

Practitioners are often charged with the details of developing and deepening relationships between members and volunteers and organizations. This may entail the detailed work of maintaining data files with names, addresses, and personal histories. The tracking may also involve recognition, matching levels of involvement with appropriate rewards: receipts, thank you letters, certificates, plaques, T-shirts, pins, invitations, and even planning annual special celebrations.

The task of informing these stakeholders may also fall to the practitioner. Social media sites, print and digital newsletters, direct mail, magazines, Web sites, personal visits, telephone calls, meetings, and special events may all be used by practitioners to ensure that members and volunteers are kept up to date about the activities and accomplishments of the organization. If the relationship is to deepen, such regular and personal contact is vital.

However, it is also critical for the practitioner to devise means for soliciting input from the stakeholders so that it does not appear that they are exploited for the resources they can bring with them to the organization. Such methods may be informal: a Twitter stream throughout a special event, a short digital video delivered through e-mail, personal debriefings after a special project or event, or occasional visits by a representative board. For example, many colleges and universities maintain alumni councils that gather once or twice a year to plan alumni events but also to respond to questions or to ask questions of administrative leaders. The popularity and availability of e-mail and social networking has made it easier for organizations to design links from a Web site for questions or comments to be directed to public relations or management personnel, or for those who are committed to similar causes to link together in an electronic community. A Facebook group of volunteers may provide a great opportunity for personal networking but also for practitioners to gain new perspectives on the opinions, beliefs, and attitudes of those actively participating.

More formal methods for stimulating input and feedback may also be used. Surveys or focus groups may yield important results. In-depth interviews are also helpful in obtaining the opinions and attitudes of stakeholders. Members or volunteers who are empowered to affect change by offering their insights will be far more likely to continue the relationship than those who are not allowed to become part of the strategic enterprise of the organization. However the feedback and/or input is generated, sharing some of that with other members or volunteers underscores the seriousness with which the practitioners and management are considering it. Responding quickly to a posted question or concern or having a question-and-answer period at monthly or quarterly meetings with responses stressed and demonstrated are just some ways that management may demonstrate its commitment to the two-way communication flow.

BALANCING INTERESTS

The relationships are not always positive or easy. Some membership groups become so closely knit that they are not open to newcomers or to input from newcomers. Balancing organizational commitment, which is a positive attribute of these relationships, with a need to maintain openness may demand action from the practitioner. For example, what orientation is offered to newcomers? Involving veterans in that process may help demonstrate the need for inclusion.

Occasionally, some gifts of involvement, time, or money come with implicit or explicit conditions. Practitioners may need to lead management to establish and then publicize policies concerning such gifts and the like before sensitive situations develop.

Policies for recruiting and involving members and volunteers need to be developed to help manage other issues as well. Will volunteers be required to complete specialized training or have a formal background check? The organization may need to establish standards for dependability and performance; even though the volunteer is not an official employee, some method may be needed to ensure that each individual meets the requirements of the various tasks. Legal issues involving liability and privacy should also be addressed. Using the image of a volunteer or member in a publication may require signed consent, for example, and certainly using the image of a nonprofit's client might require such. Membership organizations may need very detailed descriptions as to who qualifies. If there are educational, geographic or accomplishment requirements, for example, they need to be publicized clearly.

Practitioners and their organizations should also have policies that address the ethical and legal concerns of clients or volunteers. For example, how may the service accomplishments of a health care organization be publicized without invading the privacy of clients or patients or their families? In a litigious culture, volunteers or the organization may require specialized education about the legal issues involved in their activities. Agencies that solicit donations for children or other protected groups may need policies regarding volunteer access to knowing the identities or other private information about those in the groups. One temptation in fundraising may be to overly emotionalize those who benefit from the donations. In a nonprofit environment filled with organizations that may all have equally worthy missions and yet must vie against each other for the available time, money, and effort of volunteers and members, practitioners may find the competition so tough that it may be easy to argue that the end justifies the means. However, whether the practitioner is one within a nonprofit organization or one within an agency contemplating charitable pro bono work, ethical practice would be characterized by a commitment to contextually truthful presentation of information that treats donors and the recipients of services with the same levels of dignity and respect.

The cases in this chapter explore the relationships of donors, volunteers, and the nonprofits that depend on their support. Several cases raise issues of law, ethics, and responsibility; others provide examples of public/private partnerships. As you research these cases, ask yourself: What motivates lead members of the public to become involved? Are the nonprofits' relationships with their key stakeholders consistent with their missions? How can these stakeholders work together even more effectively to accomplish their common purposes?

ADDITIONAL READINGS

Austin, Erica W., & Pinkleton, Bruce E. (2015). *Strategic public relations management: Planning and managing effective communication programs.* (3rd ed.) New York: Routledge.

Bonk, Kathy, Tynes, Emily, Griggs, Henry, & Sparks, Phil. (2008). *Strategic communications for nonprofits: A Step-by-Step guide to working with the media.* New York: Jossey-Bass.
Kelly, Kathleen S. (1996). *Effective fund-raising management.* Mahwah, NJ: Lawrence Erlbaum Associates.
Radtke, Janel. (2008). *Strategic communications for nonprofit organizations: Seven steps to creating a successful plan.* New York: Wiley.

CASE 24: DESIGNATED DONATIONS? THE AMERICAN RED CROSS AND THE LIBERTY FUND

September 11, 2001: Virtually every household in the United States and millions across the globe shared in the fear, the anger, the disbelief, and the sorrow resulting from the terrorist attacks on Washington, D.C., and New York City. Many wanted to do something to reach out to the thousands of victims and their families and to offer assistance to those who were actively giving support.

Creation of the Liberty Fund

The American Red Cross quickly responded to the disaster and perhaps just as quickly created the Liberty Fund, a special opportunity for donations that would go to support the aid and recovery efforts. The creation of a special fund was unexpected. Traditionally, when soliciting funds, the Red Cross had asked donors to give to its Disaster Relief Fund where money raised could be used in connection with whatever disasters arose. By the end of October, the Liberty Fund had received $547 million in pledges.

The Associated Press reported that the Red Cross had spent more than $140 million on terrorism-related efforts. Nearly $44 million was used through the Family Gift Program to help cover the costs of housing, food, child care, and other expenses for more than 2,200 affected families in New York and Washington. *The Toronto Star* reported on November 7 that victims' families had received an average of $25,000 for three-months' living expenses from the fund, meaning that only about one-third of the amount raised in the Liberty Fund had gone directly to victims and their families. The Associated Press said about $67 million was spent on immediate disaster-relief needs such as shelter, on-site food, on-site counseling, and other support for victims' families and rescue workers. More than $11.5 million went to blood-donor programs, $14.7 million to nationwide community outreach, and another $2.5 million to indirect support costs.

Too Much Support?

There was just one problem. The Red Cross said all the money in the Liberty Fund would not be required to address the needs. Red Cross CEO

Bernadine Healy reported that $200 million of the fund would be used to support other Red Cross efforts, an announcement that spawned a negative uproar and prompted two Congressional hearings. When donors found out that up to half of the Liberty Fund was going to be used to support other projects, national reaction was swift. Some people felt they had been misled. They had given money believing it would be used to support the victims or the survivors of the disasters, and they wanted the funds to be used in that way.

The uproar led to changes at the Red Cross. Dr. Healy resigned as CEO on October 26, citing differences with the governing board. She was allowed to keep the title of president until the end of 2001.

Harold Decker, who had served as the organization's deputy general counsel since February 2001 and general counsel since September 2001, was named interim CEO in October.

One of his first actions was to announce that as of October 31, the Red Cross would cease soliciting donations for the Liberty Fund. Contributions received from that point on would be added to the group's Disaster Relief Fund unless donors specifically targeted the Liberty Fund for their donations. Accounting firm KPMG was hired to audit the Liberty Fund.

In the November 14, 2001, release announcing the change, Decker said:

> Americans have spoken loudly and clearly that they want our relief efforts directed at the people affected by the September 11 tragedies. We deeply regret that our activities over the past eight weeks have not been as sharply focused as America wants, nor as focused as the victims of this tragedy deserve. The people affected by this terrible tragedy have been our first priority, and beginning today, they will be the only priority of the Liberty Fund.

David T. McLaughlin, chair of the Red Cross Board of Governors, said in the release:

> The people of this country have given the Red Cross their hard-earned dollars, their trust and very clear direction for our September 11 relief efforts. Regrettably, it took us too long to hear their message. Now we must change course to restore the faith of our donors and the trust of Americans and, most importantly, to devote 100 percent of our energy and resources in helping the victims of the terrorist attacks.

Former Senate Majority Leader George Mitchell was named as the "independent overseer" of the fund in January 2002. The former senator had become known for his leadership in the negotiations to foster peace in Ireland and in the Middle East. He was charged with helping to develop a plan for use of the Liberty Fund monies. Mitchell led the group to declare that 90 percent of the $360 million dedicated for victims would be spent by the first anniversary of the attacks, with the remainder to be earmarked for long-term aid.

The Red Cross also created a "Celebrity Cabinet" in February 2002 to promote its work. Celebrities such as actors Jennifer Love Hewitt and Jane Seymour and Mets catcher Mike Piazza were included in the first group.

New guidelines for the Liberty Fund were developed. Families who had members killed or seriously injured in the attacks were to receive financial support through the Family Gift Program for one year, an extension of the initial three-month funding period. The Red Cross said in a November 2001 release.

The remaining needs of the families would be studied, the Red Cross said in a November 2001 release, and some financial support might be offered even longer. In addition, the names of the 25,000 families it had supported would be shared in a database with other relief agencies in an effort to help coordinate relief.

In addition to its decision to extend longer-term help to victims' families, the Red Cross said it would charge operating costs for the Liberty Fund and such services as the toll-free information lines to the interest earned on the fund balance, rather than directly to the fund itself. An additional 200 caseworkers were being hired, and more full-time staff members were moved to the Long-Time Disaster Recovery Unit.

The Red Cross said it expected to spend about $300 million in 2003 to further these efforts, and the remaining $200 million-plus would be held in trust for later help to victims. The Red Cross said it was also contacting the victims of the postal-anthrax attacks and had already given money to the families of three anthrax victims.

The Changes Prompt Praise and Criticism

According to a Red Cross news release on November 14, 2001, the Oversight and Investigations Subcommittee of the U.S. House Energy and Commerce Committee endorsed the Red Cross's decision to use all the Liberty Fund donations to support the needs of people affected by the terrorist attacks. Appearing with the Red Cross officials, Committee chair Rep. James C. Greenwood (R-Pa.) was quoted on National Public Radio's (NPR) *All Things Considered* endorsing the changes. He said this was a "first-rate response" from the group. Other members of the Oversight Committee promised continuing scrutiny. Rep. Bart Stupak (D-Mich.) said the news conference alone was not enough. He told *All*

Things Considered on NPR: "This is really just the beginning of it. We will continue our oversight of the American Red Cross. We'll continue to make sure that donors' intent and wishes are followed through."

Reacting to the controversy, Daniel Borochoff, president of the American Institute of Philanthropy, a charity-watchdog group, told Knight Ridder Washington Bureau reporter Kevin Murphy, on November 15, 2001, that when the Red Cross set up the Liberty Fund, "The message in most people's minds was that 100 percent would go to victims' families and relief work." The earlier decision to use the fund to help support other Red Cross efforts may offer a lesson, however:

> People understand the important role the Red Cross plays in disaster relief, but I think it will lead to some healthy skepticism. It won't be enough for them to say, "give us some money for this disaster." People will want to know how much do you really have, how much do you need, what are you doing with it?

Paul Clolery, editor-in-chief of the *NonProfit Times*, a bimonthly trade paper, told Knight Ridder, "It is the first time I know of that they set up a separate fund, and therein was their huge mistake." Before when they responded to disasters with appeals, "They always couched it in phrases like 'for this and other disasters,' which is the correct way because you never know how much money you are going to need."

Lasting Changes at the Red Cross

Following this controversy, the Red Cross said it would remove references to a specific crisis from its advertising and make a public announcement at the point when it had received enough money to cover a relief effort. NPR reported in June 2002 that a system for double-checking to ensure designated gifts are used where the donor intended would also be instituted. According to a June story in the *Atlanta Journal-Constitution*, all disaster-related appeals would contain this statement:

> You can help the victims of (this disaster) and thousands of other disasters across the country each year by making a financial gift to the American Red Cross Disaster Relief Fund, which enables the Red Cross to provide shelter, food, counseling and other assistance to those in need.

Donations to the general Disaster Relief Fund also dropped in the months following the terrorist attacks. Chief Financial Officer Jack Campbell told the Associated Press in October 2001 that the disaster fund held about $26 million as of September 30, whereas its target goal had been $57 million. In March 2002, the *Dallas Morning News* reported that the

Wise Giving Alliance of the Better Business Bureau had removed its seal of approval for the Red Cross, saying it would not be restored until the charity demonstrated it was meeting all standards for good management.

However, Alliance President Art Taylor commended the changes in fund-raising announced in June by the Red Cross. He was quoted in the *Atlanta Journal-Constitution* in June: "We believe that donors, beneficiaries and the charity itself all benefit when there is a clear understanding of how donations will be used."

Across the country, the controversy affected giving to local chapters. "There are 1,100 chapters across the U.S., and we're all suffering to some degree from the national negative publicity about the organization," Greg Hill, director of communications and marketing at the Dallas chapter told Todd Gillman of the *Dallas Morning News*. "And whether it's justified or not doesn't matter." The St. Louis chapter cut 14 jobs and closed two offices after a drop in donations, and chapters from North Carolina to Maine reported troubles in fund-raising. At the national headquarters, some 30 communication and marketing department employees were expected to be laid off by summer 2002, according to *PRWeek*, and a hiring freeze was in place while interim CEO Decker conducted an internal reorganization.

Yet by March 2002, Red Cross national spokeswoman Devorah Goldberg told the *Dallas Morning News*: "It's obviously settled down quite a bit. . . . Controversies come and go. We respond to more than 67,000 disasters every year. We're still there, we're still serving communities nationwide."

In August 2002, the Red Cross named Rear Admiral Marsha Evans as CEO, who had been heading the Girl Scouts of the USA. Darren Irby, the Red Cross director of external communications, told *PRWeek* in August 2002:

> Some people criticized us for not being as up front as we could be about where their donation was going, so we took a real hard look, and our commitment now is to be the leader in transparency and accountability.

Irby said tactics needed included clearer and simpler statements about how donations will be used because most Americans don't understand the work of charities.

He also said recruiting more third parties to speak for the organization and better cross-training of volunteers would help. "All we can do is be a leader in responding to the lessons we learned, and hope that other nonprofits will learn from that," Irby told *PRWeek*.

Yet, controversy arose again in spring 2003 when tax documents released by the Red Cross showed that during her last six months of employment as CEO and president of the Red Cross from July through December 2001, Healey had received some $1.3 million in deferred compensation, almost $300,000 in salary, an additional $228,929 in severance pay, $50,000 in expense allowances, and $5,622 in benefits. The documents also revealed that her chief of staff, Catharine "Kate" Berry, who was fired 11 days after Healy' s resignation, received $73,602 in salary and benefits, $132,509 in severance pay, and $403,473 in deferred compensation during that time period. The compensation Healy received during the last six months of 2001 was more than twice what she had received during her first 22 months at the Red Cross and exceeded the highest salary of $690,000 listed by *The Chronicle of Philanthropy*'s October 2002 report, which said 34 of 282 large nonprofits paid their CEOs more than $500,000.

Other September 11-Related Charities Also Come Under Criticism

The Red Cross was not the only charity to be questioned about its disbursement of terrorism-related donations. According to a report in the June 23, 2002, *New York Times*, the September 11 Fund, a joint project of the New York City United Way and the New York Community Trust, had distributed less than half of the $456 million it had received. The Robin Hood Relief Fund in Manhattan had $23 million in undistributed donations, the World Trade Center Relief Fund had $29 million of its $65 million remaining, and the Uniformed Firefighters Association was reported to be negotiating about how to distribute its $60 million. Many of the charities' leaders reported that the immediate needs of victims had been met, and they were dealing with how to finance longer-term needs such as mental-health counseling and job training.

Questions for Reflection

1. What characterizes a mutually beneficial relationship between a charitable organization and its donors or members? What duties or responsibilities do nonprofits or charities owe to their donors and their clients?
2. What responsibility do governments and regulators have in overseeing the operations of nonprofit, fund-raising organizations?
3. What environmental factors may have contributed to this crisis for the American Red Cross?
4. The American Red Cross and other agencies have responded to many natural disasters such as hurricanes or earthquakes and other terrorism-related crises like the Boston Marathon

Bombing since 2001. What suggestions do you have for agencies seeking to address the needs of a particular crisis? What are the best communication practices for these agencies?

Information for this case came from the following: Blaul, B. (October 30, 2001). American Red Cross names Harold Decker interim CEO. American Red Cross Release. *PR Newswire*; Flaherty, M.P., & Gaul, G.M. (November 19, 2001). Red Cross has pattern of diverting donations. *The Washington Post*, p. A1; Gillman, T.J. (March 11, 2002). Red Cross faces continuing queries about Sept. 11 funds. *The Dallas Morning News*; Irby, D. (November 14, 2001). Red Cross announces major changes in Liberty Fund. American Red Cross News Release. *US Newswire*; Irby, D. (November 14, 2001). Members of Congress praise Red Cross for policy changes with Liberty disaster fund. American Red Cross Release. *PR Newswire*; Mollison, A. (June 6, 2002). Red Cross changes the way it solicits funds. *The Atlanta Journal-Constitution*, p. A14; Mollison, A. (April 19, 2003). Red Cross chief got $1.9 million gold parachute. *The Atlanta Journal-Constitution*, pp. A1, A13; Murphy, K. (November 15, 2001). Charity watchdog agency wants Red Cross to be more candid about donations. Knight Ridder Washington Bureau; Quenqua, D. (August 25, 2002). Cross purpose. *PRWeek*, p. 19; Rabin, P. (May 6, 2002). Red Cross reorganization results in comms cutback. *PRWeek*, p. 2; (November 15, 2001). Red Cross "correction" redirects reserve funds. *The Washington Times*; Seabrook, A. (June 5, 2002). American Red Cross makes changes in money solicitation. *NPR All Things Considered*; Seabrook, A. (November 14, 2001). Red Cross announces all donations to its Liberty Fund will be used for victims of Sept.11. *NPR All Things Considered*; Strom, S. (June 21, 2002). Charitable contributions in 2001 reached $212 billion. *The New York Times*. www.nytimes.com; Strom, S. (June 23, 2002). Families fret as charities hold a billion dollars in 9/11 aid. *The New York Times*. www/nytimes.com; Strom, S. (February 2, 2003). With a lawsuit pending, charities are divided over disclosure. *The New York Times*. www.nytimes.com; Superville, D. (October 30, 2001). Red Cross to cease solicitations for Sept. 11 disaster relief fund, introduces interim CEO. *Associated Press*; (December 27, 2001). "Mitchell heads WTC Red Cross fund. *United Press International*; Walker, W. (November 7, 2001). U.S. Red Cross may double victims' payout. *The Toronto Star*, p. A8; Zepeda, P. (February 3, 2003). Senator Mitchell praises Red Cross for its "excellent service to America." Red Cross News Release at www.redcross.org/press/.

CASE 25: "GATHER YOUR FRIENDS. DO WHAT YOU LOVE": THE ALZHEIMER'S ASSOCIATION

Figure 7.1 In a 2011 Photo, Tennessee Women's basketball coach Pat Summitt sits next to her son, Tyler Summitt, at her Knoxville, Tennessee, home after announcing that she had been diagnosed with early onset dementia—Alzheimer's type—over the summer. (AP Photo: University of Tennessee by Debby Jennings.)

The summer solstice, the longest day of each year, has become a day designated for fund-raising and support for the Alzheimer's Association and the services it provides.

The mission of the Alzheimer's Association is simple: "To eliminate Alzheimer's disease through the advancement of research, to provide and enhance care and support for all affected; and to reduce the risk of dementia through the promotion of brain health." The task is not simple, however. The association reports that more than 5 million Americans now live with the disease, with one of three senior adults dying from the results of Alzheimer's or other dementia-related diseases.

"For people with Alzheimer's disease and their caregivers, every day is the longest day," Angela Geiger, chief strategy officer for the Alzheimer's Association, told *USA Today*. "It made sense to connect that to the longest day of the year and . . . give people a chance to make a difference."

Partnering to Make a Difference

During The Longest Day event, advocates are encouraged to form teams to spend the 16 hours of daylight in activities, with each participant being asked to raise at least $100 an hour for the Alzheimer's Association. The day concludes with a sunset celebration. Team members may participate in a one-hour block or in longer segments. Leading individual and team fund-raisers are noted on The Longest Day Web site. Individuals who raise at least $1,600 are recognized as an "all-day hero." Teams that garner $5,000 or more are called a "team of heroes." Funds raised through The Longest Day and other such events go toward the care and support, research, and advocacy efforts of the association. Volunteer participants raised more than $315 million in 2013.

Supporters are encouraged to "Gather your friends. Do what you love" during the event. Suggested activities range from dancing, hiking, cycling, quilting, walking, and swimming to musical and theater performances to sky diving to playing card games. The association provides a variety of tools to help team members raise funds, and all team members receive a T-shirt to wear during their "Longest Day" activities. Sample e-mail requests and tweets are provided, and useful fund-raising tools are available on Facebook. A Web page designed to help solicit donations is customizable for each team. Various designs for posters are available.

The association partnered with PepsiCo, EnAble, NuStep, Inc., and the American Contract Bridge League in 2014 to promote involvement during the June event. More than 2,700 participants and 1,100 teams signed up to participate. Posts on the association's blog detail the personal stories of team members who often participate in honor or memory of a loved one with Alzheimer's.

An Inspirational Example

Among those is Pat Summitt, former coach of the University of Tennessee women's basketball team, whose teams have won eight National Collegiate Athletic Association (NCAA) championships while acquiring 1,098 victories. The announcement from Coach Summitt in August 2011 that she had been diagnosed with early onset Alzheimer's sent "shockwaves around the country," according to ABC newscaster Robin Roberts, bringing renewed attention to the disease. While Summitt was able to continue to coach the team during that academic year, she retired at the end of the season as head coach emeritus.

Summitt and her son, Tyler, formed The Pat Summitt Foundation Fund, part of the Community Foundation of Middle Tennessee, to support the fight against Alzheimer's by funding grants to support families, spread awareness, and advance research. Her coaching career and her health were the focus of an ESPN documentary, *Pat XO*, produced as part of nine documentary films about sports women that aired on the sports network during the 40th anniversary of the Title IX legislation.

Summitt and her son, Tyler, were presented the Sargent and Eunice Shiver Profiles in Dignity Award at the Alzheimer's Association National Dinner on April 24, 2012.

Harry Johns, the president and CEO of the Alzheimer's Association, noted:

> The Alzheimer's Association applauds Coach Summitt for courageously sharing her diagnosis and helping to raise awareness of the sixth leading cause of death in the U.S. The courage and dignity with which she lives on and off the court will help eliminate the stigma often associated with the disease.

Questions for Reflection

1. Cause-related nonprofits face the challenge of creating public awareness and distinction for their mission and purpose. Evaluate the value of special events such as "The Longest Day" for such groups.
2. What motivates volunteers to participate in fund-raising and awareness-raising events? How does the Alzheimer's Association appeal to some of these motivations?
3. What's the value of a group/event T-shirt?
4. Summitt's honesty and courage in facing her illness have inspired many, illustrating the power of a celebrity in helping publicize a cause. Offer some principles that should help nonprofits balance privacy, publicity, and care in such situations.

Information for this case is drawn from http://act.alz.org/site/TR/LongestDay/TheLongestDay?pg=entry&fr_id=5860; Araton, Harvey. (December 11, 2011). Summitt still inspires, often in silence. *The New York Times*; ESPN.com. (July 8, 2013). Director's Moment: *Pat XO*. Espn.go.com/vido/clip?id=9460768; ESPN.com. (March 5, 2013). "Sum it up": Robin Roberts interviews Summitt. Espn.go.com/video/clip?id-9018423; Friedman, Lindsay. (June 20, 2013). Samaritans honor those with Alzheimer's on longest day. *USA Today*. http://www.usatoday.com/story/news/nation/2013/06/20/alzheimers-disease-longest-day/2439507/; Heintz, Erin. (April 23, 2012). Alzheimer's Association to honor legendary University of Tennessee Lady Vols head coach emeritus Pat Summitt and son Tyler at National Alzheimer's dinner. Release. Alzheimer's Association. www.alz.org.

CASE 26: "I'M A MORMON" CAMPAIGN TARGETS PUBLIC PERCEPTIONS

When the Church of Jesus Christ of Latter-day Saints (the Mormons) decided to hire well-known public relations agencies Ogilvy & Mather and Hall & Partners in 2011 to explore the general public opinion of the church, it wasn't an unusual move. In fact, the church, along with other denominations, had long been active in using commercials, newspapers, and billboards to inform and attract interest. However, it seemed to be time for a different approach. Research suggested that Mormonism was possibly the most misunderstood religious organization in America, despite garnering a tremendous amount of popular culture attention through Broadway musicals, a reality television program, and some highly covered news events.

Researching a Church's Image

The first step in the public relations plan was to find out just what people thought of Mormons. National trends over the previous decade had shown a general decline in affiliation with any organized religious groups, especially among 20 and 30 year olds. But after the agencies conducted focus groups and surveys, the leaders of the church were surprised to learn that it wasn't just apathy affecting their outreach efforts, but something more negative. If respondents had an opinion at all about Mormons, they tended to use words such as "sexist," or "anti-gay," which wouldn't necessarily distinguish them from opinions of other religious groups. But, when respondents also used adjectives such as "cultish," "secretive," "controlling, and pushy," the leaders were taken aback.

"We're not secretive," Stephen B. Allen, managing director of the church's missionary department and in charge of the campaign, said in an interview that appeared in *The New York Times*. "And we're not scared of what people think of us. If you don't recognize the problem, you can't solve the problem. If nobody tells you you have spinach in your teeth, how would you know?"

Sharing Personal Stories through a Multimedia Campaign

In an effort to change the reported negative views of the church, the innovative "I'm a Mormon" campaign kicked off in 2010—a campaign that sought to demystify the faith group by using a highly personalized approach. The multi-million-dollar, multimedia campaign involved television, billboards, and online media with messages that invited visitors to a new enhanced Web site. The site featured 50,000 profiles of individual church members, each telling a personal story and talking about their faith and defying the negative stereotypes expressed by the respondents. Featured video testimonies included profiles of interracial couples, young women with eating disorders who overcame their adversity, single mothers, immigrants, and soldiers. (Visitors to the new church YouTube channel could also access the videos.)

The Web site opens with an array of photographs of men and women of different ages and races and a written invitation: "While our backgrounds and experiences are diverse, we share a deep commitment to Jesus Christ, to each other, and our neighbors. Watch these stories of faith in the everyday lives of Mormons. You can also meet Mormons here," with a link to another page that offered even more images. A pull-down menu on the site allows visitors to search for Mormons by gender, age or ethnicity, and another link allows one to search for a congregation.

One example: when one clicks on the picture, a headline reads, "Hi, I'm Christopher," and offers essentially a 140-character description of Christopher: "I'm a professional ballet dancer and a ballet master. I have shared my talent and taught all over the world, and I'm a Mormon."

The accompanying video is titled "I'm a Mormon, Adoptee, and a Ballet Dancer." The video features Christopher in a dance studio teaching young ballerinas to dance. He tells his story by describing his professional ballet career since the age of 14, which includes several appointments with international ballet companies. Audiences meet the white family who adopted him—a self-described white, Puerto Rican, West Indian family. Christopher shares the initial adversity he faced in the dancing industry as a person of color. Viewers meet his wife and child in the video as well. A pop-up link at the end of the video offers one a chance to view Christopher's profile where he describes why he is a Mormon and how he lives his faith.

Campaign Expands Its Reach

The campaign was first launched in nine U.S. cities and expanded to 13 more U.S. cities the next year, with a major push in New York City, just blocks away from the Broadway theater where "The Book of Mormon" was playing to packed crowds. Later, the campaign was extended to the United Kingdom.

"As a religion, branding a religion, I can't recall [another one] offhand," Rosanna Fisk, CEO of the PRSA in New York, told a reporter for ABC News as the campaign launched in New York City in June 2011. "What I see in this, however, has similarities of other kinds. It's quite a testimonial. [The campaign] shows how different people come from different backgrounds and are all joined by the same, common belief."

Viewing statistics in the first year were impressive. One million people initiated online chats with Mormons. According to an article in

The New York Times, Mia B. Love's video prompted a man to write her a personal letter thanking her for helping the man's wife decide to join the church. The mayor of Saratoga Springs, Utah, and the daughter of Haitian immigrants, Love said the church has always been involved in missionary work, and the ads are just an extension of that work. "They wanted to get the word out that we're not a cult, we're not sitting in the mountains here with five wives," she said. "They wanted to let people know that we're normal."

The Web site was recognized as a 2011 "Top Ten Website of the Year" by Interactive Media Awards.

The Mormon Presidential Candidate

The image campaign was an interesting outcome of the opinion research, but the image campaign efforts were magnified when prominent Mormons (frontrunner and eventual nominee Mitt Romney and candidate John Huntsman) entered the 2012 presidential campaign, and a nexus of public relations nuances arose. While some in the press and on social media questioned the planning, organizers called the timing of the "I'm a Mormon" campaign with the presidential campaigning season a coincidence. To discourage the perception that the campaign was politically motivated, the promotional ads were not aired in states that had early primaries.

A Tradition of Promotion and "Making Friends"

Public relations groundbreaker Edward Bernays outlined publicity efforts that were common in religious organizations in his 1928 book, *Propaganda*. He wrote:

> Many churches have made paid advertising and organized propaganda a part of their regular activities. They have developed church advertising committees, which make use of newspapers and the billboards as well as of the pamphlet. Many denominations maintain their own periodicals. The Methodist Board of Publication and Information systematically gives announcements and releases to the press and the magazines.

Early religious public relations practitioners debated what the purpose of their activities really was: Was it to educate or to persuade? In 1929, representatives of several protestant denominations met to form what eventually became the Religion Communicators Council. By the mid-1940s, members of the council made a distinction among public relations, promotion, and publicity. They defined public relations as the strategic planning, as determined by public opinion, to promote the church. Promotion was the act of seeking volunteers, prayers, or financial contributions. Publicity was about creating favorable feeling about the church.

In the 1950s and 1960s, public relations came to be understood by council members to be about "doing whatever contributes toward making a church deserve and receive the confidence and cooperation of increasing numbers of people—in still simpler form: making friends for Christ and his Church" (Ralph Stoody, cited in Cannon 2008). Over the next 50 years, many religious groups developed sophisticated communication programs, although some critics question whether such efforts are appropriate.

In her book *Brand of Faith*, media studies scholar Mara Epstein said: "Marketing is sort of a necessary evil. It's part of our culture at this point, and if faiths want to be part of the culture, they're going to have to do marketing, or they'll get lost in the conversation."

Questions for Reflection

1. In what ways did the individual focus of the "I'm a Mormon" campaign help strengthen stakeholder relations?
2. What are the ethical considerations and implications of marketing a religious organization or a religion? Should religious organizations be held to a different standard of ethical behavior when it comes to public relations? Explain.
3. The campaign was developed following extensive research. How might the ongoing impact of the campaign be assessed?

Information drawn from http://www.mormon.org/people; Bernays, E. (1928). *Propaganda.* Routledge; Bulik, B. (May 11, 2009). Churches get religion on marketing. *Advertising Age, 80*, 17; Campbell, D., Green J., & Monson, J. (May 18, 2012). The stained glass ceiling: Social contact and Mitt Romney's "religion problem." *Political Behavior, 34*, 277–299; Cannon, D. (2011). Not conformed to this world: How U.S. Religion communicators describe public relations. *Public Relations Journal, 5*, 3. http://www.prsa.org/intelligence/prjournal/documents/2011cannon.pdf; Cannon, D.F. (2008). *Speaking of faith: Public relations practice among religion communicators in the United States* (Doctoral Dissertation.) Retrieved from ProQuest, 0549968601; Collins, C.A., & Rothmyer, S. (1981). The church and PSA's. *Religious Communication Today, 4* (1), 32–36; Epstein, M. (2008) *Brands of faith: Marketing religion in a commercial age.* Abingdon, Oxon, U.K.: Routledge; Goodstein, L. (November 17, 2011). Mormon's ad campaign may play out on the '12 campaign trail. *The New York Times.* http://www.nytimes.com/2011/11/18/us/mormon-ad-campaign-seeks-to-improve-perceptions.html?pagewanted=all&_r=0; Kirkland, Lyman. (June 17, 2011). Mormon.org selected as winner of prestigious web award. News release. www.mormonnewsroom.org/

article/mormon-org-winner-prestigious-web-award; Pew Research. (2008). Religious landscape survey. http://religions.pewforum.org/reports; Riparbelli, Laura. (June 21, 2011). Mormon NYC ad campaign "very savvy branding." ABC News. http://abcnews.go.com/Business/mormon-nyc-ad-campaign-savvy-branding/story?id=13888304&singlePage=true; Stoody, R. (1958). *A handbook of church public relations.* New York; Abingdon Press.

CASE 27: HABITAT FOR HUMANITY: BUILDING CORPORATE BRIDGES AND AFFORDABLE HOUSES

Habitat for Humanity, a nonprofit Christian ministry with operational headquarters in Americus, Georgia, and administrative headquarters in Atlanta, has united volunteers in an effort to build affordable decent housing for low-income residents across the globe. Its mission, according to its Web site: "Seeking to put God's love into action, Habitat for Humanity brings people together to build homes, communities and hope." Founded by Millard and Linda Fuller in 1976, Habitat for Humanity International and its affiliates in more than 3,000 communities in 70 nations have built or repaired more than 800,000 houses that are then sold to partner families with no-profit, zero-interest mortgages. Since its inception, Habitat affiliate members have served more than 4 million people. In 2013 alone, more than 100,000 families were served.

The Foundation is Laid

Habitat for Humanity International has more than 1,400 active U.S. affiliates and about 80 other national organizations around the world. Habitat saw a dramatic increase in growth after former U.S. President Jimmy Carter and his wife, Rosalynn, took their first Habitat work trip, the Jimmy Carter Work Project (JCWP), to New York City in 1984. Their personal involvement in Habitat's ministry brought the organization national visibility

The former president's work continues to bring media, corporate, and volunteer attention to Habitat. The Carters have participated in Habitat builds not only in many locations in the United States but in other nations, from South Africa to the Philippines. In 2013, for the 30th consecutive year, the Carters led builds in Oakland and San Jose, California; Denver, Colorado; New York City; and Union Beach, New Jersey.

As quoted on the Habitat Web site, President Carter endorses the Habitat model:

> Habitat has successfully removed the stigma of charity by substituting it with a sense of partnership. The people who will live in the homes work side by side with the volunteers, so they feel very much that they are on an equal level.

The Structure is Developed

Habitat houses are affordable to low-income people because they are sold at no profit, with a no-interest mortgage. Using volunteer labor and donations, Habitat builds and/or refurbishes houses with the help of the homeowner (partner) families. The houses are then sold to partner families at no profit, financed through affordable, no-interest loans. A down payment and mortgage payments are required, and partners are required to put "Sweat Equity" into building their house and the houses of others. Mortgages run 7 to 30 years, and the monthly mortgage payments are used to build other houses.

Habitat for Humanity International's headquarters provides information, training, and a variety of other support services to Habitat affiliates worldwide. Habitat for Humanity's work is accomplished at the community level by affiliates, independent, locally run, nonprofit organizations. Each affiliate coordinates all aspects of Habitat home building in its local area: fund-raising, building site selection, partner family selection and support, house construction, and mortgage servicing.

All Habitat affiliates are asked to "tithe"—to give 10 percent of their contributions to fund house-building work in other nations. Tithing provides funds for international building and gives affiliates the opportunity to demonstrate the spirit of partnership. In 2011, affiliates tithed $13 million to support Habitat's work around the world.

In recent years, increased emphasis has been placed on helping communities recover from disasters. After Superstorm Sandy hit the New Jersey and New York shores, Habitat Disaster Corp volunteers spent more than 1,400 hours working to help repair homes in 11 deployments. Funds to help support this work were raised by rock icon Bruce Springsteen and President Carter, who recorded a public service announcement urging people to support Habitat for Humanity in the Sandy recovery efforts.

Volunteers and Donors Raise the Walls

The organization seeks volunteers from many stakeholder groups: corporations; communities; religious groups (although Habitat and its affiliates do not proselytize); private philanthropy; cause marketers; media and entertainment groups. These volunteers are engaged in work in local communities in the United States and in nations around the world. In May 2014, more than 8,600 women volunteered at Habitat builds in all 50

U.S. states. The second annual Habitat Youth BUILD in 2013 engaged 14,000 volunteers with builds across 42 sites in seven Asian countries: China, Cambodia, India, Indonesia, Japan, Nepal, and the Philippines.

Habitat and AmeriCorps have been strong partners since 1994, and more than 8,000 volunteers with AmeriCorps have offered more than 13 million hours of service with Habitat. A 2013 initiative involved veterans and AmeriCorps members in a very public build on the Mall in Washington, D.C. During the five-day Veterans Build on the Mall, seven houses were framed; the houses were then given to capital-area affiliates to be completed. In May 2014, more than 400 Habitat AmeriCorps workers gathered to build 10 new homes and repair others in Iowa, North Carolina, and Wisconsin.

Habitat for Humanity International's Corporate Sponsorship program challenges corporations to join with Habitat in working to ensure that all people have decent, affordable shelter. Companies form partnerships with Habitat in a variety of ways, through product donations, financial support, and by encouraging employees to work as Habitat volunteers. The leading corporate and foundation partners noted on Habitat's Web site are recognized according to contribution levels, from Bank of America and Thrivent Financial, which give $10 million annually, and Dow, Valspar, and Whirlpool, which give between $5 million and $10 million annually. Other multi-million dollar annual corporate donors include the Home Depot Foundation, Lowe's, Nissan, Schneider Electric, PG&E, HILTI Foundation, City Foundation, Delta, GAF, GM Foundation, JP Morgan Chase, and Yale.

Although numerous corporations and businesses have joined in partnership with Habitat, examine just a few:

- Since 2006, Nissan has contributed more than $12 million to Habitat for Humanity, and its employees have helped to build more than 55 homes across the United States. The corporation has also donated 120 vehicles. Beginning in 2011, Nissan has also sponsored a "Heisman House Build" in recognition of its sponsorship of The Heisman Memorial Trophy, involving many former Heisman winners in supporting Habitat. In a Habitat release, Nissan Marketing Vice President Jon Brancheau explained: "Together with Habitat for Humanity and the Heisman Trust, we're continuing our mission to improve the communities where our employees and customers live, and we're grateful to these athletes for joining in this one-of-a-kind partnership to build this house."
- Whirlpool Home Appliances, which has been a corporate sponsor since 2004, has donated more than 140,000 appliances for

new Habitat Homes, more than $78 million in value, and the corporation has recently renewed its commitment to provide a range and refrigerator in every new Habitat home. Employees have participated in the Carter Builds since 2003. Beginning in 2006, Whirlpool began recognizing an outstanding U.S. Habitat for Humanity affiliate and its relationship with its local community by holding a build in the affiliate's community. The "Building Blocks" Builds have been held in Nashville, Phoenix, Dallas and Atlanta, and 43 homes have been constructed.

- Lowe's has been a consistent Habitat partner, contributing nearly $63 million to Habitat since 2003. Since 2004, Lowe's has been the corporate underwriter of the Women Build, offering free training clinics for women as well as financial support. In a release, Larry Stone, chairman of Lowe's Charitable and Educational Foundation, said: "Lowe's involvement with Women Build is much more than a financial arrangement—it is a reflection of our commitment to address the nationwide issue of substandard housing. We are helping to build homes everyone can take pride in—our employees, the volunteers, the partner families and the communities."
- Novelis, the world's leading producer of rolled aluminum products, is headquartered in Atlanta, where it has worked closely with the Atlanta Habitat affiliate on local projects while continuing to work with Habitat Humanity International in international projects. In 2013, Novelis sponsored a Blitz Build in an Atlanta subdivision; the build was completely run by employees, who did fund-raising and construction. Novelis has contributed to Habitat's Global Mission Fund and its India BUILD initiative, and Novelis Asia donated funds and volunteer hours to construct a home in Korea.
- Employees at Atlanta-based AT&T Digital Life built a house in Atlanta in 2014, the first of five builds that have been pledged. Other homes will be built in Dallas, Los Angeles, New York and Seattle, supported by donations from Digital Life and more than 100 AT&T volunteers. Kevin Petersen, senior vice president, Digital Life, Inc., described the corporation's commitment: "We're all about giving homeowners peace of mind. As a result, we're compelled to work with Habitat for Humanity to help those who need the security that owning a home can provide. Giving back through home builds across the country and in our hometown of Atlanta feels right."
- Delta Air Lines has been a consistent Habitat partner. Delta's "Force for Global Good" encourages employees to work together

to make a difference. Working with Habitat, more than 9,800 Delta employees have offered more than 92,000 volunteer hours to help construct 115 houses in eight countries. In March 2013, volunteers from 16 cities in the United States and Canada built 10 homes in Quezon City, Philippines. Delta also donated use of two airplanes to fly volunteers to Haiti for the 28th annual Carter Work Project in 2011.

Questions for Reflection

1. Habitat partnerships offer individuals and corporations a variety of philanthropic options. What objectives might be addressed through different types of involvement?
2. What are the strategic motivations for corporations and foundations to become involved with an international social service agency? What are the potential liabilities of such involvement?
3. Habitat celebrates the involvement of Jimmy and Rosalynn Carter. What are some opportunities and threats presented by celebrity involvement or identification with a charitable or social service organization?
4. How do group service opportunities improve employee morale?

Information for this case was drawn from the following: the Habitat Web site at www.habitat.org; news releases, including: Habitat for Humanity partners with Delta Air Lines for 28th annual Jimmy and Rosalynn Carter Work Project. (November 3, 2011). http://www.habitat.org/newsroom/2014archive/3_11_2014_Delta_Skymiles; Delta volunteers build 10 homes with Habitat for Humanity in Manila, Philippines. (March 11, 2014). Release. http://news.delta.com/2014-03-11-Delta-Volunteers-Build-10-Homes-with-Habitat-for-Humanity-in-Manila-Philippines; Delta Air Lines employees to build third Habitat for Humanity home in Long Beach. Release. http://www.habitatla.org/delta-air-lines-employees-to-build-third-habitat-for-humanity-home-in-long-beach; Lowe's and Habitat for Humanity. http://www.habitat.org/wb/partnerships/wb_lowes.aspx; Nissan partners with Habitat for Humanity, Heisman Trust for weekend of Dallas-area community service activities. Release. http://www.habitat.org/newsroom/2014archive/4_24_14_Heisman_Dallas; Whirlpool and Habitat for Humanity announce 2014 partnership renewal. Release. http://www.habitat.org/newsroom/2014archive/4_01_14_Whirlpool_Partnership_Renewal; Whirlpool and Habitat for Humanity: An overview. Web site. http://Whirlpool%20Corporation%20-%20Habitat%20for%20

Humanity.htm; Novelis sponsors Blitz Build with Atlanta Habitat. (November 25, 2013). Release. http://www.habitat.org/newsroom/2013archive/10_25_2013_Novelis_Blitz_Build.aspx; Lowe's and Habitat for Humanity announce 5-year, $23.5 million partnership. Release. http://media.lowes.com/pr/2014/02/20/lowes-and-habitat-for-humanity-announce-5-year-23-5-million-partnership/; Lowe's Heroes. Release. http://responsibility.lowes.com/community/lowes-heros/; Buchoiz, B.B. (September 1996). Building morale off-site, *Crain's Small-Business-Chicago, 4*(7), 18; Gunsauley, C. (September 1, 2001). Charity projects improve employee motivation, morale. *EBN, 15* (10), 63–64; Kloer, Phil. (2012). Tied together. *Habitat World*. http://www.habitat.org/lc/hw/archived/stories/tithed-together/.

PROFESSIONAL INSIGHT How do you motivate ongoing volunteer participation?

Figure 7.2 Justin Rudd, Community Action Team, Long Beach, California

I believe that people want to do good, be involved, and help. Getting them dialed in to participate in an event or project is quite possible—if you can educate them effectively about what their involvement will be and what the outcome will look like. Motivating others to get involved is possible. Thankfully, with a wide range of events and projects (mostly youth, animal, environmental, and educational) that my nonprofit puts on annually, there is bound to be something of interest to the audience of volunteers I'm trying to recruit. I understand that every animal advocate is not going to be as passionate about spelling bees or beach cleanups. I try to get people dialed in to volunteer where their heart and mind are.

There are a few specific ways I have found that work well to get my pleas for volunteers out to the public:

- I maintain an active volunteer database and ask prospective helpers to register their e-mails with my Constant Contact database. I keep those volunteers regularly updated with e-mail messages about upcoming events.
- I use Facebook to post regular messages to my personal page and to fan pages that I've set up for each activity.

- I take advantage of invitations to speak at career days, university classrooms, scout troops, and other civic groups. I also post on my Facebook page that I appreciate opportunities to speak in front of groups of people.
- I write and send out press releases explaining the need for help at upcoming events. I'm sure to include details about arrival time, length of a volunteer shift, info about parking and refreshments. I always make sure my volunteers get free parking and snacks. Not many want to pay to volunteer.
- I depend on volunteers to tell their friends about their good experiences.

At and after an event, there are a few things I do for volunteers to thank them (and hopefully get them to help at other upcoming events):

- At the event, I am personally sure to welcome the volunteers and thank them for coming. If they feel important and valued from the start, it will show throughout the length of the project or event.
- After events, I am consciously aware to quickly post photos and videos from our events, so that others can see the fun and effect that volunteers can have while helping out. Personally, I utilize Facebook, Twitter, YouTube, and e-mail.
- I am sure to "tag" volunteers in photos on Facebook. I know that kind of validation is important in this age of social media gratification.
- For those who go the extra effort in volunteering for a particular event, I'll post a note on their Facebook wall, and/or send them a quick thank you note via e-mail.
- At some events, when practical, I'll bring extra snacks, coffee drinks, or special T-shirts for the volunteers.
- At the end of the year, I host an outstanding volunteer luncheon for my top 40–50 volunteers. I am sure to say a good word about each during a recognition ceremony during that event. Of course, the event is free.
- I am aware of others' time, especially on their weekends. If an event is long, I'll break up the volunteer shifts in shorter segments. Volunteers are more likely to participate for a 3–4 hour shift, as opposed to a 7–8 hour shift. I don't want to burn out my helpers. I want them to leave happy and satisfied, not worn out and disenfranchised.

Justin Rudd's nonprofit 501c3 Community Action Team (CAT) based in Long Beach, California produces more than 60 events, projects, and contests a year. Events include beach cleanups, spelling bees, bike parades, weight-loss contests, dog parades, beauty pageants, and 5K/10K races. Details at www.JustinRudd.com.

CHAPTER 8

Stakeholders

Government Regulators

Few organizations in the United States escape the scrutiny and influence of government regulators. From jetliners 35,000 feet above the earth's surface to miners 5,000 feet below it, most organized human activity attracts government attention. Some agencies, such as the Federal Aviation Administration (FAA), become as well known as the companies they monitor. Others, such as the Mine Safety and Health Administration, are seldom seen or heard outside their own industry.

Regulatory agencies exist because elected federal, state, and local officials create them to develop and enforce rules needed to carry out the law. In most cases, regulations focus on protecting human health and safety, the natural environment, and the free-market economic system.

THE ROLES OF PRACTITIONERS

Public relations practitioners must understand the regulations that govern their organizations' activities and anticipate how the rules might affect their own plans or those of competitors. Knowing the rules will help practitioners:

- Contribute effectively to discussion, analysis, and strategic planning.
- Understand the consequences of both compliance and noncompliance.
- Anticipate how regulations may affect customers, employees, investors, and others.
- Interpret the potential effects of newly proposed rules.
- Prepare to explain adverse regulatory decisions.

REGULATORY COMPLEXITIES

Complex regulations and high stakes have made pharmaceutical public relations a demanding specialty. The Food and Drug Administration

(FDA) strictly enforces its rules concerning the language that drug companies must use in describing the testing, efficacy, and side effects of products. News releases or other materials that run afoul of FDA rules may lead to delay, embarrassment, fines, or other sanctions.

Occasionally, regulatory agencies have overlapping responsibilities. For example, both the Federal Trade Commission (FTC) and the Federal Communications Commission (FCC) were involved in establishing the National Do-Not-Call Registry in 2003, responding to industry objections and subsequent lawsuits, and implementing the new rules.

When the federal government establishes a regulatory agency, state governments often create their own corresponding agency to govern intrastate activities, and strong state regulatory structures are common in public service utilities, such as electric-power companies and telecommunications, and in the banking industry.

Some states have consistently adopted stricter rules than their federal counterparts in certain regulated activities, earning reputations as rule-making leaders and complicating the jobs of public relations professionals. For example, the California Air Resources Board has gained recognition for setting the nation's toughest auto emissions standards since it was established more than 45 years ago.

CRITICS OF REGULATION

Regulatory efforts have attracted a large number of critics who say they simply add to the costs of producing a product or service without providing an equivalent value in benefits. The operation of free markets, the critics say, would accomplish the same good effects that government rules do.

John Stossel, an investigative reporter and co-anchor for ABC-TV's *20/20* news program who's been honored five times for excellence in consumer reporting by the National Press Club and received 19 Emmy Awards, is a tireless critic of government regulation. He explained his reasons in 2001 at a Hillsdale College seminar:

> When I started 30 years ago as a consumer reporter, I took the approach that most young reporters take today. My attitude was that capitalism is essentially cruel and unfair, and that the job of government, with the help of lawyers and the press, is to protect people from it. For years, I did stories along those lines—stories about Coffee Association ads claiming that "coffee picks you up while it calms you down," or Libby-Owens-Ford Glass Company ads touting the clarity of its product by showing cars with their windows rolled down. I and other consumer activists said, "We've got to have regulation. We've got to police these ads. We've got to have a Federal

Trade Commission." And I'm embarrassed at how long it took me to realize that these regulations make things worse, not better, for ordinary people. The damage done by regulation is so vast, it's often hard to see. The money wasted consists not only of the taxes taken directly from us to pay for the bureaucrats, but also of the indirect cost of all the lost energy that goes into filling out the forms.

PROTECTING THE POWERLESS

Regulatory advocates respond that powerful corporations, highly motivated to minimize costs and well equipped with resources needed to prevail in disputes, would not adequately protect the health of workers or the environment if the government did not supervise them closely.

Here are brief descriptions of some of the most prominent federal regulatory agencies. The descriptions are adapted from materials the agencies have published.

Consumer Product Safety Commission (CPSC)

The CPSC protects the public against unreasonable risks of injuries and deaths associated with consumer products. The agency has jurisdiction over about 15,000 types of consumer products ranging from coffee makers to toys to lawn mowers. The goals of the agency, according to the 2011–2016 Strategic Plan, are:

> Goal 1: Take a leadership role in identifying and addressing the most pressing consumer product safety priorities and mobilizing action by our partners.
> Goal 2: Engage public and private sector stakeholders to build safety into consumer products.
> Goal 3: Ensure timely and accurate detection of consumer product safety risks to inform agency priorities.
> Goal 4: Use the CPSC's full range of authorities to quickly remove hazards from the marketplace.
> Goal 5: Promote a public understanding of product risks and CPSC capabilities.

Environmental Protection Administration (EPA)

The EPA's mission is to protect human health and safeguard the natural environment on which life depends. In July 1970, the White House and Congress worked together to establish the EPA in response to growing public demand for cleaner water, air, and land. Before formation of the EPA, the federal government was not structured to make a coordinated attack on the pollutants that harm human health and degrade the environment.

Equal Employment Opportunity Commission (EEOC)

The EEOC coordinates all federal equal employment opportunity regulations, practices, and policies. The commission also interprets employment discrimination laws, monitors the federal sector equal employment opportunity program, and provides funding and support to state and local fair employment practices agencies and tribal employment rights organizations.

Federal Aviation Administration

The FAA is responsible for the safety of civil aviation. The FAA's major roles include:

- Regulating civil aviation to promote safety.
- Encouraging and developing civil aeronautics, including new aviation technology.
- Developing and operating the air traffic control system for civil and military aircraft.
- Developing and carrying out programs to control aircraft noise and other environmental effects of civil aviation.

Federal Communications Commission

The FCC operates bureaus that process applications for licenses, analyze complaints, conduct investigations, develop and implement regulatory programs, and take part in hearings. Some of the bureaus are:

- Consumer and Governmental Affairs, which educates and informs consumers about telecommunications goods and services and invites public input to help guide the work of the FCC.
- Media, which regulates AM, FM radio and television broadcast stations, as well as cable and satellite distribution.
- Wireless Telecommunications, which oversees cellular and Personal Communication Service (PCS) phones, pagers, and two-way radios.
- Wireline Competition, which regulates phone companies that mainly provide interstate services through wire-based networks including corded and cordless phones.

Federal Reserve System

The Federal Reserve, central bank of the United States, was founded in 1913 to provide the nation with a safer, more flexible, and more stable monetary and financial system.

The central bank's duties fall into four general areas:

- Conducting the nation's monetary policy.
- Supervising banking institutions and protecting the credit rights of consumers.

- Maintaining the stability of the financial system.
- Providing certain financial services to the government, public, financial institutions, and foreign official institutions.

Federal Trade Commission

The FTC works to ensure that markets are vigorous, efficient, and free of restrictions that harm consumers. Experience demonstrates that competition among firms yields products at the lowest prices, spurs innovation, and strengthens the economy. Markets also work best when consumers can make informed choices based on accurate information.

To ensure the smooth operation of the free-market system, the FTC enforces federal consumer protection laws that prevent fraud, deception, and unfair business practices. The commission also enforces federal antitrust laws that prohibit anticompetitive mergers and other business practices that restrict competition and harm consumers.

Food and Drug Administration

The FDA is responsible for protecting the public health by assuring the safety, efficacy, and security of human and veterinary drugs, biological products, medical devices, commercial food supply, cosmetics, and products that emit radiation. The FDA advances the public health by helping to speed innovations that make medicines and foods more effective, safer, and more affordable and by helping people get the accurate, science-based information they need to use medicines and foods to improve their health.

The FDA works to ensure that consumers have up-to-date, truthful information on the benefits and risks of regulated products. Its complementary roles are:

- Ensuring that the information companies provide about products is accurate and allows for their safe use.
- Communicating directly with the public concerning benefits and risks of products the FDA regulates.

Occupational Safety and Health Administration (OSHA)

OSHA's mission is to save lives, prevent injuries, and protect the health of America's workers. To accomplish this, federal and state governments work in partnership with the more than 100 million working men and women and 6.5 million employers covered by the Occupational Safety and Health Act. Nearly every working man and woman in the nation comes under OSHA's jurisdiction (with some exceptions such as miners and transportation workers).

National Highway Traffic Safety Administration (NHTSA)

NHTSA is responsible for reducing death, injury, and economic loss resulting from highway accidents. The agency sets and enforces safety standards for motor vehicles and vehicle equipment. NHTSA investigates safety defects in motor vehicles, sets and enforces fuel economy standards, helps reduce the threat of drunk drivers, promotes use of seat belts, child safety seats, and air bags, investigates odometer fraud, establishes and enforces vehicle antitheft regulations, and provides consumer information on motor vehicle safety topics.

Securities and Exchange Commission

The primary mission of the SEC is to protect investors and maintain the integrity of the securities markets. As more first-time investors turn to the markets to help secure their futures, pay for homes, and send children to college, these goals are more compelling than ever.

The world of investing is fascinating, complex, and potentially fruitful. Unlike the banking world, where deposits are guaranteed, stocks, bonds, and other securities can lose value. There are no guarantees. The principal way for investors to protect the money they put into securities is to do research and ask questions.

The main purposes of the laws creating the SEC can be summed up in two propositions:

- Companies publicly offering securities for investment dollars must tell the public the truth about their businesses, the securities they are selling, and the risks involved in investing.
- People who sell and trade securities—brokers, dealers, and exchanges—must treat investors fairly and honestly, putting investors' interests first.

U.S. Department of Agriculture (USDA)

The USDA's Food Safety Mission Area ensures that the commercial supply of meat, poultry, and egg products is safe, wholesome, and correctly labeled and packaged. The Food Safety and Inspection Service (FSIS) sets standards for food safety and inspects meat, poultry, and egg products produced domestically and imported. The FSIS inspects animals and birds at slaughter and processed products at various stages of production and analyzes products for microbiological and chemical adulterants. FSIS also informs the public about meat, poultry, and egg safety issues.

PRACTITIONERS BY MANY NAMES

Of course, some practitioners work directly for a national, state, or local government. The interpretation of what has come to be known as the "Gillette Amendment" to the 1913 Appropriations Act for the U.S. Department of Agriculture has resulted in some restrictions in the use of federal funds to support the work of overt public relations, so the titles used for such positions are carefully chosen. Practitioners may be called "information specialists" or "communication specialists" when working for agencies or "public affairs officers" in the military. Regardless of the title, the importance of the function is clear: establishing mutually beneficial relationships between the government and its citizens is a goal inherently important within a democracy.

The cases in this chapter challenge you to explore the varied motivations and practices of communicating to and with governments. As you discuss these cases, address questions such as: How do the communication strategies and tactics described here indicate the priorities of these stakeholders? In what ways do businesses and organizations seek to influence governments, and in what ways do governments seek to influence their stakeholders? Do they encourage robust involvement in open, democratic action and processes? How might these strategies and tactics be understood in light of democratic principles and communication ethics?

ADDITIONAL READINGS

Lee, Mordecai, Neeley, Grant, & Stewart, Kendra (Eds.). (2011). *The practice of government public relations*. Boca Raton, FL: CRC Press.

Lerbinger, Otto. (2005). *Corporate public affairs: Interacting with interest groups, media and government*. New York: Routledge.

Wilson, James Q. (2000). *Bureaucracy: What government agencies do and why they do it*. New York: Basic Books.

CASE 28: "LET'S MOVE!" PUTS CHILDHOOD OBESITY ON A DIET

The statistics from the Centers on Disease Control and Prevention were startling: one in three children and adolescents in the United States was obese or overweight. Childhood obesity had more than doubled, and adolescent obesity has quadrupled in the past 30 years. Children and adolescents who are overweight or obese are likely to have immediate health consequences that may persist into adulthood.

In response to these concerns, First Lady Michelle Obama unveiled a nationwide campaign in February 2010 called "Let's Move!" that sought to offer a comprehensive approach to challenge children to be more physically active, to eat more nutritiously, and to achieve better health.

Off to a Fast Start

In a February 9, 2010, White House release announcing the initiative, Ms. Obama explained:

> The physical and emotional health of an entire generation and the economic health and security of our nation is at stake. This isn't the kind of problem that can be solved overnight, but with everyone working together, it can be solved. So, let's move.

The campaign was launched at a news conference at the White House. President Obama signed a Presidential Memorandum that created the first Task Force on Childhood Obesity charged with conducting a review of all programs and policies related to child nutrition and physical activity within 90 days in order to develop a national action plan to set benchmarks and recommend how best to use federal resources to fight obesity. Several members of the president's cabinet, the mayor of Somerville, Massachutsetts, and the mayor of Hernando, Mississippi, the president of the American Academy of Pediatrics, members of the 2009 National Championship Pee-Wee football team, and former football player NBC correspondent Tiki Barber were on the conference program.

Teaming Up for Support

A new independent foundation, the Partnership for a Healthier America, was created by a coalition of other nonprofits to guide the effort. The partners include the Robert Wood Johnson Foundation, W.K. Kellogg Foundation, The Alliance for Healthier Generation, The California Endowment, Kaiser Permanente, and Nemours.

In February 2013, Ms. Obama announced an extension of the campaign, Let's Move! Active Schools, a five-year plan to persuade at least 50,000 schools to offer students 60 minutes of physical activity before, after, or during the school day. Partners in the initiative included Nike, which pledged $50 million; GENYOUth Foundation, ChildObesity180, Kaiser Permanente and the General Mills Foundation, which pledged $20 million; and the U.S. Department of Education, which pledged to direct $80 million of physical education funds to the program.

Other groups joined the movement. The American Beverage Association announced that it would develop a more uniform and clear calorie label on all containers within two years. Disney said it would require all the food and beverage products promoted on its media channels, online channels, and theme parks to align with the federal standards by 2015.

Major chains such as Walmart and Walgreens agreed to build stores in areas known as "food deserts," where more than 9 million Americans lack places to buy healthy and fresh foods. Birds Eye said it would invest at least $2 million for three years to encourage children to eat more vegetables and would distribute 50 million coupons in support of the effort.

The American Academy of Pediatrics asked doctors to monitor the body-mass index of child patients and when necessary to prescribe simple steps parents can take to promote healthier activities and eating for their children. More than 150 hospitals agreed to offer healthier fruits, vegetables, whole grains, and low-calorie selections in patient meals and in their cafeterias.

Faith and community organizations supported the effort through local wellness programs that were co-sponsored by Faith United to End Childhood Obesity and Save the Children, by planting 1,500 gardens, by helping start 7,000 farmers markets and 1,500 gardens, and by making fresh produce available to more than 5,000 food pantries.

Spreading the Message

A dynamic Web site (http://www.letsmove.gov/) was designed to support the campaign, with sections dedicated to helping children and parents "Learn the Facts"; "Eat Healthy"; "Get Active"; "Take Action"; and "Join Us." The colorful site offered information, encouragement, recipes, and opportunities to sign up and link with other organizations. A blog offered personal updates and photographs throughout the campaign. Information was available in English and Spanish.

The campaign also used social media sites to share information. Ms. Obama's @FLOTUS account sent tweets such as "'The food our kids are eating today will affect their health for decades' #KidsStateDinner #LetsMove" and "'Parents deserve to have the information they need to make healthy choices for their kids.' #LetsMove." A Facebook page for "Let's Move!" (www.facebook.com/letsmove) offered photos, recipes, comments, and graphics.

Ms. Obama promoted the campaign through appearances at schools, parks, and other events across the country and made numerous television appearances, from the *Tonight Show* to *Nickelodeon*. Kid Reporters for The Scholastic Kids Press Corps covered the campaign, writing stories about the many ways in which Ms. Obama promoted "Let's Move!"

An assortment of print, radio, and video public service announcements (PSAs) were developed each year for the campaign. Warner Brothers and Scholastic Media worked with the Ad Council and the U.S. Department of Health and Human Services to develop and run public service announcements that featured well-known pro athletes promoting "60 Minutes of Play a Day." Some featured children's television characters such as Big Bird from Sesame Street. When the 2013 NBA champion Miami Heat players visited the White House, they filmed a PSA with Ms. Obama. The PSA was then featured on ABC, CNN, ESPN, VH1, and other outlets. The YouTube video got more than 3.5 million views, and Ms. Obama's Instagram photo about the PSA got more than 27,000 "likes."

By 2012, according to a Washington Post/Kaiser Family Foundation survey, more than 80 percent of Americans said they had heard of the "Let's Move!" campaign.

The USDA developed a new Web site to host a revamped food pyramid and created an interactive database, the "Food Environment Atlas," to map healthy food environments in communities. The USDA also worked with members of the School Nutrition Association and other school food suppliers to foster participation in the Healthier U.S. School Challenge. Congress passed the Healthy, Hunger-Free Kids Act of 2010 requiring healthier food to be served in school lunchrooms, a move that stirred backlash when some children refused to eat the new options.

QUESTIONS FOR REFLECTION

1. How will the success of this campaign be evaluated? What metrics should be used in gauging the effectiveness of public information or public health campaigns?
2. This campaign engaged a wide range of stakeholders, from individual celebrities to for-profit corporations. How might a public affairs practitioner or a public information specialist best balance the needs and interests of these varied groups?
3. The campaign has faced criticism from some who see government information campaigns as too intrusive. What should the limitations be when public affairs practitioners plan and execute such campaigns?

Information for this case is drawn from Centers for Disease Control and Prevention. (February 27, 2014). Childhood obesity facts. http://www.cdc.gov/healthyyouth/obesity/facts.htm; Cohen, Elyse. (February 9, 2014). Let's Move! anniversary: Four years of showing how we're moving towards a healthier nation. Let's Move! Blog. http://www.letsmove.gov/blog/2014/02/09/let%E2%80%99s-move-anniversary-four-years-showing-how-we%E2%80%99re-moving-towards-healthier-nation; Goodin, Emily. (February 28, 2013). Michelle Obama announces expansion of "Let's Move!" anti-obesity program. The Hill. http://thehill.com/video/in-the-news/285533-michelle-obama-announces-expansion-of-lets-move-program#ixzz37x5oiv; Hosmer, Jonas. (February 10, 2010). Let's Move! to fight obesity. Scholastic News. http://www.scholastic.com/browse/article.jsp?id=3753544; Kane, Jason, & Chanoine, Saskia. (February. 9, 2012). As Michelle Obama's anti-obesity push turns 2, it's time for a check-up. *PBS Newshour*. http://www.pbs.org/newshour/rundown/second-anniversary-of-lets-move; Office of the First Lady. (February 9, 2010). First Lady Michelle Obama launches Let's Move: America's move to raise a healthier generation of kids. News Release. www.whitehouse.gov/the-press-office/first-lady-michelle-obama-launches-lets-move-americas-move-raise-a-healthier-genera; Thompson, Kirssah. (February 9, 2012). Michelle Obama keeps moving with "Let's Move." *The Washington Post*. http://www.washingtonpost.com/politics/michelle-obama-keeps-moving-with-lets-move/2012/02/09/gIQAAAQc1Q_story.html.

CASE 29: COMMEMORATING THE FIGHT FOR CANADA: THE 200TH ANNIVERSARY OF THE WAR OF 1812

From 2012 to 2015, the government of Canada sponsored a commemoration of the War of 1812 as it anticipated celebration of the 150th anniversary of its Confederation in 2017. On June 18, 1812, Americans declared war on Great Britain and its North American colonies. The December 24, 1814, peace negotiations resulted in the signing of the Treaty of Ghent, which established the border between the United States and what would become the nation of Canada—the longest undefended border in the world. The early conflict laid the groundwork for Canada's Confederation and its emergence as an independent nation. The commemoration allowed Canada to showcase the many cultures that have enriched its independence and unity.

A Tribute to History and Diversity

In a message on the commemoration Web site, Prime Minister Stephen Harper encouraged Canadians to pay tribute to the war and their diverse heritage.

> The War of 1812 was a seminal event in the making of our great country. On the occasion of its 200th anniversary, I invite all Canadians to share in our history and commemorate our proud and brave ancestors who fought and won against enormous odds. . . . June 2012 will mark 200 years since the declaration of the War of 1812—a war that saw Aboriginal peoples, local and volunteer militias, and English and French-speaking regiments fight together to save Canada from American invasion.

Activities, events, and educational experiences funded in large part by the national government's Department of Canadian Heritage marked the celebration. Offering grants through the 1812 Commemoration Fund, the department coordinated the three-year celebration, working with other federal departments and agencies, the Royal Canadian Navy, Army and Air Force, municipalities, the First Nations and Métis, and regional War of 1812 organizations.

The key images selected for celebration during the campaign were four diverse historical characters: Major-General Sir Isaac Brock, the Canadian general who defeated the Americans at Fort Detroit and was later killed during the Battle of Queenston; Shawnee Chief Tecumseh, who fought alongside Brock and led some 800 native warriors against the Americans; Charles de Salaberry, a French-speaking British soldier who defended Montreal against American advances; and Laura Secord, who made a heroic 20 mile walk from the Niagara area to warn British troops of a planned American attack.

A robust Web site helped share information about the commemoration, and banners, posters, videos, photographs, speeches, and publications carried key messages.

Celebrating Military, Political and Cultural Events

Some of the activities and events that marked the three-year-long commemoration included:

- Revitalization of historic military sites, such as the Fort York National Historic Site, which houses the largest collection of authentic 1812-era buildings in Canada. The building of a virtual heritage trail network. Artists created an interactive installation of 200 tents, called "The Encampment," to detail stories of the civilians touched by the war. In October, Fort York hosted an outdoor 1812-related film festival, a lecture series, and a Regency Ball. On April 27, 2013, First Nations representatives led a sunrise ceremony and commemorative service for The Battle of York at the fort. The next day a large military parade traveled from downtown Toronto to Fort York.
- A special traveling exhibition created by the Canadian War Museum examined the War from the perspectives of the Canadians, Americans, British, and Native Americans.
- An education campaign about the importance of the War in Canadian history, with extensive teaching and learning resources, including lesson plans, assignments, quizzes and a timeline, in both English and French for grades 5, 7–9 was available through the commemoration Web site.
- The Royal Canadian Mint created five commemorative coins in honor of the anniversary. Four of the coins honored the four key personalities selected to represent the War. The fifth commemorated the HMS Shannon, a naval vessel that lost 23 crew members while capturing a U.S. warship.
- The Canada Post issued two commemorative stamps, one featuring Chief Tecumseh and the second General Sir Isaac Brock.
- Members of the Canadian Forces, Canada Company, the Canadian National Exhibition (CNE), Exhibition Place and the Canadian International Air Show presented "By Sea, By Land and By Air" events in August and September, 2012.

- The Royal Canadian Navy 2012 presented "Operation Sail" events at locations in the Great Lakes, the Eastern seaboard, and New Orleans.
- On October 2012, participants from Fort George in Canada and Fort Niagara in the United States performed a re-enactment of the Battle of Queenston.
- Library and Archives Canada presented a virtual exhibition of rare portraits and archival documents from the period.
- The funding of *Queenston Soldiers*, a documentary film that highlights the role of African-Canadian militias in the war.
- An exhibit highlighting the Aboriginal contributions to the war offered by the Aboriginal Affairs and Northern Development Canada.
- Support for up to 100 historical re-enactments, commemorations, and other local events in municipalities across the country.

In a speech at the official launch of the commemoration in Toronto on June 18, 2012, James Moore, the minister of Canadian Heritage and Official Languages, said:

> The 200th anniversary of the War of 1812 is an opportunity for all Canadians to take pride in our traditions and our collective history. Recognizing today's anniversary, the bicentennial of the War of 1812, is an important step in recognizing our past, celebrating our heroes and understanding all those who have sacrificed so that Canada can today stand tall and proud.

Questions for Reflection

1. Who were the critical stakeholders for the Canadian government as it planned this commemoration?
2. Evaluate the communication tools used in this campaign. How do they reflect a concern for diversity?
3. Commemoration of events such as wars can unify—or divide—nations and regions. What were the strategic purposes of the Canadian commemoration?
4. What does this campaign demonstrate about effective multicultural communication practices?

Information for this case was drawn from The War of 1812 Web site at http://1812.gc.ca/eng/1305654894724/1305655293741 and from Canadian Heritage. (October 11, 2012). Harper government invests in

War of 1812 documentary film. News Release. http://pch.gc.ca/eng/1349459422266/1349460036842; Gariépy, Sébastien. (October 14, 2011). Harper government invests in legacy projects to commemorate the 200th anniversary of the War of 1812. News Release. http://1812gc.ca/eng/1318621202062; Gerard, Shane. (December 8, 2011). Toronto's War of 1812 Bicentennial program announced. City of Toronto News Release. http://wx.toronto.ca/inter/it/newsrel.nsf/11476e3d3711f56e85256616006b891f/2eb38945ad6df98d85257960005c5b5e?OpenDocument; Moore, James. (June 18, 2012). Speaking notes for the Honourable James Moore, minister of Canadian Heritage and Official Languages on the occasion of the official launch of commemorative events for the 200th anniversary of the War of 1812. Speech. http://pch.gc.ca/eng/1342616885503; Reeves, Alex. (June 18, 2012). The Royal Canadian Mint announces series of five commemorative circulation coins celebrating the 200th anniversary of the War of 1812. News Release. http://www.mint.ca/store/news/the-royal-canadian-mint-announces-series-of-five-commemorative-circulation-coins-celebrating-the-200th-anniversary-of-the-war-of-1812-5300010?cat=News+releases&nid=7000002&parentnid=600004&nodeGroup=About+the+Mint&lang=en_CA#.U6nqlvldWCK.

CASE 30: "THE RECKONING": MEMORIAL AND CEREMONY MARK 10-YEAR ANNIVERSARY OF 9/11

Figure 8.1 The World Trade Center ceremony marking the 10th anniversary of the attacks takes place at the National September 11 Memorial on September 11, 2011, in New York. (AP Photo: Mark Lennihan.)

On the 10th anniversary of the day Al Qaida terrorists flew two airplanes into the World Trade Center, one into the Pentagon, and one into a field in Pennsylvania in a failed attempt at a third target, the Ground Zero Memorial Plaza opened as part of commemoration events of the tragic events of September 11, 2001.

During the 10 years of planning for the memorial and the sad anniversary, many psychologists and many in government and the media talked of the importance of using the day to move from mourning to memorializing. Annually, the names of those killed would be called aloud, and the timing of the attack remembered with a moment of silence in New York City and many other sites across the nation.

For 230 days following the attack in New York City, workers carefully combed through debris left by the fallen towers collecting pieces of bodies and lives. No artifact was deemed too small to save and no body part was too small to save for possible identification. While the permanent memorial was planned and built, visitors to the makeshift Ground Zero Memorial could see large amounts of the personal debris saved and oddly positioned in glass casings. For example, a smudged and singed teddy bear sat next to part of a briefcase.

Planning a Permanent Memorial

Planning for a permanent memorial began early. It was clear a memorial should be at the World Trade Center site, but there was much debate about what the memorial should be and how it should be opened, centering around three major questions:

1. What would the surrounding buildings look like?
2. Would it be finished in time for the 10th anniversary?
3. Who would be invited to the ceremony and official first viewing of the memorial?

Construction of a memorial had strategic buy-in from victims, politicians, and citizens from New York, the rest of America, and global allies. There was agreement that the site had to stand as something uniquely American as well as memorializing those who died. Because the area is the heart of the business district, the memorial had not only to manage visitors, but also to allow commerce to be practiced around it.

A difficult question involved ownership of the site itself and the planning for future construction. In some ways, virtually everyone affected by the tragedy felt some emotional ownership of the World Trade Center site, and before the acrid dust had actually settled, opinions about the future of the site were being shared. It was possible for the property's legal owners and city and state politicians to sit in conference rooms to make plans for the site and discuss the outcome.

On the other hand, victims and their families, people at community meetings, and ordinary people in the streets all had desires, demands, and opinions about the memorial, and some had media contacts and political clout. Public opinion was filtering up through blogs, interviews, online comments, and polls taken by major news outlets. Larry Silverstein, the developer who owned the lease to the Twin Towers, received thousands of letters the first month after the towers fell. There were many opinions on how it should physically be rebuilt—some said it should have the latest in eco-friendly and green space design. Others asserted that it should be a park, a commercial space, or contain affordable housing. Whatever was actually built, public opinion called for it to depict good versus evil, peace and revenge, rebirth and memorial.

Blogger Andrew Sullivan posted:

> Someone sent me this small quote from a book on architecture. It's from Minoru Yamasaki, the designer of the World Trade Center. Yamasaki wrote: "The World Trade Center should, because of its importance, become a living representation of man's belief in humanity, his need for individual dignity, his belief in the co-operation of men, and through this co-operation his ability to find greatness." No wonder these demons destroyed it. I want Bush tomorrow to say that we will rebuild it—taller, bigger, stronger.

But there were opposing views. According to Greenspan's book, *Battle for Ground Zero*, philosopher Crispin Sartwell countered Yamasaki's view in an opinion piece in the *Philadelphia Inquirer*—a major daily newspaper. He wrote:

> Yamasaki's claim that the WTC represented individual dignity is laughable . . . .The gleaming glass and steel rectangles were objects of a kind of unimaginable ferocity, a human imagination so dedicated to its own annihilation that it was the opposite of anything mammalian, a kind of refutation of the human body . . . .Let's build something human . . . .Not a symbol, a real place; not a place to die, a place to live.

Greenspan called the rhetoric about the site's fate "biblical" and filled with "irreconcilable desires."

Cooperation Needed

Before any of the symbolic or physical opinions could be implemented, though, public and private cooperation was necessary in sorting who would be responsible for what would occur. Just six weeks before the September 11 attacks, Silverstein had made the biggest real estate deal in New York's history, paying $3.2 billion to the Port Authority of New

York and New Jersey for a 99-year lease on the Twin Towers. At that time, New Yorkers began speculating how Lower Manhattan would change because of the deal.

In the days immediately following the attacks, Silverstein worked out a monumental insurance claim and contacted his architect. By September 20, he announced his rebuilding plans at a press conference, a plan that would transform New York's skyline. The entire footprint would also include three other buildings that were damaged by the attacks, various memorial attractions, and a transportation hub that would be designed above and below ground. Plans were for the entire site to be completed by 2020.

Many architects became involved in the planning. An architect was hired by the Port Authority to redesign the transportation hub that had been badly damaged by the attack. More capacity would be needed to accommodate the throngs of people expected to visit the site for years to come. Different architects were engaged for the memorial plaza, the museum, and the three additional commercial buildings. For months after the attack, two large spotlights shot up from the area into the night sky and seemingly beyond as architect Michael Arad and landscape artist Peter Walker planned the memorial plaza.

Coordinating the symbolic and prosaic visions and details for such construction was difficult. It was decided that a new skyscraper would be built, 1,176 feet high with 104 floors. Even though construction teams would at times set records in how fast they could build a commercial tower, all the controversy would delay the completion of the $3.2 billion building several years past the 10th anniversary, leaving security fencing, cranes, scaffolding, and half-finished structures present at the commemorative event. Yet, the unveiling of the 9/11 memorial on the 10th anniversary brought an emblematic end to the decade-long controversy about how the physical memorial would be constructed.

Some Stakeholders Not Invited

Family members of victims of the attacks were invited to the ceremony as well as to the first viewing of the memorial the day before the ceremony. New York Mayor Michael Bloomberg's office told media the ceremony would concentrate on victims' families. Bloomberg's spokespeople said the reasons were because it was the right thing to do and there were space constraints.

However, that focus meant that first responders were not going to be invited, a decision that caused friction with the fire and police departments and advocacy groups. Spokespeople for the various groups called Bloomberg's decision a "slap in the face" and visible evidence their untreated ailments that resulted from their working in the aftermath of the attacks were going to be ignored (and not compensated) by the city. Moreover, they said they felt that being left out of the ceremony meant being left out of the "official narrative of recovery and renewal."

The Dedication Ceremony

By September 2011, the National 9/11 Memorial was complete, and the dedication took place around a plaza that has been praised widely for its memorial and ecological feats.

The plaza stands on the area where the Twin Towers stood. It covers half of the 16 acres of the original World Trade Center site and features two of the largest fountains ever built. The artificial waterfalls cascade over a square, granite fountain that is sunken into the exact imprint of the Twin Towers' foundation. The water falls from a heated and cooled (so it is always touchable) bronze edifice inscribed with the names of the fallen employees, vendors, visitors, airplane passengers, and first responders. The water falls into a reflecting pool and eventually flows into a seemingly bottomless void in the center of the fountain.

A series of 30-foot white oak trees, which were groomed for five years before being placed in the plaza, surrounds the fountains. Eventually there will be 400 trees that will double in size. The trees are an ecological masterpiece planted in the plaza, which is actually a six-foot high engineered structure designed to keep the trees watered, drained and healthy.

The ceremony began with a solemn welcome from New York City Mayor Michael Bloomberg. President Obama then read a passage from Psalm 46. Family members then began reading the names of those who were killed. At 8:46 a.m. and 9:03 a.m., bells were rung to commemorate the times when the planes hit the towers. President George W. Bush read a quotation from Abraham Lincoln. Musician Paul Simon sang the "Sound of Silence" to close the ceremony.

The ceremony was broadcast and streamed live all over the world. Split screens showed coordinated details at the other attack sites in Pennsylvania and Washington as well as other commemorations around the world such as Grosvenor Square in London.

Mourning and Memorializing as an Event

The reviews of the ceremony and the memorial were positive, despite criticism from supporters of the first responders who had not been invited. Even the failure to complete the construction was forgiven. *The New York Times* published a special commemorative section titled "The Reckoning," a term once used to denote "the settlement of a bill."

The New York Times writer Sam Anderson thought the unfinished Ground Zero was perfectly fitting for a nation that he said "prefers to be constantly under construction." He noted some of the nation's most iconic photographs are of construction projects, like the *Life* magazine photo of the construction workers having lunch as their feet dangle from a steel joist on a partly constructed Empire State Building or the one of sculptors rapelling down George Washington's nose during the construction of

Mount Rushmore. Anderson called the perpetual construction zone left in the wake of the tallest construction project in American history a more "potent symbol than any possible finished product."

Questions for Reflection

1. What were the strengths of the commemoration ceremony? How might it have been improved?
2. Were the appropriate stakeholders invited to the ceremony? Why or why not?
3. In what ways should solemn commemorations be planned differently than celebrations?
4. What are some public relations principles that help practitioners negotiate the pitfalls of high cost, high emotion planning?

Information drawn from the Web site http://www.911memorial.org/memorial and Craven, J. (n.d.) What are they building on Ground Zero?; Fountain, H. (September 11, 2011). Ground Zero now. *The New York Times.*; Greenspan, E. (2013). *Battle for Ground Zero: Inside the political struggle to rebuild the World Trade Center.* New York: Palgrave MacMillan; Hampson, R., & Moore, M. (September 11, 2011). On 10th 9/11 anniversary, wounds fresh as healing continues. *USA Today.* http://usatoday30.usatoday.com/news/nation/story/2011-09-11/september-11-10th-anniversary/50360724/1; Kennicott, P. (August 26, 2011). Review: 9/11 Memorial in New York. *The Washington Post.* http://www.washingtonpost.com/lifestyle/style/review-911-memorial-in-new-york/2011/08/04/gIQARX-ETgJ_story.html; Kleinfield, N. (September 11, 2011). Getting here from there. *The New York Times*; Moore, R. (July 30, 2011). 9/11 Ground Zero: why has its rebirth turned sour? *The Guardian*; Nakamura, David, & Lynch, Colum. (September 11, 2011). America marks 10th anniversary of Sept. 11 terror attacks. *The Washington Post.* http://www.washingtonpost.com/politics/america-marks-10th-anniversary-of-sept-11-terror-attacks/2011/09/11/gIQA9QssJK_story.html; Stein, J. (August 30, 2011). First responders decry exclusion from 9/11 ceremony. CNN.com; Sullivan, M. (September 11, 2012). How to cover the 11th anniversary of 9/11? *The New York Times*; Templeton, Ted, & Lumley T. (August 17, 2002) 9/11 in numbers. *The Guardian.* http://www.theguardian.com/world/2002/aug/18/usa.terrorism; Van Camp, S. (April 1, 2013). 6 tips for PR success with your events. *PRNews.* http://www.prnewsonline.com/water-cooler/2013/04/01/tis-the-season-6-tips-for-event-pr-success/; Hampson, R. & Moore, M.T. (September 11, 2011). On 10th 9/11 anniversary, wounds fresh as healing continues. *USA Today.* http://usatoday30.usatoday.com/news/nation/story/2011-09-11/september-11-10th-anniversary/50360724/1.

CASE 31: BRITISH PETROLEUM, THE GOVERNMENT, AND THE MEDIA INFLUENCE PUBLIC OPINION DURING AND AFTER DEEPWATER HORIZON EXPLOSION

Figure 8.2 The fire from the Deepwater horizon explosion lit the sky. (Photo: NOAA.)

Figure 8.3 National Geographic videographer Bob Perrin films an oil slick at the Deepwater Horizon site. (Photo: NOAA.)

An explosion on the Deepwater Horizon oil rig in the Gulf of Mexico on April 20, 2010, resulted in the loss of 11 lives and numerous injuries to oil workers on the rig and billions of oil leaking from the Macondo exploration well operated by the international energy firm British Petroleum (BP). For several months, the spill polluted Gulf Coast waters with untold millions of barrels of oil—the U.S. government said upward of 4 million, BP said 2.4 million—that prompted a loss of revenue and recreation for businesses, residents, and visitors to the five states bordering the Gulf.

On a dedicated Deep Horizon Web site,[1] BP offers this explanation of the accident:

> The accident involved a well integrity failure, followed by a loss of hydrostatic control of the well. This was followed by a failure to control the flow from the well with the blowout preventer (BOP) equipment, which allowed the release and subsequent ignition of hydrocarbons. Ultimately, the BOP emergency functions failed to seal the well after the initial explosions.

An apology follows: "We regret the impacts on the environment and livelihoods of those in the communities affected. We have, and continue to, put in place measures to help ensure it does not happen again."

Media Coverage Provides Multiple Images

The disaster offered haunting images: Fire burning on the oil rig. Beaches covered with thick, dark oil. Testimony at Congressional hearings. Coverage, particularly on television, was intensive for more than three months and continued for years as legal battles ensued. Polls conducted by the Pew Research Center for the People & the Press reported that between 50 percent and 60 percent of Americans said they were following the story "very closely" throughout the summer.

While numerous story lines were presented by the coverage, the Pew Center for Journalism, which studied media coverage of the ongoing story, concluded three major storylines were depicted: corporate responsibility; the government's role; and the environmental and social impact/clean-up and containment, which got the largest amount of coverage. The report concluded:

> They largely avoided the temptation to turn the disaster into a full-blown political finger-pointing story. The Obama White House generated decidedly mixed media coverage for its role in the spill saga, but questions about its role diminished over time—in part thanks to a Republican misfire. And the administration fared considerably better than BP and its CEO Tony Hayward, who on balance were portrayed as the villains of the story.

BP Responds to the Crisis

While later investigations showed that the energy corporation, its rig owner TransOcean, and cement contractor Halliburton all shared some responsibility for the disaster, oil giant BP was the center of government investigation and public ire. CEO Tony Hayward became the face of the crisis to such an extent that *The New York Times* concluded, "If there's a public villain of the Gulf of Mexico oil spill—one person who, rightly or not, will be remembered for the deadly blowout, the black slick and all that followed—it's probably Tony Hayward."

During the early weeks of the crisis, according to Reuters, BP sought to shift responsibility for the spill to the other agents. However, negative media coverage and political pressure led BP to change tactics. CEO Hayward became more direct, seeking to explain the various actions being taken by BP to cap the well.

BP launched a public relations offensive in May 2010, investing what some said was $50 million. The campaign hired Anne Kolton, a former spokesperson for former Vice President Dick Cheney. Reportedly, the corporation purchased ads on Google attempting to drive anyone searching for information related to the oil spill to its Web site. A BP ad campaign was launched on television and in major U.S. newspapers in June 2010. The video commercial shows Hayward apologizing for the oil spill and explaining what BP was doing to respond to the environmental disaster. In the commercial, Hayward says: "We know it is our responsibility to keep you informed. And do everything we can so this never happens again. We will get this done. We will make this right."

However, his public image was not strong. In late May, his quote, "I'd like my life back," was widely replayed on news and social media to wildly negative response. He apologized for the comment on June 2 in a statement posted on the BP Facebook page, saying:

> I made a hurtful and thoughtless comment on Sunday when I said that "I wanted my life back." When I read that recently, I was appalled. I apologize, especially to the families of the 11 men who lost their lives in this tragic accident. Those words don't represent how I feel about this tragedy, and certainly don't represent the hearts of the people of BP—many of whom live and work in the Gulf—who are doing everything they can to make things right. My first priority is doing all we can to restore the lives of the people of the Gulf region and their families—to restore their lives, not mine.

Comments posted in response were largely negative.

The next day, Hayward and BP Chairman Carl-Henric Svanberg told shareholders in a release that the Gulf spill was the corporation's "top priority, along with rebuilding trust and confidence in BP and ensuring that such an accident never happens again." More than $1 billion had already been spent in direct costs for the cleanup, according to the release.

Hayward testified before a Congressional committee on June 17 where he and the corporation were sharply criticized; some media commentators criticized his testimony for seeming unconcerned or callous. And, when he went to the Isle of Wight in England to watch his yacht race only a few days after the testimony, it seemed to media audiences that he was either unaware or uncaring of the impacts of the spill.

In October 2010, Hayward was replaced as CEO. In the release announcing the management change, Hayward stated: "The Gulf of Mexico explosion was a terrible tragedy for which—as the man in charge of BP when it happened—I will always feel a deep responsibility, regardless of where blame is ultimately found to lie."

The Government Reacts

The federal government was faced with several critical problems—how to help cap the well so the oil would stop flowing; how to stem the environmental and economic damage from the spill; how to fairly investigate its cause and then seek judicial responses as needed; and what regulatory actions should be taken to prevent other such accidents. Federal responses to the oil spill and the recovery efforts were cataloged on a Web site, http://www.restorethegulf.gov/.

In his role as the nation's spokesperson, President Obama's statements and actions were scrutinized. After an independent commission was commissioned in May to investigate the explosion, at a June 1 news conference in the Rose Garden at the White House, he pledged that investigators would have freedom to "follow the facts wherever they may lead, without fear or favor." A few days later in a speech, he called on Congress to pass a climate change bill, which some criticized as an opportunistic move to link his agenda to the crisis and others praised as an appropriate response to public concerns about the environment.

But as the oil continued to spill and the economic impact resulting from oily beaches and sea animals grew, many pressed for Obama to direct actions to ease the crisis. In a speech from the Oval Office on June 15, Obama outlined the government's position, recounting the appointment of a special commission to investigate the causes of the spill and to seek changes to ensure one would not occur again, and a federal commitment to coastal reconstruction. He said:

> But make no mistake: We will fight this spill with everything we've got for as long as it takes. We will make BP pay for the damage their company has caused. And we will do whatever's necessary to help the Gulf Coast and its people recover from this tragedy.

Obama assured residents of the area of his faith that the area would recover from the crisis, saying: "We pray for the people of the Gulf. And we pray that a hand may guide us through the storm towards a brighter day."

Unfortunately, it would be many months before the damage from the spill was cleaned up, and lawsuits resulting from the disaster continued for years, which kept the issue on the public agenda. Bob Garfield, writing in *Advertising Age*, said the crisis had highlighted both "greenwashing" and "godwashing." He concluded: "Words matter. Images matter, and when you contaminate them you despoil your own communications environment." Somber words to describe a sobering crisis.

NOTE

1. http://www.bp.com/en/global/corporate/gulf-of-mexico-restoration/deepwater-horizon-accident-and-response.html.

Questions for Reflection

1. Did Tony Hayward "make it right" as promised in the company's public relations advertising campaign? Why or why not? How important is the role of top leadership in communication during a crisis?
2. When managing a crisis, what are some of the most important public relations communication principles organizations should follow?
3. When managing a crisis, what are some of the most important public relations ethical guidelines organizations should follow?
4. Crises that last over many months pose particular challenges for organizations. How can organizations evaluate the effectiveness of communication during and after a long-term crisis?

Information for this case was drawn from Associated Press (September 19, 2013) BP oil spill: federal judge accepts Halliburton guilty plea agreement. *The Guardian.* http://www.theguardian.com/environment/2013/sep/19/bp-oil-spill-halliburton-pleads-guilty; Bergin, Tom. (June 1, 2010). Special report: Inside BP's war room. Reuters. http://www.reuters.com/article/2010/06/01/us-oil-spill-bp-idUSTRE65059M20100601; BP. (June 3, 2010). Chairman and CEO give assurance that BP will meet its obligations in Gulf of Mexico. Release. http://www.bp.com/en/global/corporate/press/press-releases/chairman-and-ceo-give-assurance-that-bp-will-meet-its-obligations-in-gulf-of-mexico.html; BP. (July 27, 2010). BP CEO Tony Hayward to step down and be succeeded by Robert Dudley. Release. http://www.bp.com/en/global/corporate/press/press-releases/bp-ceo-tony-hayward-to-step-down-and-be-succeeded-by-robert-dudley.html; BP. (n.d.).

Deep Water Horizon accident and response. http://www.bp.com/en/global/corporate/gulf-of-mexico-restoration/deepwater-horizon-accident-and-response.html; (June 17, 2010). http://www.cbsnews.com/news/rep-joe-barton-apologizes-to-bps-tony-hayward-for-white-house-shake-down-video/; BP oil spill by the numbers (September 14, 2010). *The Independent.* http://www.independent.co.uk/environment/bp-oil-spill-disaster-by-numbers-2078396.html; Courson, P. (September 27, 2010) Public perception of BP affected spill response, Allen says. CNN.com. http://www.cnn.com/2010/US/09/27/gulf.oil.disaster/; Durando, Jessica. (June 1, 2010). BP's Tony Hayward: "I'd like my life back." *USA Today.* http://content.usatoday.com/communities/greenhouse/post/2010/06/bp-tony-hayward-apology/1#.U-86q_ldWAU; Eilperin, Juliet, & Farenholdt, David. (May 22, 2010). Graham, Reilly to lead investigation of oil spill. *The Washington Post.* http://www.washingtonpost.com/wpdyn/content/article/2010/05/21/AR2010052102403.html; Garfield, B. (June 21, 2010). From greenwashing to godwashing, BP and Obama fail at image control. *Advertising Age, 81*, 25; Jacobson, M. (July 9, 2013). By the numbers: The oil spill and BP's legal troubles. *PBS Newshour.* http://www.pbs.org/newshour/rundown/gulf-oil-spill-by-the-numbers/; Krauss, Clifford, & Schwartz, John. (November 15, 2012). BP will plead guilty and pay over $4 billion. *The New York Times.* http://www.nytimes.com/2012/11/16/business/global/16iht-bp16.html?pagewanted=all; Martinez, Michael. (February 14, 2013). Transocean pleads guilty, fined 2nd-biggest penalty for Gulf spill.CNN.com. http://www.cnn.com/2013/02/14/justice/transocean-deepwater-fine/; Mufson, Stefen, & Shear, Michael D. (June 3, 2010). Obama hopes oil spill boosts support for climate bill. *The Washington Post.* http://www.washingtonpost.com/wpdyn/content/article/2010/06/02/AR2010060200380.html?sid=ST2010060104078; Obama, Barack. (June 15, 2010). Remarks by the President to the Nation on the BP Oil Spill. http://www.whitehouse.gov/the-press-office/remarks-president-nation-bp-oil-spill; Pew Center (2010). *100 Days of Gushing Oil: Eight Things to Know About How the Media Covered the Gulf Disaster.* Report. http://www.journalism.org/2010/08/25/100-days-gushing-oil/); Poll: 70% say BP handling oil spill badly. CBS News. http://www.cbsnews.com/news/poll-70-say-bp-handling-oil-spill-badly/; Reed, Stanley. (September 1, 2012). Tony Hayward gets his life back. *The New York Times*, p. BU1; Reuters. (July 26, 2013). Halliburton pleads guilty to destroying Gulf oil spill evidence. http://www.reuters.com/article/2013/07/25/us-gulf-spill-halliburton-idUSBRE96O1HF20130725; Ryan, Kevin. (June 10, 2010). Don't blame BP for advertising on Google. Ad Age. http://adage.com/article/digital-next/blame-bp-advertising-google/144567/; Shear, Michael D. (June 1, 2010). Obama meets with leaders of new oil spill commission. *The*

Washington Post. http://www.washingtonpost.com/wpdyn/content/article/2010/06/01/AR2010060101416.html?sid=ST2010060104078; Zak, Dan. (June 3, 2010). As oil spread, did BP battle to contain the media? *The Washington Post*. http://www.washingtonpost.com/wp-dyn/content/article/2010/06/03/AR2010060300848.html.

CASE 32: CRYPTOKIDS®: CRACKING THE GOVERNMENT CODE?

The site welcomes visitors with this message:

> Hi Kids! We're the CryptoKids® and we love cryptology. What's cryptology? Cryptology is making and breaking codes. It's so cool. We make codes so we can send secret messages to our friends. And we try to figure out what other people are writing about by breaking their codes. It's a lot of fun.

Animal Characters with Special Skills

The CryptoKids® are an assortment of nine animal characters with special interests and skills who are featured in a series of games and activities on the children's page. There's Crypto Cat® who grew up on a Navajo reservation and created a code based on the Navajo language. Her best friend is Decipher Dog®, whose stepmom works as a network engineer and whose dad is a police officer. Along with his time as a junior varsity quarterback, D-Dog works on the wireless computer network he's built for his home and cracks codes with his friends. Rosetta Stone®, the child of two archeologists, is home schooled so she can travel with her parents to digs and explore hieroglyphics.

The turtle, T-Top®, is a computer wizard, an interest he gained from his uncle who works for a computer company. Joules®, a squirrel, plays saxophone in the school band when she's not building sand castles with her family or working in electronics like her parent. The snow leopard twins, Cy® and Cindi®, whose dad is an army computer scientist and whose mom is a government engineer, make videos. These animals have formed a club called CryptoKids, and they are helped by Sergeant Sam®, an eagle who is a member of the U.S. military who visited their school to talk about coding.

Challenging Children to Stay Involved

The games and activities offered on the page are challenging. Logic puzzles, math challenges, and cypher and coding activities engage visitors to the page to spend time strengthening and practicing critical thinking and computation skills. Other links take visitors to the National Cryptologic

Museum site and to information about high school and college math programs such as the Math Education Partnership Program and the High-School Work Study Program (http://www.nsa.gov/academia/early_opportunities/index.shtml) and career and internship opportunities.

The site and its multiple opportunities for learning about cryptology have been offered to children (and other visitors) by the National Security Agency (NSA), whose vision is to achieve "global cryptologic dominance through responsive presence and network advantage," according to its Web site (www.nsa.gov), since 2005. The site includes a note to parents and teachers that explains, "Our goal was to provide a safe, educational, and fun place for kids to visit related to cryptology" (http://www.nsa.gov/kids/notices/notic00002.shtml).

The NSA site was developed by its public relations office, which used input from a variety of focus groups of children, teachers, and parents to craft content for the site. The number and variety of characters and activities on the NSA have been updated since the page's launch. The kids' page is likely designed to support the agency's third goal, as noted on its own site, to "attract, develop and engage an exceptional, diverse workforce prepared to overcome our cryptologic challenges."

Other Agencies Open Kids Zones

Similarly, the Central Intelligence Agency launched its own Kids Zone page in 2007 (https://www.cia.gov/kids-page). Its page invites visitors to learn about the agency through solving puzzles or playing games—and to "see some top secret things you won't find anywhere else." The games range from puzzles, concentration, word find, to photo analyses, world geography, aerial analysis, and coloring pages. Visitors who land on the site read:

> The CIA is an independent US government agency that provides national security "intelligence" to key US leaders so they can make important, informed decisions. CIA employees gather intelligence (or information) in a variety of ways, not just by "spying" like you see in the movies or on TV *(though we do some of that, too).*

The CIA page offers lesson plans, information resources and discussion points to help students learn more about the agency and its history (https://www.cia.gov/kids-page/parents-teachers).

The National Counterterrorism Center's Kids Zone page (http://www.nctc.gov/site/kids/) offers animated characters, a coloring book, music, and games such as "Liberty Tic-Tac-Toe" and "Geo's Map Match" and links to other federal security agencies' children's Web sites.

The federal Web sites were developed in response to a 1997 order from President Clinton, who instructed all government agencies to find ways to educate children about how the government works. The memo told agencies to:

> Focus on the identification and development of high-quality educational resources that promote high standards of teaching and learning in core subjects. Of particular importance are resources that will help students read well and independently by 4th grade, and master challenging mathematics, including algebra and geometry, by 8th grade.

Questions for Reflection

1. What key publics do Web sites like these seek to engage? What type of measurements would you suggest these agencies use in assessing the value of the Web sites?
2. Do the game-based sites now available on government-funded Web sites meet educational objectives—or are they more persuasive than informative?
3. Many corporations have also created game-filled Web sites to attract children and young adults. What type of cautions or warnings—if any—should Web-based game sites designed to attract children and young people for persuasive or educational purposes be required to display?

Information for this case is drawn from Clinton, William J. (April 18, 1997). Memorandum for the heads of executive departments and agencies. http://www.nrojr.gov/whmemo.txt; Parnass, Sarah. (November 4, 2011). CIA and NSA Web sites invite children. ABC News. http://abcnews.go.com/blogs/politics/2011/11/cia-and-nsa-websites-invite-children/; Schmidt, Michael. (January 25, 2014). On children's Web site, N.S.A. puts a furry, smiley face on its mission. *The New York Times*, A10; Vicens, A.J. (June 7, 2013). Spy kids: The NSA is looking for the next generation of sneaky geeks. Mother Jones. http://www.motherjones.com/mojo/2013/06/nsa-cryptokids-spy-kids.

PROFESSIONAL INSIGHT How can governments and government institutions seek to persuade citizens?

Figure 8.4 Dwain McIntosh, Retired Public Information Specialist

Managing stakeholders when you work for a state or federal institution is sometimes tricky business. In a government institution, a public relations practitioner's job is to provide information more than to persuade anybody of anything. However, the stakes also are often high and must hold up under intense media and public scrutiny. It is tempting for those not well versed in public relations ethics and ideals to withhold information. It can be a rude awakening for newly minted public relations practitioners when they encounter administrative personnel who would seek to keep public affairs officers out of the loop.

To me the first thing one must do when seeking to persuade citizens is to persuade administrators that honest, upfront information is often the easiest way to avoid trouble. Additionally, as a former reporter, communications officer in a state government, a communications point person for a political campaign and a public relations practitioner for a regional state university, I have found the collective experience leads me to believe you persuade citizens by honest information exchange and healthy media relationships. Citizens, media, and regulators all respond more sympathetically when provided with accurate, timely information. When they are not met with that information at the door of the governor's mansion for instance, they feel betrayed and seek information at the backdoor. The practitioner loses credibility and control of the rhetorical situation.

On most days, working for a government institution can be about promotion—celebrations and commemorations. About 95 percent of what you do is not controversial. It is just providing information to your publics. For instance, as a university director of public relations, I got requests on campus to do stories about lectures, concerts, art exhibits, or on some faculty member who had distinguished himself. You often hear the gatekeepers refer to that as fluff, because there is no controversy. However, by getting that information right—accurate, format friendly, timely—when something does happen on campus that could have implications those gatekeepers know you can be trusted. You build relationship capital with "the fluff."

However, the business of government institutions is to serve people, so transparent conveyance of actions taken is an important part of daily business as well. Historically, traditional media outlets like newspaper, radio, and television were meant to do just that: provide information so citizens could make informed decisions. In some ways, practitioners involved in government business still practice Ivy Lee's brand of public relations, which is why public relations offices are often called "office of communication" or "public information/affairs" or "information services."

Not only does persuasion "happen" when transparency is practiced, but also persuasion often comes in the form of educating citizens. Most regulations and regulating bodies are meant to do the same thing that all government institutions are supposed to do: protect the ordinary citizen. They are not meant to be scary authorities that only take punitive action, which is often the perception. Even government officials look to obfuscate because they are anxious about what regulators might find. Sometimes it takes educating all stakeholders in the purpose of regulation and government.

If citizens, regulators and government officials remember the mission (to protect) and all seek to be transparent, even when punishment is due it can be defused with honesty and a credible relationship.

Dwain McIntosh spent more than 20 years as the director of information services at Murray State University in Kentucky. Before his work in higher education, McIntosh worked on two political campaigns for Kentucky governor candidates. He was a communication specialist in the Department of Public Information in the Kentucky State Capital and was promoted to Assistant News Director. He began his career as an ace reporter for the Paducah Sun Democrat.

CHAPTER 9

Stakeholders

Activists

Activists are saints, sinners, and sometimes both. It depends on your perspective of the public issue on which activists have focused. Because issues seldom have only two sides, several activist organizations may get involved in a public discussion or controversy and try to influence its eventual outcome. Not only would the groups voice a range of viewpoints, but they also might use a variety of methods to grab attention and get support for their preferred outcome.

Activist groups generally adopt conventional behaviors, conforming to public expectations because there's little reward in intentionally annoying people. Some groups are more colorful or aggressive, especially if they have a hard time getting noticed. A small number are deliberately destructive and engage in illegal acts.

PURPOSES OF ACTIVISM

In democracies, activism contributes to the process of public life. Activists have influenced social acceptance of diverse lifestyles, social restraints on tobacco use, popular attitudes on animal rights, public debate on gun control, reproductive rights, alcohol consumption, and much more.

Activist groups, often called special-interest groups or advocacy groups, usually try to:

- Influence popular opinion.
- Promote changes in public policy.
- Exert pressure on corporations.
- Remedy social problems.
- Affect personal behavior.

In big cities and small towns around the world, community activism has been used successfully to spotlight social problems and propose solutions. Activists have organized campaigns against drug abuse, teen pregnancy, neighborhood deterioration, domestic violence, and homelessness.

They have formed programs to promote mass transit, historical preservation, youth activities, and fairness in hiring and housing.

GAINING PUBLIC ATTENTION

While some activism occurs quietly—riverkeepers checking the safety of local waters or urban farmers tending their lawn crops—often activism seeks a public stage, hoping to use media attention to focus attention on their cause and to arouse greater support. Actions such as marches, boycotts, even acts of civil disobedience, are planned and carefully executed.

Seeking celebrity involvement in activist campaigns is a longstanding tactic of groups who want more publicity. Videos or photos of a beautiful Hollywood actress testifying before a Congressional committee or a musician linking arms with those opposing construction of nuclear power plants may find a more prominent place in the news cycle than less well-known participants.

After purchasing shares in public corporations, activists gain the right to make statements and offer resolutions at annual meetings attended by investors. Shareholder resolutions proposed by activists not only draw public attention to the group's central concern, but also affect corporate decision making on sensitive issues. Even when the resolutions are voted down, corporate officers may later modify the practices that antagonized critics to avoid future confrontations.

The FrameWorks Institute offers a toolkit, Framing Public Issues,[1] that provides a research-based strategic approach for establishing issues as part of the public agenda that will be familiar to students of public relations. In explaining message development, the toolkit offers advice on framing messages and suggests six elements of the frame: context, numbers, messengers, visuals, metaphors, and tone.

DIGITAL MEDIA TAKE ACTIVISM GLOBAL

The popularity of social media has raised activism to a global scale. For example, in May 2014, when First Lady Michelle Obama tweeted a photo of herself holding a sign reading "#BringBackOurGirls," she brought international attention to a social media movement aimed at highlighting the need for intervening to protect Nigerian girls who had been kidnapped from a boarding school. However, her message was then recontextualized by activists opposed to the use of military drones—illustrating the multiple frames used by activists seeking public attention and public action.

Web sites that host petitions provide an easy option for those seeking to gain attention for a cause or for those who want to express support. Similarly, "liking" a cause-related Facebook page, retweeting a message, or commenting on a YouTube video has become as common as a bumper sticker on an automobile or a slogan-branded T-shirt.

Social protests such as Occupy Wall Street and the political revolts that came to be known as the Arab Spring that often relied on social media exchanges to spread messages about meetings, strikes, marches, and resistance, illustrate the speed and the reach of digital communication.

AN UNDEREXAMINED ROLE

Some public relations scholars have said that the study and practice of public relations have focused too much on examining the discipline from the standpoint of a practitioner working in or for a large organization. More work is needed, they've said, to understand relationships from the activists' perspectives and to listen to voices in the community that have been completely left out of discussions on public issues. In some circumstances, arriving at a win–win solution may simply mean that the quiet voices of small groups or unaffiliated individuals have been ignored.

In contrast, some critics have said that carefully orchestrated activist campaigns often distort the true dimensions of popular opinion. Some campaigns, critics say, hijack the public agenda by using conflict to lure the news media to a shallow pool of controversy and then claim it's the mainstream of public thought.

The CEO of Daimler-Chrysler's Chrysler Group said, "You might call it the difference between natural public opinion and synthetic public opinion."

As you consider these cases, seek to identify the public relations problem or opportunity, the methods and tools used to resolve the situation, and how one might evaluate the success or failure of the public relations efforts. Explore these questions: What would characterize a mutually beneficial relationship between an organization and an activist group in this circumstance? How would you define the objectives of the activists in each case? Those of the business or organization? Could better communication practices have helped resolve this situation more quickly? And if so, what should have been done, and when? What are the most appropriate ways to evaluate the success of an activist campaign? What ethical principles should underlie communication among activists, organizations, and their other stakeholders?

NOTE

1. Available at http://www.frameworksinstitute.org/assets/files/PDF/FramingPublicIssuesfinal.pdf.

ADDITIONAL READINGS

Alinksy, Saul. (1989). *Rules for radicals: A practical primer for realistic radicals.* Vancouver, WA: Vintage Books.

Best, Joel. (2001). *Damned lies and statistics: Untangling numbers from the media, politicians, and activists.* Berkeley: University of California Press.

Bornstein, David. (2007). *How to change the world: Social entrepreneurs and the power of new idea.* London: Oxford University Press.
Demetrious, Kristen. (2013). *Public relations, activism, and social change.* New York: Routledge.
Keck, Margaret E., & Sikkink, Kathryn. (1998). *Activists beyond borders: Advocacy networks in international politics.* Ithaca, NY: Cornell University Press.
Shaw, Randy. (1999). *Reclaiming America: Nike, clean air, and the new national activism.* Berkeley: University of California Press.
Tarrow, Sydney. (2005). *The new transnational activism.* Cambridge: Cambridge University Press.

CASE 33: PETA SERVES UP "HOLOCAUST ON YOUR PLATE" CAMPAIGN

Eight panels, each 6 feet high and 10 feet long, paired bigger-than-life photographs of Holocaust victims with images of livestock to support the Holocaust on Your Plate campaign created by People for the Ethical Treatment of Animals (PETA). A typical panel showed a five-foot-square photo of concentration camp inmates, crowded into three-tiered bunk beds, and a same-sized image of chickens in cramped cages. Across the panel's top, big block lettering said, "To animals, all people are Nazis." PETA sent sets of the panels for public display across the nation and around the world in 2003 to raise awareness of animal rights.

The campaign also sought to include television ads as part of the media plan. PETA reported that one TV station in Richmond, Virginia, did agree to air a commercial in October that had been rejected by stations in other states. The ad showed someone looking through slits in the side of a truck with a voice-over using the tagline: "Each age has its own atrocities. End the animals' holocaust. Please become a vegetarian."

The Advocates Face Protests

The United States Holocaust Memorial Museum protested the exhibit, as did the Anti-Defamation League. The museum had sold copies of the photos to the group unknowingly, it said. Spokeswoman Mary Morrison told the *New York Daily News* that the request to use the photographs came from a private e-mail account. The project was described as one that would be "comparing the atrocities of the Holocaust to other forms of oppression throughout history."

The Anti-Defamation League denounced the project. In a February 24 release, Abraham H. Foxman, the Anti-Defamation League national director and a survivor of the Holocaust, said:

> The effort by PETA to compare the deliberate systematic murder of millions of Jews to the issue of animal rights is abhorrent. PETA's effort to seek "approval" for their "Holocaust on your Plate" campaign is outrageous, offensive and takes chutzpah to new heights.

PETA Responds

PETA defended its use of the photographs in the exhibits and ads. An October 9, 2003, PETA release announcing the exhibition's display in New York City explained its purpose this way:

> PETA wants to stimulate contemplation of how the victimization of Jews, Gypsies, homosexuals, and others characterized as "life unworthy of life" during the Holocaust parallels the way that modern society abuses and justifies the slaughter of animals. Just as the Nazis tried to "dehumanize" Jews by forcing them to live in filthy, crowded conditions, tearing children away from their mothers, and killing them in assembly-line fashion, animals on today's factory farms are stripped of all that is enjoyable and natural to them and treated as nothing more than meat-, egg-, and milk-producing "machines."

Campaign Coordinator Matt Prescott, who PETA explained had family members who had been murdered by the Nazis, was quoted as saying:

> The very same mindset that made the Holocaust possible—that we can do anything we want to those we decide are "different" or "inferior"—is what allows us to commit atrocities against animals every single day. We are asking people to allow understanding into their hearts and compassion onto their tables by embracing a nonviolent, vegan diet that respects other forms of life.

Despite criticism, PETA maintained the campaign. For almost two years, the exhibit traveled throughout the United States and into other countries and was frequently met with protesters.

A Sudden Apology

Then, on May 5, 2005, PETA President Ingrid Newkirk sent an e-mail message to many Jewish media outlets and Jewish rights groups. The message read: "I have decided to apologize for the pain caused by the 'Holocaust on Your Plate' campaign."

In response, the Anti-Defamation League said while it "would have preferred that the apology had come earlier, it welcomes the letter and expressed hope that PETA would no longer engage in efforts to compare the slaughter of animals to human suffering in the Holocaust."

Another Controversial Campaign

However, soon PETA unveiled a new campaign composed of 12 large panels that showed pictures of animals next to images of black men and women being abused as slaves or former slaves. The photos were graphic and horrifying. One panel in the exhibit showed a black civil rights protester at a lunch counter being beaten next to a photo of a seal being bludgeoned. Another panel paired the photograph of a lynching with that of a cow hanging in a slaughterhouse. Another panel showed a photograph of a chained slave's foot next to a photo of the chained foot of an elephant. The title of the exhibit: "Are Animals the New Slaves?"

PETA had planned a 10-week, 42-city national tour. However, reaction to the exhibit was quick and heated. Newspapers wrote editorials criticizing the campaign. Groups such as the National Association for the Advancement of Colored People and the American Jewish Congress protested.

On August 15, 2005, PETA said it would suspend the campaign. Dawn Carr, a PETA spokesperson, told the Associated Press: "We're not continuing right now while we evaluate. We're reviewing feedback we've received—most of it overwhelmingly positive and some of it quite negative."

Questions for Reflection

1. What would motivate PETA to plan such extreme exhibits?
2. How would you have advised the groups, such as the Anti-Defamation League and the National Association for the Advancement of Colored People, to respond to the exhibits they opposed?
3. Identify the ethical issues raised by these two campaigns. How might these campaigns have been more persuasive in fostering a commitment to vegetarianism?
4. PETA has been criticized for some past campaigns as well as its Holocaust and slavery efforts. Why would PETA favor campaigns that shock and offend?

Information for this case was drawn from Anti-Defamation League. (February 24, 2003; updated May 5, 005). ADL denounces PETA for its "Holocaust on your plate" campaign; calls appeal for Jewish community support "the height of chutzpah." ADL release. www.adl.org/PresRele/HolNa_52/4235_52; Center for Consumer Freedom. (September 1, 2005). PETA flops with race card. www.consumerfreedom.com; Katz, C.

(March 4, 2003). D.C. Holocaust Museum outraged by PETA pix. *New York Daily News*, p. 15; Mnookin, S. (March 10, 2003). Ads: A plate of controversy. *Newsweek,* p. 10; Morgante, M. (February 28, 2003). Animal-rights comparison to Holocaust draws fire. The Associated Press; Prescott, M. (October 9, 2003). Grandson of celebrated Jewish author brings giant graphic display to show how today's victims languish in Nazi-style concentration camps; PETA release. www.peta.org/mc/NewsItem.asp?ie=3021; Prescott, M. (September 30, 2003). Group asks Holocaust Museum to consider today's victims of factory farming. PETA release. www.peta.org/mc/NewsItem.asp?id=2946; Smith, W.J. (May 6, 2005). PETA's non-apology apology. National Review Online. www.nationalreview.com; Tolerance.org Staff. (May 6, 2005). PETA apologizes for Holocaust on your plate campaign. www.tolerance.org/news/article_tol.jsp?id=1207; Tolerance.org Staff. (August 15, 2005). PETA rethinks "slavery" exhibit. www.tolerance.org/news/article_tol.jsp?id=1266; Walker, D. (August 13, 2005). PETA reconsiders campaign after complaints of racism. Associated Press; Willoughby, B. (March 7, 2003). PETA turns Holocaust into pig pen. Teaching Tolerance. www.tolerance.org/new/article_hate.jsp?id=724.

CASE 34: STANDING OUT IN A FIELD OF PINK

Figure 9.1 A pink Breast Cancer Awareness ribbon adorns the turf at Detroit's Ford Field in the first quarter of an NFL football game between the Detroit Lions and the Cincinnati Bengals on Sunday, October 20, 2013. (AP Photo: Paul Sancya.)

As Pat Garofalo noted in his *U.S. News & World Report* blog on October 27, 2013:

> If you tuned into a National Football League game during the last month, you surely noticed that there was pink everywhere, from the gear worn by the players and coaches right down to the penalty flags. The stadiums are pink, the fields are pink. Even the goalposts are pink.

Garofalo was describing the visual impact of the NFL's A Crucial Catch campaign in support of the National Breast Cancer Awareness Month. From pink shoes to pink referee's whistles, even to pink padding around the goal posts, it was difficult to watch a game in October without getting reminded of the campaign. In fact, the NFL did find that the pink penalty flags were so hard to distinguish on the field that it had to go back to using the traditional yellow penalty flag.

A Crucial Catch

According to the www.nfl.com/pink Web site, all the pink clothing worn by the teams' players and coaches and the other pink equipment used during games are auctioned off through the NFL Action Web site, and the proceeds go to support the American Cancer Society's Community Health Advocates National Grants for Empowerment program. Other NFL pink items are available for retail purchase. The "CHANGE" program gives support to underserved communities to provide screening programs and outreach. Fans are also asked to donate $10 directly to the American Cancer Society through text messaging.

The NFL reports that since 2009, about $4.5 million has been given to the American Cancer Society, 100 percent of the net proceeds from Pink products that are auctioned or sold. How the net proceeds are calculated by the league is explained on its Web site. Merchandisers who create and sell the Pink products pay a royalty to the league for the use of its logos. The costs of promoting the A Crucial Catch campaign are deducted from the total royalties, and that net amount is what is donated. Writing for Business Insider, Gaines calculated that $11.25 of every $100 in pink merchandise sold goes to the American Cancer Society.

Dig Pink!

Other sports organizations have also gone pink. The Side-Out Foundation (www.side-out.org) has used a Dig Pink initiative to involve middle school, high school, and college volleyball teams in fund-raising through games and tournaments on local, city, or state levels while raising awareness of the disease among younger athletes. The organization was founded by Rick Dunetz, who was the volleyball coach at West Springfield High School in Virginia. During his first season as coach, he says the team lacked focus, and he as the coach was distracted as well because his mother had been diagnosed with breast cancer for the second time. When his team became aware of the diagnosis, it became a rallying point for team unity.

As noted on the Side-Out Web site: "It was indeed a 'miracle season,' as the team described it. They walked off the court that last day of the season proud of their achievements, but more importantly, inspired to face adversity without fear of failing." Convinced of the powerful nature of the connection of teams with cancer patients, Donetz developed a way for teams to use their sport to provide support for others and unity for themselves.

The foundation offers several opportunities for team members and other volunteers to become involved in raising support. Rock the Pink Festivals have featured state tournaments in Maryland, Nebraska, New York, Texas, and Virginia. Its 2013 "Dig Pink Rally" goals were to involve at least 500 college teams and 1,500 younger teams in efforts to raise at least $2 million, surpassing the $1.1 million raised by 1,088 teams in the 2012 rally. Teams are encouraged to dedicate a portion of the funds raised for local needs. Foundation funds have been used to fund research through the National Institutes of Health, George Mason University, Translational Genomics Research Institute (TGen), and the Mayo Clinic.

The personal experiences of another coach led to the creation of Coaches vs. Cancer, a collaboration of the National Association of Basketball Coaches and the American Cancer Society. Then University of Missouri basketball coach Norm Stewart was diagnosed with cancer in 1989. While undergoing treatment, he asked Missouri fans to pledge money to the American Cancer Society for every three points the team scored during the 1989–1990 season. That effort worked so well that Stewart was motivated to advocate for a national coalition.

More than 500 NCAA basketball coaches are involved, as well as some high school coaches. Membership has now grown to include coaches across many sports. The Web site says,

> The Coaches vs. Cancer program presents an excellent opportunity for you, as a community leader and role model for youth and adults alike, to involve your community and create a positive image for the coaching staff, your school or league, and your sports program.

The Coaches vs. Cancer Council that provides oversight includes the coaches from well-known programs across the United States, including Mike Krzyzwewski, Duke University; Bruce Weber, Kansas State University; and Tubby Smith, Texas Tech University. Tournaments and galas are used to raise funds, up to $87 million so far. One event was announced in a June 2014 release from the organization heralding the Coaches vs. Cancer Classic Championship scheduled for the Barclays Center, Brooklyn, New York, in November 2014. Teams from Stanford, University of Nevada Las Vegas, Temple, and Duke have committed to playing.

Bright Pink!

Of course, one way to stand out among the "pink" activists is to go Bright! Lindsay Avner launched the Bright Pink organization in 2007. According to the charity's Web site (brightpink.org), Avner was the youngest American to undergo a double mastectomy with reconstruction to combat the risk of developing breast cancer after she discovered she carried a mutation on the BRCA 1 gene. Her great-grandmother and grandmother had died of breast cancer and her mother had experienced ovarian cancer and breast cancer.

The Bright Pink group seeks to offer support to women between ages 18 and 45 by offering "Brighten Up" Educational Workshops and Emerging Medical Professional Workshops. The sessions teach ovarian and breast cancer basics and strategies for early detection and for reducing risks. In 2013, 90 education workshops were conducted at sites as varied as Macy's, Morgan Stanley, The University of Texas at Austin, and the University of Southern California. Workshop leaders receive training by attending the "Bright Pink University." Ms. Avner says, "Bring Bright Pink is all about being bright . . . being smart, being positive, and being in control of your breast and ovarian health."

Funds are raised through special events, individual and corporate contributions, grants and cause-related marketing. According to information on the Bright Pink Web site, more than $7.5 million has been raised since 2008, and about $3.5 million was invested in Bright Pink programs. The Chicago Bulls, eBay, General Mills, *aerie*, and Westfield are among the corporate sponsors. Churchill Downs became a partner in 2014 as part of its sixth annual Pink Out campaign by donating $50,000. According to a story in nfocuslouisville.com, guests attending the Longines Kentucky Oaks on May 2 who contributed directly to the organization were given a pink lapel ribbon, and Vineyard Vines donated 30 percent of the proceeds from the sale of its Kentucky Derby Collection Pink Lilies ties, tote bag, and pocket square to Bright Pink.

Partnering for a Purpose

These sports-related campaigns have offered opportunities for those not directly at high risk for the disease to demonstrate concern and support. Numerous charitable organizations and for-profit corporations have tied the ribbon of support since 1992 when associates at Estee Lauder counters first distributed 1.5 million ribbons in an effort to develop nationwide awareness of the disease and the need to fund research to discover a cure. In 1993, the Avon Corp. began selling a version of the ribbon as a piece of jewelry, and $10 million of the pink-ribbon pins were sold in the first two years. (Avon has gone on to become the largest private donor to community-based nonprofit breast cancer programs, raising more than $815 million since 1992.)

The American Cancer Society offers National Partner status to corporations who commit to raising or donating at least $200,000 by forming "Making Strides Against Breast Cancer" teams for events, sponsoring "Making Strides" events, or through direct donations. Corporations from Athena to Tanger Outlets are recognized on the American Cancer Society Web site.

A 2011 article in *Marie Claire* noted, "All told, an estimated $6 billion is raised every year in the name of breast cancer."

Time Out?

The growing number of "pink ribbon" campaigns and efforts has led some to suggest the efforts constitute "pinkwashing," a cosmetic campaign more intended to benefit a brand than to support the socially responsible cause. A headline in the October 11, 2010, *New York Times* suggested consumers and advocates may be suffering from "Pink Ribbon Fatigue." Medical sociologist Dr. Gayle Sulik, author of the 2010 book, *Pink Ribbon Blues: How Breast Cancer Culture Undermines Women's Health,* suggests on her Web site (http://gaylesulik.com) that "the pink ribbon is itself wrapped in a system that uses advocacy, culture, mass media, and the medical industry for its own purposes, to create a festive culture of consumption that wrests in profitable complacency."

Many challenges remain for public relations practitioners and groups seeking to help in the campaign against breast cancer. Transparency in fund-raising and funding expenditures, clarifying what amount of donated or retail funds will actually flow through organizations or corporations to what type of efforts will help promote trust. Most fund-raising totals are publicly available, although the amounts of money that actually go to support research, treatment, support, or information campaigns may be more difficult to determine. The research grants offered may be tracked, as is the number of patients and family members who receive direct support from the various organizations. Yet the results of some of the awareness and information campaigns are more difficult to measure.

Charity Navigator, a nonprofit advocacy watchdog, seeks to provide information about the various campaigns in an easily used database.

It offers its highest rating (4-Stars) to the Dana-Farber Cancer Institute; Susan G. Komen for the Cure; the Breast Cancer Research Foundation; The Rose; Breast Cancer Connections: National Breast Cancer Foundation; Living Beyond Breast Cancer; Breastcancer.org; Lynn Sage Cancer Research Foundation; and Sharsheret.

Devising appropriate methods to track awareness and response would provide evidence of the positive impact of campaigns. Beyond that impact analysis, however, ongoing creativity in event planning and solicitation may help these campaigns score points that will help them stand out in the field of pink.

Questions for Reflection

1. Breast cancer research, prevention, and treatment are causes that evoke strong empathetic responses from consumers and donors. What are the advantages and disadvantages when a corporation or a nonprofit aligns its cause-related sponsorships with such an emotion-laden topic?
2. What are the advantages and disadvantages when a sports organization or a coach commits to a pink-ribbon or breast cancer awareness campaign?
3. What metrics would you suggest practitioners use to assess the impact of the awareness and information campaigns that often accompany fund-raising campaigns?
4. How might corporations and nonprofits that become involved in social health campaigns or sustainability campaigns counter the criticisms that they are "pinkwashing" or "greenwashing"? How should they respond if they receive such criticisms in social media or in the mass media?

Information for this case was drawn from the Bright Pink Web site at www.brightpink.com and the American Cancer Society. About Coaches vs. Cancer. http://www.cancer.org/involved/participate/coachesvscancer/about-coaches-vs-cancer; Avon Foundation for Women. The Avon breast cancer crusade. http://www.avonfoundation.org/causes/breast-cancer-crusade/; Cancer Navigator. Charities working to prevent and cure breast cancer. http://www.charitynavigator.org/index.cfm?bay=content.view&cpid=497#.U80r0PldWCk; Coaches vs. Cancer. http://www.coachesvscancer.org/; Gaines, Cork. (October 15, 2013). A shockingly small amount of money from Pink NFL merchandise sales goes to breast cancer research. Business Insider. http://www.businessinsider.com/small-amount-of-money-from-pink-nfl-merchandise-goes-to-breast-cancer-research-2013-10; Gaines, Cork. (October 2, 2012). The NFL is turning everything pink for breast cancer awareness. Business Insider.

http://www.businessinsider.com/nfl-goes-pink-for-breast-cancer-awareness-2012-10?op=1#ixzz38TZtM9d8; Garofalo, Pat. (October 27, 2013). The NFL's pinkwashing problem. *U.S. News & World Report.* http://www/usnews/com/opinion/blogs/pat-garofalo/2013/10/27/is-the-nfls-pink-breast-cancer-campaing-doing-more-harm-than-good; Godfrey, Amber, Leddy, Rick, & Gulish, Brian. (June 25, 2014). 2014 Coaches vs. Cancer Classic Championship round matchups set. Release. http://cvclassic.com; Goldman, Lea. (September 14, 2011). The big business of breast cancer. *Marie Claire.* http://www.marieclaire.com/world-reports/news/breast-cancer-business-scams; Lerner, Barron H. (October 11, 2010). Pink ribbon fatigue. *The New York Times.* http://well.blogs.nytimes.com/2010/10/11/pink-ribbon-fatigue/; Patient Resource. These days, Mizzou's Norm Stewart Is "Stormin" Against Cancer. https://www.patientresource.com/Colorectal_Survivor_Story1.aspx; Side-Out Foundation. (2013). Annual Report. http://www.side-out.org/about-side-out/annual-report/; Side-Out Foundation. Our story. http://www.side-out.org/about-side-out/our-story/; Snider, Laura. (March 27, 2014). Bright Pink. Nfocuslouisville.com, p. 41; Sternberg, Josh. (October 8, 2013). The NFL flagged for "pinkwashing." Blog. http://digiday.com/author/jost-sternberg/).

CASE 35: GREENPEACE PRESSURES RUSSIA TO STOP DRILLING ARCTIC OIL

To oil companies, the Arctic appears to be the final frontier. As climate change has melted parts of the Arctic ice shelf, rich sources of oil, gas, iron ore, and minerals have become attainable. Shell Oil says the Arctic holds 400 billion barrels of untapped oil and 30 percent of the world's untapped natural gas. The Arctic stretches across foreign borders in Canada, Russia, America (Alaska), Denmark (Greenland), Norway, Sweden, Finland, and Iceland.

When large areas of the Arctic ice in Russian waters melted, State-run Gazprom-Neft was the first company to place an offshore oil rig to tap into those resources. The rig was supposed to begin drilling in early 2012, but the operation was delayed until spring 2013 because of safety concerns.

Greenpeace Sets Sail to Protest

The Arctic contains a unique and fragile ecosystem—an ecosystem that some activists would like to protect. The largest independent environmental organization, Greenpeace, with its focus on protecting ecosystems, took note of the Prirazlomnaya platform. Soon after Gazprom began drilling, Greenpeace set sail in its 39-year-old 946-ton icebreaker ship, the *Arctic Sunrise*, to the remote site to begin peacefully protesting drilling in the Arctic in general and specifically to protest Gazprom's lack of a safety plan to prevent spills.

The ship contained 28 activists and two journalists. The activists came from all over the world, including Argentina, Australia, Brazil, Britain, Canada, Denmark, Finland, France, Italy, the Netherlands, New Zealand, Poland, Russia, Sweden, Switzerland, Turkey, Ukraine, and the United States.

When the *Arctic Sunrise* reached the drilling platform, inflatable boats were launched toward the platform, and three crew members attempted to scale the platform. In turn, the Russian Coast Guard detained the three who boarded the platform. They then seized the crew and ship and charged the Greenpeace activists with piracy, which carries a 15-year prison sentence.

Arrests Prompt International Attention

Foreign leaders asked Russian officials to release the activists, saying they clearly weren't pirates. The Netherlands petitioned the International Tribunal for the Law of the Sea to request the authorities dismiss the charges and free the activists. Russia countered the tribunal, saying the matter was not international since the offense was against Russian property.

But media attention did not abate. As cameras and protests were trained on the Greenpeace incident, conferences such as The Society of Petroleum Engineer's Arctic and Extreme Environments were held in Russia. Engineers and executives from all over the world and from companies such as ExxonMobil, Chevron, and Total met to "discuss, debate and develop the future potential of the Arctic frontier."

Impact of the Protests

After three months of international protests, Russia released the crew members. Ten months after its seizure, the *Arctic Sunrise* was given back to Greenpeace. After a month of repairing the damage inflicted by the Russian Coast Guard, the ship began its trip back to the Netherlands on August 1, 2014.

While the Greenpeace crisis had been resolved, the incident has had some effect. Even Russian President Vladimir Putin recognized the need to build economic bridges with some of the same countries that protested the arrests of the *Arctic Sunrise* crew. He has added some safety and environmental comments when speaking about "carrying out intensive work in the Arctic regions to explore and develop new oil and gas fields and minerals deposits," according to a Kremlin transcript obtained by *The Christian Science Monitor*.

> It is absolutely clear now that the climate is changing. The Arctic is a very vulnerable region in terms of maintaining the environmental balance and the need to keep this balance, and so we must be very careful about how we go about our economic activity in the region.

Clearly, the future of the Arctic has not been resolved. Viktor Boyarsky, an Arctic explorer and director of the State Museum of the Arctic and Antarctic in St. Petersburg, told *The Christian Science Monitor* that he supports economic development in the Arctic and thinks Russian border guards acted correctly in arresting the Greenpeace activists.

"The Arctic does not tolerate heroism," he said. "This was just a PR stunt, and they have to be punished. Stiff fines would be just the thing for them."

Questions for Reflection

1. Do countries or large corporations have an obligation to be environmentally friendly? Why or why not?
2. If this was "just a PR stunt," was it effective? Why or why not?
3. Explain the ethical implications of Greenpeace's actions.
4. Explain the ethical implications of Russia's actions.

Information drawn from Alkandari, K. (May 2014). Activist and post-modern public relations: Greenpeace and Arctic exploration leads to jail time. Unpublished graduate student paper; Elferink, A. (January 7, 2014). The Arctic Sunrise incident and the International Law of the Sea. K.G. Jebsen Centre for the Law of the Sea blog. http://uit.no/Content/361427/The%20Arctic%20Sunrise%20Incident%20and%20ITLOS_final.pdf; Greenpeace International. http://www.greenpeace.org/international/en/about/; Shell Global. Shell in the Arctic. http://www.shell.com/global/future-energy/arctic.html; Society of Professional Engineers. http://www.arcticoilgas.com/en/; Weir, F. (September 26, 2013). Drill, comrade, drill: Why the Kremlin's Arctic plan worries activists. http://www.csmonitor.com/World/2013/0926/Drill-comrade-drill-Why-the-Kremlin-s-Arctic-plan-worries-activists-video; Williams, C. (August 1, 2014).Greenpeace protest ship released by Russia after 10 months. http://www.latimes.com/world/europe/la-fg-russia-greenpeace-arctic-sunrise-20140801-story.html.

CASE 36: ACTIVISTS KEEP NIKE ON THE RUN

Written by Larry F. Lamb

Nike knows how to compete. It won its position atop the world's shoe industry a generation ago and remains the leader. It received acclaim twice as Advertiser of the Year—in 1994 and 2003—at France's Cannes Lion festival, sometimes called the Olympics of Advertising. It's the company whose 1996 ads said: "You don't win silver. You lose gold." Nike has repeatedly bested rivals like Adidas, New Balance, and Reebok in the athletic-shoe footrace. In the United States, its market share is about 40 percent.

Yet, clear-cut victory has eluded Nike in its marathon contest with activists and media critics who have run the company ragged on the issue of worker abuse in overseas production facilities. Even when Nike asked the U.S. Supreme Court in 2003 to affirm the company's First Amendment right to speak publicly on the issue, the court refused to take a position on the question. No gold, no silver, no bronze.

Code of Conduct

Nike, headquartered in Beaverton, Oregon, doesn't own or operate shoe production plants overseas. Instead, it hires subcontractors in low-wage countries such as China, Indonesia, South Korea, and Vietnam to produce shoes to Nike specifications. To assure workers' rights there, Nike requires its subcontractors to adopt Nike's Code of Conduct and allow unannounced visits by inspectors chosen by Nike. Adopted in 1992, the code required compliance in four areas of employee welfare:

- Health and safety.
- Pay and benefits.
- Terms of work.
- Management–workers relations.

Yet, some critics have said that Nike's worker-protection program is little more than window dressing for sweatshop operations, and others say that the company's public statements on the issue have been misleading and incomplete. Complaints about overseas labor abuse began plaguing Nike in the 1980s, and the reports reached a wide audience in the 1990s in media such as *The Economist* and *The New York Times*. CBS News reported in 1996 that workers making Nike shoes in Southeast Asia were poorly paid, exposed to hazardous chemicals, and mistreated by managers.

Columnist Provokes CEO Letter

In a single week in June 1996, *The New York Times* columnist Bob Herbert twice used his commentary to take a swipe at Nike; its cofounder and chief executive, Philip H. Knight; and the famous professional athletes making millions from Nike contracts. Citing Indonesia as an example, Mr. Herbert said thousands of workers producing Nike products earned $2.20 a day.

"Philip Knight has an extraordinary racket going for him," the columnist wrote on June 10.

> There is absolutely no better way to get rich than to exploit both the worker and the consumers. If you can get your product made for next to nothing, and get people to buy it at exorbitant prices, you get to live at the top of the pyramid.

Four days later, Mr. Herbert added:

> Nike is the most vulnerable to criticism of the athletic footwear corporations because it is the biggest, the most visible and by far the most hypocritical. No amount of charitable contributions or of idealized commercial images can hide the fact that Indonesia is Nike's kind of place. The exploitation of cheap Asian labor has been a focus of its top executive, Philip Knight, for more than three decades.

Mr. Knight, in a letter to *The New York Times* one week later, responded:

> Nike has paid, on average, double the minimum wage as defined in countries where its products are produced under contract. This is in addition to free meals, housing and health care and transportation subsidies. Underdeveloped countries must trade or see deeper declines in living standards. History shows that the best way out of poverty for such countries is through exports of light manufactured goods that provide the base for more skilled production.

Nike continued to answer its critics with information on its inspection and enforcement program as well as economic arguments about international trade, comparative advantage, and global competition.

Tongue-Tied Public Relations

The Wall Street Journal, under the headline "Nike Inc.'s Golden Image Is Tarnished As Problems in Asia Pose PR Challenge," asked in 1997:

How has Nike, a brand renowned for its global marketing finesse, found itself in this situation? It's because the athletic-shoe maker has remained tongue-tied, public relations experts say, in the face of a loose-knit but efficient attack that combines the speed of the Internet with good old-fashioned rabble-rousing.

On college campuses, student activists were questioning deals arranged by Nike and its competitors to provide big universities not just with footwear and apparel for varsity teams but also logo-licensed products for sale to the public. The activists said that, through the multiyear contracts, university administrators were complicit in the abuse of foreign laborers because universities assured a future market for goods produced under exploitation. To coordinate anti-exploitation campaigns emerging on more than 100 college campuses, activists formed the United Students Against Sweatshops.

At the University of North Carolina (UNC) at Chapel Hill, student activists tried to persuade administrators to cancel a Nike contract in 1997 with a campaign featuring "Just Don't Do It" leaflets that accused the shoe company of unfair labor practices.

According to *The Wall Street Journal*,

> In 1997, Nike signed an $11.6 million deal with UNC's athletic department to outfit most of its sports teams and to manufacture UNC-logo sweatshirts and T-shirts, which in turn would generate $6 million to $8 million in annual sales for the company.

Nike's Campus Visit

As the activist campaign gained attention at UNC, Nike responded with a combination of ads in the *Daily Tar Heel* student newspaper, campus visits by a public relations team, and personal contact by Nike representatives with the members of the activist group. Before the fall semester ended, the company had offered an expense-paid trip to Southeast Asia for a faculty member and three students, including a *Daily Tar Heel* reporter. Under the plan, the four would tour facilities to see for themselves the conditions in which Nike shoes were made.

The plan was scrapped, however, when some UNC faculty members objected, and a regular undergraduate course on environment and labor in the global economy was established instead. Nike executives were invited to attend the class, and one who did in April 1998 was Nike chief executive Philip Knight.

An Activist Sues

Marc Kasky, a San Francisco activist interested in humanitarian causes, watched the give-and-take between the company and its critics, and he grew angry over Nike statements that he considered misleading or downright false. At about the same time that Mr. Knight visited the Chapel Hill classroom, Mr. Kasky filed a complaint in California Superior Court, accusing the company of unfair business practices, negligent misrepresentation, fraud, and deceit.

In his lawsuit, Mr. Kasky cited nine instances in which Nike issued positive statements about its labor practices that conflicted with information from other sources. The nine instances included:

1. A letter from Nike to university presidents and athletic directors.
2. A 30-page brochure on Nike labor policies.
3. A news release on its labor practices.
4. Material on the Nike Web site concerning its code of conduct.
5. A document offering Nike's perspective on the labor controversy.
6. A news release responding to sweatshop allegations.
7. A letter from Nike to the YWCA of America.
8. A letter from Nike to the International Restructuring Education Network Europe.
9. Mr. Knight's letter to *The New York Times.*

Facts in Conflict

For example, Mr. Kasky challenged Nike's claim that it paid double the minimum-wage rate in Southeast Asian countries. He said that Ernst & Young, an auditing firm that Nike hired to inspect a Vietnamese factory, found that workers received an average wage of $45 monthly, $5 above the minimum wage. He called Nike's claim "deceitful."

Noting that Nike's Code of Conduct forbids the use of corporal punishment or harassment of any kind in worker discipline, Mr. Kasky said the CBS News *48 Hours* program reported that 45 Vietnamese workers were forced by supervisors to kneel with their hands held in the air for 25 minutes. The same program, he said, reported that a supervisor hit 15 Vietnamese women on the head as a penalty for poor sewing.

Nike's letter to university officials included assurances of compliance with health and safety regulations, according to Mr. Kasky, but the Ernst & Young inspection found that thousands of women between the ages of 18 and 24 were exposed to high levels of toluene fumes and chemical dust in a Vietnamese plant.

In his lawsuit, Mr. Kasky said a central purpose of Nike's Code of Conduct was "to entice consumers who do not want to purchase products made in sweatshop and/or under unsafe and/or inhuman conditions." He said that the letters and other communications were marketing tools used by the company to attract customers.

Public Debate or Commercial Speech?

Nike disagreed. The company told the court that it was engaged in a public discussion of controversial issues, such as globalization and international trade, which had sparked comment in a number of quarters. The letters, news releases, Web pages, and other communications represented the company's voice in an open debate on matters of public policy, according to Nike, and its participation in public discussion was protected absolutely by the First Amendment.

The decision of the California Superior Court favored Nike. When Mr. Kasky appealed to the California Court of Appeal, his argument was rejected again. Mr. Kasky persisted, and the California Supreme Court reversed the earlier decisions in May 2002.

The California judges said:

> Because the messages in question were directed by a commercial speaker to a commercial audience, and because they made representations of fact about the speaker's own business operations for the purpose of promoting sales of its products . . . [Nike's] messages are commercial speech,

The court did not say that Nike had misled anyone, deceived consumers, or misrepresented its practices. In fact, the lower courts had not attempted such an evaluation because they judged Nike's statements were entitled to full protection of the First Amendment.

Breathing Space in Public Debate

In public policy discussions, the courts generally say that the First Amendment protects the expression of views, even if incorrect or exaggerated, as long as they contain no deliberate or reckless falsehoods. Full and robust debate flourishes when speakers have the liberty to voice ideas, however unconventional or unpopular, without fear that they may be hauled into court to explain errors, misstatements, misinterpretations, or shades of meaning.

Commercial speech is a different animal, the courts say, and the First Amendment affords it limited protection because its fundamental purpose is to promote a transaction rather than to contribute ideas to public debate.

The California Supreme Court explained:

> Our holding in no way prohibits any business enterprise from speaking out on issues of public importance or from vigorously defending its own labor practices. It means only that when a business enterprise makes factual representations about its own products or its own operations, it must speak truthfully.

Five months after the California court ruled that Nike's statements were commercial speech, the company filed an appeal with the U.S. Supreme Court, asking it to review the decision. Nike's attorneys said the California verdict would curtail businesses' participation in public discussion and deprive the general public of a full spectrum of views.

U.S. Supreme Court Accepts Case

In January 2003, the high court agreed to hear Nike's appeal. Many First Amendment scholars, news organizations, and others supported Nike and filed friend-of-the-court briefs to oppose California's apparent expansion of the commercial-speech umbrella. Among the briefs was one filed by the PRSA.

"Those of us who assist companies in gathering and disseminating information related to their businesses have always relied on the same First Amendment protections as those who openly criticize Nike and other corporations," PRSA President Reed Byrum said. "Without that protection, there will be a serious impact on all aspects of corporate communications from business, to corporate crisis communications and even to philanthropic and community-outreach programs."

Sonia Arrison, a First Amendment Fellow of the National Press Club, wrote a newspaper commentary that said:

> Laws that were meant to stop false claims such as "orange juice cures cancer" should not be distorted and used as political weapons. And surely in an established democracy, the government does not allow one side in a debate to summarily stifle its opponents' viewpoints.

A Mix of Debate and Marketing

When the Supreme Court heard attorneys for Kasky and Nike in April 2003, several justices seemed to see elements of both commercial speech and noncommercial speech in the Nike communications. According to a *New York Times* account of the hearings, Justice Stephen G. Breyer told the attorneys, "The truth of the matter is, I think it's both," and later he added, "I think the First Amendment was designed to protect all the participants in a public debate, and a debate consists of facts. Once you've tied a party's hands behind his back with respect to the facts, you've silenced him."

The Supreme Court handed down its order in June 2003 and left many who had looked forward to a landmark ruling in stunned silence or heated indignation. "Improvidently granted," said the court, meaning that it had changed its mind about taking the case. Six voted to dismiss, and three would have rendered a verdict.

Nike faced the prospect of returning to the California court system, where it would have to defend its communications as commercial speech. The company would be going back in 2003 to the future it had first faced in 1998.

Settlement Reached

Less than three months after the U.S. Supreme Court decided not to decide, Nike and Marc Kasky settled their differences out of court. Nike agreed to give $1.5 million to programs of the Fair Labor Association (FLA). With the funds, the FLA planned to support:

- Improvements in independent monitoring of workplace conditions in manufacturing countries.
- Worker development programs that focus on education and economic opportunity.
- Collaboration to formulate a global standard for measuring and reporting corporate responsibility performance.

The FLA was formed in 1999 by a diverse group, including Nike and other apparel manufacturers, colleges and universities, human rights organizations, and activists. It promotes its code of conduct, monitors practices in factories that make products for Nike and other brands, and coordinates public reports on monitoring results.

In the Bloomberg News service reports on the settlement, a law professor at George Washington University said Nike's payout was a sensible alternative to further litigation. The professor, Jonathan Turley, said, "Any trial in this case would have been a bloody nightmare—the type of press that a company like Nike would never welcome."

Attorneys for Mr. Kasky issued a statement saying that their client was "satisfied that this settlement reflects Nike's commitment to positive changes where factory workers are concerned."

Questions for Reflection

1. In what ways did Nike's communications focus on marketing and sales? In what ways did they focus on public debate about international trade and economic growth?
2. Nike doesn't operate shoe production facilities in the United States or elsewhere. Why would some consumers hold the company responsible for working conditions in facilities where its shoes are made?
3. Most footwear companies hire subcontractors in developing countries to make their shoes. Why would Nike attract a lion's share of the criticism?

4. Nike has said it will refrain from public debate about overseas working conditions in the future. Is this a good idea or a bad idea?

Information for this case was drawn from the following: the Nike Web site at http://www.nike.com/nikebiz/nikebiz.jhtml?page=0; Arrison, S. (January 22, 2003). Letting Nike speak. *The News & Observer*, p. A25; Carter, R. (April 30, 2002). ABC: Athletics, Business & Carolina. *The Daily Tar Heel*, p. 1. (April 20, 1998). Complaint, *Kasky* v. *Nike*, Superior Court of the State of California; Herbert, B. (June 14, 1996). In America: Nike's bad neighborhood. *The New York Times*, p. 25; Herbert, B. (June 10, 1996). In America: Nike's pyramid scheme. *The New York Times*, p. 27; Knight, P. (June 21, 1996). Letter: Nike pays good wages to foreign workers. *The New York Times*, p. A29; Marshall, S. (September 26, 1997). Nike Inc.'s gold image is tarnished as problems in Asia pose PR challenge. *The Wall Street Journal*, p. B1; McCarthy, M. (June 15, 2003). Wake up consumers? Nike's brash CEO dares to just do it. *USA Today*, p. B1; (June 26, 2003). Opinion, *Nike* v. *Kasky*, U.S. Supreme Court; (March 3, 2003). PRSA presses Supreme Court to protect free speech right for American business. PRSA news release; Savage, D. (January 11, 2003). Justices to hear Nike free-speech claim. *The Los Angeles Times*, p. C1; Stancill, J. (November 15, 1997). Nike offers tour of Asian factories to UNC critics. *The News & Observer*, p. B1; Tkacik, M. (January 10, 2003). High court may decide to hear whether Nike's PR statements to media, others are protected. *The Wall Street Journal*, p. B1.

CASE 37: REFUGEES INTERNATIONAL LOBBIES FOR ASYLUM SEEKERS

The United Nations High Commission for Refugees (UNHCR) reported there were 10.4 million refugees who were of concern to the commission. Refugees, under U.S. law, are defined as people located outside of the country who are "of special humanitarian concern . . . and who have demonstrated they were persecuted or in fear of persecution because of peace, religion, nationality, social group or political opinion in their own country."

An International Problem

Many times fleeing refugees leave in large waves, usually because of violent conflicts. Provisions are scarce and permission is rarely sought prior to mass movements. Many countries have laws that require refugees to verify their claims of persecution before such permission can be granted. Efficient asylum systems are often in place to assure fast and fair determination of a situation and so truly persecuted people reach safety—and those who are not won't be inclined to go to the trouble to apply.

But what happens when groups of asylum seekers show up on borders? Around the world, asylum seekers and the authorities who meet them at the borders may not know what actions to take. Send them back? House them until their situation can be determined? And, if so, house them where?

Refugees International, an organization that "advocates for lifesaving assistance and protection for displaced people and promotes solution to displacement crises," describes examples of the global problems affecting residents from the Congo to Mexico to Burma to Afghanistan that may prompt or result from refugee movement. National and international policies may not be enforced, or the policies may be inadequate to protect the rights of displaced individuals and groups. Through its advocacy, Refugee International wants to help governments, other non-governmental organizations, and individuals provide solutions.

Organizing for Advocacy

Founded in 1979, Refugees International "advocates for lifesaving assistance and protection for displaced people and promotes solutions to displacement crises," according to its Web site at refugeesinternational.org. It is independent, accepting no funds from the United Nations or any government. It sponsors about 12 field missions a year in countries across the globe, with three areas of focus: climate displacement, women and girls, humanitarian response; protection and security; and statelessness. "Whether working with stateless, internally-displaced, or refugee women and children, we stand committed to advocating for improved protection and prevention mechanisms," the organization reports on its Web site.

The organization advocates for policy change and government intervention in critical areas around the world. Examples of successes cited on its Web site include persuading the United Nations in 2013 to provide aid to displaced people in the Democratic Republic of Congo even though they were not living in the official U.S. camps. After a report cataloged "huge gaps" in aid to the Central African Republic and area nations, the U.S. government responded with more than $50 million in humanitarian aid.

Information and Persuasion Tactics

The Bacon Center for the Study of Climate Displacement was created by Refugees International in 2009 to investigate the relationships among weather disasters, climate change and environmental damage, and the displacement of peoples. Such in-depth reports and field reports serve as a useful tactic for the advocacy organization across topic areas. The reports provide information that can be used in advocacy letters, testimony before governmental bodies, blog posts, and in media statements. Information is shared through social media networks such as Facebook and Twitter. Individuals are encouraged to give to support Refugees International's efforts, but also to become engaged in persuading lawmakers and policy makers through personal correspondence and advocacy.

At its annual anniversary dinner, a major fund-raising and publicity raising event, the organization recognizes outstanding social activists with the McCall-Pierpaoli Humanitarian Award. Recipients have included entrepreneur Ted Turner, actor Forrest Whitaker, and Nobel Peace Laureate José Ramos-Orta.

Strategies for Advocacy

However, Refugees International often finds the battle to help refugees a lonely one. There may be very little public reaction to incidents of harsh and illegal government reactions to asylum-seeking refugees, and the sheer number of displacements—whether from weather-related natural disasters, civil unrest, or war—may appear overwhelming even for those who do care deeply.

In a July 28, 2014, Refugees International blog post, Jeff Crisp, the senior director for policy and advocacy, acknowledged the deep challenges faced by the organization. He writes, "In the current climate, sticking up for refugee protection might seem to be an uphill and even futile task. But it can and it must be done." He suggested a three-prong strategy for fostering governmental and public attention and action:

1. Celebrate the millions of lives that have been saved because they were allowed to seek refuge in another country for a short period or a longer period. "We need to hear more about these success stories," Crisp writes.
2. Remind governments and citizens that laws governing refugees were developed by those states, not by non-governmental organizations like Refugees International. Many such laws were developed in order to avoid repetition of the horrors of the Holocaust. Regulations provide the opportunity for a "principled and humane response," according to Crisp.
3. Ask politicians and the public to identify with the displaced and to ask how they would want to be treated if they were in that situation. Such an identification may alleviate some of the resentment, anger, and fear that refugees may now face.

Committed to bringing field-based knowledge to the public agenda in order to move governments and aid groups to action, Refugees International remains committed to its work: "Where there are needs, we witness what is lacking, we present solutions and we demand action."

Questions for Reflection

1. Are Refugees International's three message strategies effective public communication strategies? Why or why not?
2. Fund-raising is of particular concern for a non-governmental organization that does not accept governmental support. Why would such financial independence be important to an advocacy group?
3. How do organizations like Refugees International reconcile their own organizational goals with the unique cultural situations for which they advocate?

Information drawn from www.refugeesinternational.org; Crisp, J. (July 28, 2014). Sticking up for refugee protection. Blog. http://refugeesinternational.org/blog/sticking-refugee-protection; Gamboa, S., & Dann, C. (June 30, 2014). Children at the border raise question of who is a refugee. NBC News. http://www.nbcnews.com/storyline/immigration-border-crisis/children-border-raise-question-who-refugee-n144696; Libal, K., & Harding, S. (2007). The politics of refugee advocacy and humanitarian assistance. *Middle East Report*, 244. http://www.merip.org/mer/mer244/politics-refugee-advocacy-humanitarian-assistance; http://en.wikipedia.org/wiki/Nauru.

PROFESSIONAL INSIGHT Can publics become too active?

Figure 9.2 Shana Glickfield, Partner, BeeKeeper Group

Vocal activists can be an organization's greatest asset. Not only do they provide a personal, human voice to what is often communicated through fact sheets and press releases, but they are the true champions of carrying messages to other likely supporters. They will hold your sign up at a rally in front of a state capitol building and share the latest favorable article via their social media channels.

In today's transparent world, it is not enough to present a position through a "front group" purporting to represent a base of supporters. You need to show the people that you claim to represent authenticity, credibility, and, ultimately, success. But do these activists always work to your advantage? Not always.

While an organization can thrive thanks to the words and actions of its supporters, these same activists can also work to its detriment if they present extreme language and actions even implicitly on behalf of the organization. This is very much the case with PETA, where extreme actions of individuals have brought more attention to these actions than the good work of the organization itself.

Loss of control of a message can be detrimental, but message dilution and fatigue can be even more critical. The newsworthiness and success of campaign activities can lose steam and significance if not carefully curated when tied to your brand. For example, the color pink has become very closely associated with breast cancer awareness activities, thanks to the successful efforts of numerous nonprofit organizations over the years. But the term "pinkwashing" has come to refer to the oversaturation and brand confusion that has come from the prevalence of pink in events and messages, with or without consent of official breast cancer nonprofit support.

Despite any disadvantageous work of some activists, it is the vocal majority that an organization must embrace and amplify. Part of the growth and success of public activism is making sure that grassroots participants feel like their actions and messages are making an impact. It is up to the organization to provide opportunities for showcasing their voices of support and then demonstrating causation between their activities and any favorable outcomes.

In tough issue debates, your public activists will be your arsenal in the arms race for voices on your side of the issue. In awareness campaigns and calls for funding, your public activists will fight for attention for your message above the hundreds of other messages people receive each day. While it is rare that these publics will work against the organizations they seek to support, it helps to provide clearly defined calls to action, and then make those actions and messages diverse and interesting enough to maintain both their interest and that of public.

As a partner at BeeKeeper Group, Glickfield helps a wide array of clients with their communications and advocacy strategies, focusing on social media and online community building. Prior to launching BeeKeeper Group, she was the online community director for NextGenWeb.org, the online community of USTelecom. Before that, she was the director of strategic communications at Amplify Public Affairs and did advocacy work in-house at several national nonprofit organizations. She holds a law degree from Temple University.

CHAPTER 10

Stakeholders

Global Citizens

Globalism. Multiculturalism. Transnationalism. Regardless of the way it's described, the world has become a smaller arena for public relations and public communications. As markets for products and services connect countries and cultures around the world, organizations with multinational operations need public relations practitioners who can manage communication programs across borders, understand the risks of dynamic situations, and adapt quickly to either opportunities or problems.

Most of the time, public relations professionals in the United States have taken for granted the predictability and convenience of life in a free-market economy with political stability. Of course, increasing numbers of nations match the U.S. standard of living, and a few others are rapidly closing the gap. Some still lag behind.

Where living standards approach America's norm, differences in culture and media may complicate a public relations process that would seem simple in the United States. Even nations that share as much as the United States and Great Britain still contain remarkable differences.

Language is one example. Though English is spoken by almost everyone in both countries, the meaning of the same word may differ depending on where it's said. In Great Britain, businesspeople commonly use the word *turnover* to mean total revenues for a financial period, but Americans use the word *sales* to express the same idea. Americans often expect the noun *scheme* to mean a cunning or devious plot, but in Great Britain it's commonly used as a synonym for plan or program (or programme, as it would be spelled in London).

CULTURAL DIFFERENCES

Almost as variable as language, attitudes toward the use of time vary widely from culture to culture. To many in other nations, Americans appear to rush everything—even leisure. A business dinner that might last

75 minutes in a United States restaurant could take twice as long in some European cities.

The meals themselves—the food, when it's eaten, how it's eaten—also change from country to country. An English breakfast is large and varied, and afternoon tea remains a tradition. In Italy, the first meal of the day may be a bun and espresso, and other meals are likely to include pasta as a side dish but not a main dish. In Russia, breakfast foods—meats and cheeses—resemble what some Americans eat for lunch. Evening meals in many nations are later than they would be in the United States.

For public relations professionals, arranging media receptions or special events that feature food involves meticulous planning and selection to please guests. In an unfamiliar culture, only local expertise can ensure that an important event will succeed rather than embarrass.

GET LOCAL HELP

Respected authorities in international public relations strongly advise practitioners working in cultures other than their own to:

- Avoid the ethnocentrism that overvalues American habits and methods.
- Get advice and assistance from established public relations consultants in the locations where goodwill is needed.
- Allow more time to complete arrangements and obtain delivery of needed materials.

Americans sometimes believe that what works at home will surely work in other countries. Adapting tactics that have worked famously in U.S. cities, they plunge ahead, expecting similar results. Sometimes they are lucky and get what they want, but often they confuse, mystify, or offend their target publics or miss them altogether.

Local consultants can provide help with language, customs, regulations, media contacts, local transportation, and last-minute supplies or modifications. They can identify stakeholders and opinion leaders whose views will count the most. By including on-site consultants in early planning for an international program, practitioners can save time and money and also achieve a better outcome. Learning more about the ways in which varied governmental and societal institutions successfully inform and persuade their stakeholder groups will prove valuable to practitioners seeking to establish and maintain relationships within new cultures.

OVERCOMING LANGUAGE BARRIERS

In international efforts, language often represents the single most troublesome challenge. Not only are the words and sentence structure different, but also the alphabet may be entirely unfamiliar or—just as bad—misleadingly similar. In Russia, the Cyrillic alphabet is used, and the letters *BP*, the name of the petroleum giant, would sound like *VR* if strict pronunciation were used.

Sometimes, the problem is a common phrase in one language that conveys the wrong message when spoken in another. According to *The New York Times*, an expensive Italian restaurant gave Shanghai residents reason to smile when it opened under the name Va Bene, which means "go well" in Italian. In Shanghai dialect, it sounded like "not cheap."

Translation is essential, but it often slows things down. When a speaker and translator take turns, the speaker's remarks double in length, risking both boredom and misunderstanding. To avoid the need for clumsy sequential translation of a speaker's remarks through a translator, a practitioner might team up with a local consultant who learns the intricacies of a public relations program's platform and key messages well enough to handle media interviews and similar tasks independently.

Some multinational corporations are large enough to have full-time public relations professionals in countries where they operate, or they train managers in other departments to handle public relations as needed. In either case, the staffers should come from the local population. Executives at corporate headquarters also should listen carefully to public relations advice they get from consultants or qualified staff working in another country and adjust plans or responses to issues accordingly. Listening to local voices is essential regardless of where the headquarters might be.

INTERNATIONAL EXPERTISE

Practitioners around the globe may find helpful advice from professional colleagues through organizations such as the International Public Relations Association (IPRA), formed in 1955 in London, and the Global Alliance, formed in 2002. The IPRA offers a code of ethics for international communications known as the Code of Athens.

Many nations have professional associations, such as the Chartered Institute of Public Relations, a British organization, and the Korean Public Relations Association.

While the organizations may differ somewhat in structure, they seek to foster recognition of the public relations profession, to offer opportunities for skill enhancement, and to advance ethical performance. For example, according to its Web site, the vision of the Global Alliance is to:

> enhance the role and value of public relations and communication management to organizations, and to global society. We pursue this vision through leadership and service to the profession while defining universal principles that unite our professional associations and their members while embracing a diversity that enables different applications in different parts of our global community.

CRITICS OF GLOBALIZATION

Although globalization probably ranks as the leading economic force of the new century, it has attracted its share of critics. Some say globalization is a movement that exploits poor workers in weak and underdeveloped countries to provide inexpensive consumer goods for individuals who are privileged to live in prosperous countries.

Activist groups like the Mobilization for Global Justice have held rallies and marches to draw attention to the poverty of many workers in Latin America and Asia. The groups have performed street-theater skits outside offices of Citibank, the International Monetary Fund, Monsanto, Occidental Petroleum, and the World Bank. Radical protesters resorted to violence and vandalism at demonstrations in Seattle and Geneva.

Business Week pointed out that:

> Anti-globalization groups speak in the name of Third World countries, but democratically elected governments in countries such as Mexico and India often disagree with them. They want more corporate investment, not less; freer trade, not more restricted markets; and the enforcement of local labor laws, not the imposition of foreign ones.

ADJUST TO GLOBAL THREATS

The global practice of public relations has gained new urgency with the increase in geopolitical tensions between the United States and other nations. Fears of terrorism and anti-American violence have caused U.S. companies to add more security at overseas operations, reexamine relationships in vulnerable locations, and rely more on operational leadership chosen from local populations.

Reviewing the anxious situation, *PRWeek* magazine said that multinational companies should:

- Step up employee communications activities for workers in stressful regions.
- Emphasize long-term relationships and high-ranking local managers.
- Focus on the company's local history, employment, and contributions.

"Stick to talking about who your company is and what its products offer," the magazine recommended, "and don't get caught up in political issues or side-taking."

The cases in this chapter will ask you to consider how organizations, citizens groups, and governmental agencies can best respond to the opportunities and challenges posed by a global system. As you read each one, ask yourself: How can this organization best achieve mutually beneficial relationships with its critical stakeholders despite cultural, language, or economic differences? How may organizations best present messages to diverse groups? What ethical principles should guide communications with groups that may have strong national differences?

ADDITIONAL READINGS

Casmir, Fred L. (1997). *Ethics in intercultural and international communication.* Mahwah, NJ: Lawrence Erlbaum Associates.

Curtin, Patricia. A., & Gaither, T. Kenn. (2007). *Negotiating culture, identity, and power.* Thousand Oaks, CA: Sage.

Freitag, Alan R., & Stokes, Ashli Quesinberry. (2009). *Global public relations: Spanning borders, spanning cultures.* Abingdon, Oxon, U.K.: Routledge.

Higgins, Richard. (2000). *Best practices in global investor relations.* Westport, CT: Greenwood.

Tilson, Donn J., & Alozie, Emmanuel C. (2004). *Toward the common good: Perspectives in international public relations.* Boston: Pearson Education.

CASE 38: TUNISIAN GOVERNMENT COURTS U.S. AND EUROPEAN INVESTMENT

Tunisia, the northern most country in Africa, experienced the first revolution in what would become a series of nations with citizens protesting autocratic governments in favor of democracy in 2010. The Arab Spring, as the revolutions were called as a whole, came in response to what was seen as decades of repression of free speech and human rights, as well as economic mismanagement, corruption, and political dissent.

The tipping point for the protests arrived as nearly two-thirds of the people in the region were under the age of 30, widely educated, underemployed, and equipped with intimate knowledge of social media like Twitter, Facebook and YouTube, while the establishment had little knowledge of the tools as producers or receivers. The youth organizers collected support via social media, sought non-violent instruction and partners among laborers, and then shared their expertise with others in the region.

The Jasmine Revolution

Tunisia's revolution, often referred to as the Jasmine Revolution, began after a 26-year-old fruit vendor set himself on fire as an act of political protest. Mohammed Bouazizi pushed a vegetable and fruit cart around the town of Sidi Bouzid. On December 17, 2010, a policewoman confiscated his cart because he was unlicensed. After a confrontation where the policewoman slapped him, spat on him, and insulted his dead father,

Bouazizi, humiliated and disheartened, went to complain to local municipality officials about the $10 fine—$3 more than he takes home a day to support his family of eight—to no avail.

Bouazizi wasn't the first or the last to practice self-immolation in protest of political oppression, but he was the right person at the right time to spark an uprising. Just 35 days later, President Zine el Abidine Ben Ali, the dictator, fled the country, bringing an end to his 23-year rule, and Bouazizi was memorialized in graffiti art around town.

Transitioning to Democracy

Tunisia's transition to democracy has not come without issues. Instituting democratic elections and new leaders are often fraught with threats and miscalculations. However, the elected officials in Tunisia have uniquely shown the ability to compromise. Also, officials and citizens approved a new constitution that offered equal rights for men and women, a right rarely seen in the Arab word. The constitution does not cite Islam as a source of legislation.

Also setting the new democracy apart were its efforts to market itself as a place that could attract foreign business and tourism. President Moncef Marzouki, a former human rights activist who was largely responsible for bringing together Islamists and secular parties to formulate the constitution, recognizes the need for security so the ensuing stability can attract national and foreign investors as well as tourists. And it is working. America and European countries have pledged funds to help maintain stability and encourage investment. Tunisia has become internationally respected for hosting nearly one million refugees during the revolution in Libya, and it has built an economic and social bridge with the neighboring country, which had a revolution of its own during the tumultuous spring.

Promoting Investment

The Ministry of Industry, Energy and Mines has helped create The Foreign Investment Promotion Agency (FIPA-Tunisia). Its main functions are to attract and promote foreign direct investment, provide information and awareness within the international business community, and roll out the welcome wagon to foreign investors. Using online media, international forums, and studies, FIPA touts Tunisia's tax breaks and incentives, its uncomplicated bureaucracy, diverse opportunities, and its educated and enthusiastic workforce.

FIPA's Web site, investintunisia.tn, asks "why invest in Tunisia?" and provides many answers. Using lists, brochures, fliers, studies, a FAQ list, and releases, the site seeks to inform and reassure potential investors about the country's resources and stability. Promotion videos are available on Tunisia's YouTube channel. Videos such as *New Tunisia,*

New Opportunities (http://www.youtube.com/watch?v=Xbbko4KKSSw) include testimonials from corporations who have opened manufacturing and research sites in the country.

This strategy is particularly effective because Tunisia has a large online society. Traditional media has mostly been state owned, therefore the large and youthful population got most of its media culture from social networking opportunities. Digital advertising is relatively inexpensive.

Finally, FIPA tells potential investors about the growing infrastructure and the more than 1,400 flights between Europe and the nine airports in the 63,170 square-mile country—that's slightly smaller than the state of Florida—which leads to another of Tunisia's important assets: its location as an African, Arab, Mediterranean vacation spot. While tourism is still down as much as 80 percent in some regions compared to its pre-revolution numbers, a strong tourism infrastructure remains in Tunisia, especially around the seaports and Roman ruins.

Political unrest in the Middle East during 2014 offered challenges to Tunisia's emerging democracy. But its ability to invite foreign businesses to "invest in democracy" offered backers a unique opportunity to help and Tunisians an opportunity to achieve what the revolutionaries envisioned.

Questions for Reflection

1. How do Tunisia's Web communication tools and research options, like studies and forums, help promote the country?
2. What are some unique advantages to the strategy of calling foreign businesses to "invest in democracy" rather than just inviting them to open a business in Tunisia?
3. What are the risks of this type of campaign?

Information drawn from Abouzeid, R. (January 21, 2011). Bouazizi: The man who set himself and Tunisia on fire. *Time*. http://content.time.com/time/magazine/article/0,9171,2044723,00.html; Agency for the Promotion of Industry and Innovation. http://www.tunisieindustrie.nat.tn/en/home.asp; Embassy of the U.S.-Tunisia. http://tunisia.usembassy.gov/the-foreign-investment-promotion-agency-forum-to-tunisia-investment-forum-2013.html; FIPA-Tunisia. www.investintunisia.com; Murphy, C. (2012). The Arab Spring: The uprising and its Significance. http://www.trinitydc.edu/magazine-2012/; Plus Media Solutions (August 4, 2014). Washington: National Security Advisor Rice. Africa and America: Partners in a shared future. www.lexisnexis.com; Press release (February 5, 2014). Tunisia: UK 'willing to work to promote tourism, investment in Tunisia' —Stephen O'Brien. http://allafrica.com/stories/201402061017.html#ixzz39nfs9OfG; Ryan, Y. (January 26, 2011).

How Tunisia's revolution began. http://www.aljazeera.com/indepth/features/2011/01/2011126121815985483.html; Sherwood, S. (April, 5 2012). Tunisia after the revolution. http://www.nytimes.com/2012/04/08/travel/tunisia-after-the-revolution.html?_r=0&pagewanted=1; Smialek, J., & Rastello, S. (August 5, 2014). Tunisia needs U.S. support as Arab democracy hope, Marzouki says. http://www.bloomberg.com/news/2014-08-05/tunisia-needs-u-s-support-as-arab-democracy-hope-marzouki-says.html; Tunisia's Tourism Strategy for the year 2016. http://www.oecd.org/cfe/leed/46761318.pdf.

CASE 39: MARITIME TRAGEDY COMPOUNDED BY CULTURAL DIFFERENCES

Written by Larry F. Lamb

Figure 10.1 U.S. Defense Secretary Donald Rumsfeld (center) confers with Japanese Senior Vice Minister of Foreign Affairs Seishiro Eto (right), Ambassador to the United States Shunji Yanai (left) and U.S.N. Chief of Naval Operations Vern Clark. (DoD photo by R.D. Ward.)

People throughout Japan angrily condemned the U.S. Navy when a submarine accidentally rammed and sank a Japanese fishing vessel in the open ocean off Hawaii on Friday, February 9, 2001. Over the weekend, anger over the collision and relief at the rescue of 26 aboard paled beside anxiety over 9 still missing, including 4 teenagers.

As Navy officers and Japanese survivors provided more details, people everywhere were astonished to learn that the sub's maneuvers had been arranged to impress 16 civilian guests on board and that some guests had handled critical controls before the accident.

"It's outrageous and unforgivable," one resident of Uwajima, the fishing vessel's home, told BBC News. "It sounds like they were fooling around. It's very upsetting for the people in this town."

Additionally, Japanese survivors said the submarine had rescued no one but instead waited for the U.S. Coast Guard to arrive and lift them from their life rafts. Confirming their tale, the Navy said waves had been too high to risk opening the sub's hatches or approaching the small rafts.

The Navy began investigating the collision immediately and relieved the sub's commanding officer. As he prepared for a court of inquiry, he asked to testify under immunity and initially declined to speak publicly about the incident. In the United States, high rates of litigation and gigantic jury awards have conditioned people to proceed cautiously as the facts of an accident are collected and assessed, especially when criminal charges might result.

The *Yomiuri Shimbun*, Japan's largest daily newspaper, expressed disapproval: "In Japan, the person responsible for such an accident would be bound to personally apologize for their actions and accept full responsibility."

Pieces of the Puzzle

Eventually, investigators pieced together events that led to the collision. The *Ehime-Maru*, a 180-foot trawler, was heading south at 11 knots on February 9 with the open Pacific ahead and the coastline of Oahu just visible nine miles off the stern. It had departed Honolulu 90 minutes earlier, at noontime, carrying a crew of 20 as well as 13 students and 2 teachers from the Uwajima Marine Products High School. Skies were overcast, and haze made visibility no better than fair; but it was a warm day; the air was 78 degrees and the ocean was 77. The surface was choppy, rolling with swells of four to six feet.

Built in 1996 and weighing 500 tons, the *Ehime-Maru* functioned as a floating classroom, with accommodations for up to 45 students, where Japanese teens could learn the skills they'd need in the maritime trades. The trawler was bound for a fishing area 435 nautical miles distant. High above the white hull and bridge, surface search radar scanned the vicinity for traffic.

Four hours before the trawler left Honolulu, the USS *Greeneville* had put to sea at 8 a.m. from the Naval Station at Pearl Harbor, just a few miles to the west. On board were 106 officers and enlisted men.

Distinguished Civilians Aboard

Also on the *Greeneville* were 16 civilians, men and women who were the Navy's guests for the day, expecting to return to port before nightfall. The Navy arranged such visits to the *Greeneville* and other ships as part of its community relations program. The purpose was to demonstrate:

- The Navy and Marine Corps team as a unique and capable instrument of national policy.
- Resource requirements for the nation's maritime security strategy.
- Prudent stewardship of taxpayer investments in naval platforms and systems.
- The proficiency, pride, and professionalism of sailors and Marines and the need to recruit and retain them.

"The Greeneville's sole mission on 9 February," according to a Navy document, "was to conduct a public affairs 'distinguished visitor' (DV) embark for 16 civilian guests."

Assigned to a large operations area south of Oahu, the 362-foot sub proceeded on the surface for the first two hours, with the commanding officer taking groups of guests up to the bridge. Then, the *Greeneville* submerged at 10:17 a.m. During this maneuver, guests operated some of the dive controls under close supervision of the crew, and the sub continued south until noon and then reversed course. The sub's sonar array first detected the *Ehime-Maru* at about 12:30 p.m. Due to error, initial calculations showed that the distance between the two vessels was increasing rather than closing.

Demonstration of Maneuvers

As the *Greeneville* continued north, the commanding officer put the 6,000-ton submarine through a series of up-and-down angles and high-speed turns to demonstrate its tactical maneuverability. He also planned to execute a rapid dive to a depth of 400 feet as well as an emergency surfacing drill. Navy rules require a submarine to rise to periscope depth before an emergency surfacing maneuver so that officers can look in all directions to eliminate any danger of collision. Only after this inspection of the surface is complete will a submarine descend to practice the rapid ascent.

As prescribed, the *Greeneville* scanned the surface through its periscopes, but the officers and crew saw nothing. The seas were high; a white haze reduced visibility; the trawler's hull was white; its angle of approach reduced its profile; and the sub's surface search procedure was short. At the time, the *Ehime-Maru* was less than two miles away from the *Greeneville*, and the sub's detection equipment confirmed the trawler's presence, its distance, its speed, and its course. Because of earlier miscalculations and inadequate crew communications on the sub, the danger went unnoticed.

Approaching the Fatal Moment

After 66 seconds at periscope depth, the *Greeneville* began its dive and reached 400 feet about two minutes later. The commanding officer invited one visitor to sit at the helm, another to operate ballast actuator valves, and a third to sound a klaxon horn during the emergency drill. All three guests were under close crew supervision. The *Ehime-Maru*, unnoticed and unsuspecting, was less than a mile away.

It took the *Greeneville* less than a minute to get from 400 feet to the surface. As it shot out of the waves, its rudder sliced the *Ehime-Maru* from starboard to port. The trawler captain gave immediate orders to get everyone on deck for a headcount. Even before the count could be completed, waves washed across the deck and began sweeping people into the sea. The vessel was gone in less than 10 minutes.

The trawler's life rafts deployed automatically, and the crew and students struggled through waves, diesel fuel, and flotsam to reach them. Within minutes, the rafts held 26 survivors. Missing were four 17-year-old students, three crew members, and both teachers.

On the *Greeneville*, the officers and crew were surprised by the noise and shudder caused by the collision. Using the periscopes, they examined the surroundings and were surprised to see a fishing vessel sinking and its people tumbling into the water. The sub itself had suffered some damage but nothing that would threaten its seaworthiness.

The *Greeneville* immediately called the U.S. Coast Guard for rescue assistance, but the high seas prevented the submarine itself from taking survivors on board. Water washing across the deck would have poured into any open hatch as the cylindrical hull rolled with the waves. The officers also were concerned that the sub's rolling motion might swamp or capsize the rafts if the vessel got too close.

Survivors Evacuated to Honolulu

Coast Guard watercraft arrived at the scene about one hour later and by 4:15 p.m. had moved all survivors to Honolulu. Surface vessels and aircraft from the Coast Guard and Navy continued to search for the nine missing Japanese for days but had no success.

Tragic as the collision was, the Navy's embarrassment grew as it acknowledged over succeeding days, first, that the sub was impotent in the rescue efforts; second, that a sizeable guest contingent was aboard; third, that civilians handled controls in the drills; and then, that the sole purpose of the cruise was public relations.

By Sunday, apologies and condolences had been extended to Japan by the commander in chief of the U.S. Pacific Fleet, the ambassador to Japan, the Secretary of State, and the new U.S. president, inaugurated less than a month earlier. The Japanese prime minister lodged an official protest and warned that the United States might have to raise the trawler from the ocean floor, 2,000 feet beneath the waves (Figure 10.2), if the missing nine were not found.

Figure 10.2 USS Greeneville sits atop blocks in dry dock at Pearl Harbor naval shipyard following a collision at sea with the Japanese fishing vessel *Ehime*. (DoD photo.)

In Japan, people were far from satisfied by the expressions of regret, and the news media there kept insisting that the United States and the submarine's commander should extend "sincere" apologies.

A Contrast in Cultures

Japanese writer Shin-ya Fujiware, commenting in *The New York Times*, said:

> The nonappearance of the commander of the Greeneville—his failure to meet the families of the victims to express his feelings of apology and mourning—is shocking, even incomprehensible to a people whose culture stresses decorum and form. Such decorum is not merely "formal" in the American sense; it is the shape in which common humanity finds expression.

One month after the accident, the sub commander arranged to meet face to face with relatives of the victims who were lost. In a closed-doors gathering in March, he bowed formally before them and tearfully expressed his regrets.

In June, the Navy acceded to the wishes of the missing victims' families and began a salvage effort to lift the trawler from the ocean floor and move it to shallower waters where divers could search the vessel's interior for bodies. All but one of the missing nine were found by November (Figure 10.3).

Figure 10.3 During the final ceremony of the *Ehime Maru* aboard JDS *Chihaya*, representatives from three crew members' families threw flowers in the air to honor their loved ones. (USN photo by Keith W. DeVinney.)

Navy Gets Cultural Guidance

During the salvage operations, the Navy turned to a professor of religion at the University of Hawaii for guidance in observing cultural norms to show proper respect in the recovery of remains. Professor George J. Tanabe, Jr., reflecting on the entire episode for *The New York Times*, said:

> You couldn't have constructed a better scenario for the uncorking of the darker side of Japan's love-hate relationship with the United States. . . . It was one humiliation after another for Japan, a reinforcement of deeply resented stereotypes of the relationship between the two countries as tough guys versus wimps.

Cultural differences represent more than the manners and preferences of peoples. They represent perceptions of what is right and wrong and what deserves respect and how to show it, as well as the power of symbols, the need for dignity, and the expectation of truth revealed promptly and thoroughly.

Questions for Reflection

1. Some reporters said that the Navy's slow release of details in the first week after the accident provided a steady flow of damaging news. What were the alternatives?
2. Was the Navy obligated to shield the "distinguished visitors" from the media's intrusiveness?
3. What steps were available to the Navy to address the anger in Japan and make sincere apologies?
4. How would you balance the concerns about litigation in the United States with demands in Japan for full accountability and openness?

Information for this case was drawn from the following: the U.S. Navy Web site at http://www.cpf.navy.mil/greeneville; Cushman, J. (February 11, 2001). Sub in collision was conducting drill, Navy says. *The New York Times*, p. A1; French, H. (November 5, 2001). U.S. makes amends to Japan for sinking of ship. *The New York Times*, p. A6; Jehl, D. (February 12, 2001). Clues sought in sub accident; some Japanese fault rescue. *The New York Times*, p. A1; Kakuchi, S. (March 7, 2001). Apologies do little to ease grief over sea tragedy. *Asia Times*, p. 7; Marquis, C. (February 10, 2001). 9 are missing off Pearl Harbor after U.S. submarine collides with Japanese vessel. *The New York Times*, p. A16; Shin-ya, F. (February 17, 2001). In Japan, waiting for the captain to appear. *The New York Times*, p. A17; (February 16, 2001). Sub tragedy leaves Japanese town bitter. BBC News. http://www.bbc.co.uk/1/hi/world/asia-pacific/; (April 13, 2001). Transcript of USN Court of Inquiry into circumstances of collision.

CASE 40: A PRESIDENT, PRAISE LEADER, AND PROTESTER COMMUNICATE GENDER DIVERSITY TO WIN THE NOBEL PEACE PRIZE

"We cannot achieve democracy and lasting peace in the world unless women obtain the same opportunities as men to influence developments at all levels of society," according to the citation read by the head of the 2011 Nobel Prize committee in announcing the three recipients of the Peace Prize. The recipients were Ellen Johnson Sirleaf and Leymah

Gbowee for their ongoing peaceful solutions in Liberia and Tawakkul Karman, a pro-democracy advocate and demonstrator in Yemen.

What made the combination of these three women the right choice for the 2011 prize? The selection of Peace Prize winners may offer an international commentary on practical and cultural levels. Sometimes a powerful wave of how one communicates and what one communicates provides the right strategic message: it was going to take women to make peace in Africa and the Middle East.

Africa and Arab Spotlight

As a harbinger for peace, the Nobel Peace Prize grows from local efforts that eventually reach the global stage. By awarding Johnson Sirleaf, Gbowee, and Karman the prize together, a three-fold frame emerged to provide a strategy for peace in Africa and the Middle East:

1. Prize winners were from two hotspots for democratic movement, Africa and the Middle East.
2. All laureates were women, the first time since Wangari Muta Maathai won in 2004 for her contribution to sustainable development, democracy, and peace.
3. The three women used three different communication tools to promote peace.

The three Nobel Peace Prize winners were among good company. Of the 250 nominees, several Middle Eastern actors in the Arab Spring protests were rumored to be nominated. As a sign of the times, speculation also circulated that bloggers and social network activists would rise to the top of the list. The three women represented these areas and more. For instance, Karman was a female journalist who has staged peaceful protests in Yemen. She led a human rights advocacy group called Women Journalists Without Chains that planned a successful street protest. She was briefly arrested, but that arrest prompted others to take to the streets. The activities led to her nickname, the Mother of Revolution. She was protesting before the more media-attuned protests of Tunisia and Egypt began.

In a *New York Times* interview, Nadia Mostafa, a professor of international relations at Cairo University, explained the selection's political significance. "Islam has always been associated with radical terrorism, intolerance and more," she said:

> Giving it to a woman and an Islamist? That means a sort of re-evaluation. It means Islam is not against peace, it's not against women, and Islamists can be women activists, and they can fight for human rights, freedom and democracy.

The African women winners were similarly considered catalysts for turning the tide of global perception of Liberia. Gbowee was recognized for uniting Christian and Muslim women against her country's warlords. As head of the Women for Peace movement, she organized women across ethnic and religious divides and safeguarded women's participation in elections. She was also a supporter of Johnson Sirleaf for president.

Johnson Sirleaf was perhaps the most well-known among the three and was widely considered the most likely to be the sole winner of the prize in 2011. As president of Liberia, she was credited with stabilizing the country and stopping violence that was once widespread. As a Harvard graduate in economics, Johnson Sirleaf is also credited for economic development in the country, although her most ardent supporters are outside of the country and her fervent critics are local constituents, punctuating the struggle of slow local progress and inspirational global meaning. In her country, she is criticized for spending money to engage an American public relations firm to improve Liberia's once brutal international image and not moving the country out of poverty and an unemployment crisis quickly enough. However, Liberians widely acknowledge her efforts to maintain peace and security. She is also praised for securing forgiveness for billions of dollars of Liberian debt.

The Positive Peace of Women

Beyond the spotlight on the region, the Nobel Prize committee also highlighted gender diversity with the 2011 award. According to *The New York Times*, "most of the recipients in the award's 110-year history have been men, and [2011's] decision seemed designed to give impetus to the fight for women's rights around the world."

The award itself may frame a message. Researchers have noted a rhetoric of gender-specific peace. Male prizewinners' citations come from being associated with war—stopping war, bringing peace to border disputes, etc.—while female prize winners are framed as human rights peacemakers—protecting children or participating in non-violent protests or providing nourishing peace, like sustainability.

"This whole process of three women receiving the Nobel Peace Prize is really overwhelming," Ms. Gbowee said in an interview with *The New York Times*. "It's finally a recognition that we can't ignore the other half of the world's population. We cannot ignore their unique skills."

Unique Communication Skills Promote Change

Those unique skills and alternative communication tools are underlined in why the three women were nominated in the first place. President Johnson Sirleaf maintained peace for the first time in 14 years during her first tenure in office. She repaired Liberia's external reputation and has been a picture of peace throughout her life, having been educated, elected (Senate), incarcerated, and elected (president) again.

Gbowee prayed and sang her way into the peace movement. After years of education in social work and trauma healing, studying non-violent protests and peace-building leaders, and raising five children, Gbowee said her catapult into leading women into peaceful activism was a dream in which God told her to gather women and pray for peace. In her book, *Mighty Be Our Powers*, Gbowee wrote she and a Mandingo-Muslim woman named Asatu, began by "going to the mosques on Friday at noon after prayers, to the markets on Saturday morning, to two churches every Sunday," and distributing fliers that read: "We are tired! We are tired of our children being killed! We are tired of being raped! Women, wake up – you have a voice in the peace process!" Additionally, they distributed simple drawings explaining their purpose to women who couldn't read.

Later she led a group of women to the fish market on Sundays where they publicly prayed and sang. They also held non-violent demonstrations and sit-ins protesting President Charles Taylor. They implemented a sex strike and a curse. She wrote in her book: "The strike lasted, on and off, for a few months. It had little or no practical effect, but it was extremely valuable in getting us media attention."

In Yemen, Karman began her activism as a journalist advocating for the freedom of the press. She gained fame when she opposed the calls for violence during the 2005 Muhammad Cartoons Controversy, writing, "We are not to call for tyranny and bans on freedom." In public appearances, Karman exchanged her traditional *niqab* for the more colorful *hijabs*, which also showed her face. Her human rights stances included advocating for laws that would prevent women from getting married under the age of 17.

She calls herself a citizen of the world, "earth my country and humanity my nation." During the Yemeni revolution she was detained by authorities, which only added fuel to the fire of protesters. Besides protesting in the streets, she wrote opinion pieces for *The New York Times* and gave media interviews all over the world. After winning the Nobel Peace Prize, reporters interviewed her in a blue tent as she participated in an anti-government sit-in. She called the prize a victory for women everywhere, but especially for Arab women.

According to Human Rights Watch researcher Nadya Khalife: "Fortunately, these three woman have shown that with patience and perseverance anything can really happen," she said. "They really have set an example that the whole world can learn from."

And by awarding the prize to them, the Nobel committee sends a message to inspire not only the women of the Middle East and Africa but women everywhere to bring about change on a global scale.

Questions for Reflection

1. In what ways are nontraditional forms of communication sometimes more effective than traditional means?
2. The communication strategies used by the three Nobel laureates in this case sought to mobilize public action in ways that demonstrate sensitivity to and challenges to cultural norms. Identify the tactics used and explain why each either adheres to or challenges cultural norms.
3. Discuss the public relations significance of international and national awards. What strategic purpose do they offer the organization granting the awards? The recipients?

Information drawn from Alaga, E. (June 2010). Challenges for women in peacebuilding in West Africa. African Institute of South Africa Policy brief. 18. http://www.ai.org.za/wpcontent/uploads/downloads/2011/11/No-18.-Challenges-for-Women-in-Peacebuilding-in-West-Africa.pdf; Butty, J. (March 17, 2014). Liberian lawmakers demand answers on foreign lobbying fees. *Voice of America.* http://allafrica.com/stories/201403170715.html; Cowell, A., Kasinof, L., & Nossiter, A. (October 7, 2011). Nobel Peace Prize awarded to three activist women. *The New York Times.* http://www.nytimes.com/2011/10/08/world/nobel-peace-prize-johnson-sirleaf-gbowee-karman.html?pagewanted=all&_r=0; Ford, T., & Allen B. (March 19, 2012). Nobel peace prize winner defends law criminalizing homosexuality in Liberia. *The Guardian.* http://www.theguardian.com/world/2012/mar/19/nobel-peace-prize-law-homosexuality. Gbowee, L. (2011). *Mighty be our powers: How sisterhood, prayer, and sex changed a nation at war.* New York: Beast Books; Newsom, V., & Lee, W. (September 1, 2009). On nourishing peace: The performativity of activism through the Nobel Peace Prize. *Global Media Journal: Am Ed*, 8, 15; Willis, P. (March 1, 2012). Engaging communities: Ostrom's economic commons, social capital and public relations. *Public Relations Review, 38*, 1.

CASE 41: REPRESENTING CONTROVERSIAL GLOBAL CLIENTS

Photos of the first lady holding a reception for mothers on Mother's Day; congratulating children who've won academic honors; working with an autistic boy; comforting grieving mothers. Photos of the president working with advisors; visiting a school; signing documents. Typical White House publicity? In this case, the photos are available on the "syrianpresidency"

Instagram account of Syrian President Bahar al Assad, which offers a stream of photos and captions of the president and his beautiful wife, Asma—all while the Syrian state is engaged in a bitter internal conflict that has resulted in thousands of deaths and displacements.

PR Firm Represents Syrian Government

According to Syrian government documents revealed by WikiLeaks in 2012, the Assad government had placed public relations firm Brown Lloyd James on a $5,000 a month retainer to help improve the image of the president and his regime (Alpert, 2012); the fees were reported to the U.S. government as required by the U.S Foreign Agents Registration Act.

The firm successfully elicited positive coverage of the Assads. *Vogue* published a profile of Ms. Assad titled "A Rose in the Desert" that described the first lady as "glamorous, young, and very chic—the freshest and most magnetic of first ladies." The complimentary coverage of the regime met with criticism, and *Vogue* later apparently removed the article from its Web site. Similar complimentary articles had also appeared in the French *Elle*, *Paris Match* and on the Huffington Post.

The agency's BLJ Worldwide Web site (http://www.bljworldwide.com/) describes its work:

> BLJ crafts high-impact communication strategies that move diplomacy forward. Often, the most effective method for advancing diplomatic goals is to get out of the ambassador's office and get into classrooms, community centers, newspapers, and business gatherings. BLJ's innovative approach recognizes that there are many tools available for crafting diplomacy that are often overlooked. From expanding trade to driving tourism, sharing cultures and improving people-to-people interactions, our work connects world leaders, diplomats, businesses, media, academics and the general public across borders to enhance understanding, goodwill, and cooperation.

The firm ended its work with the Syrian government in December 2010. But among the leaked documents was a May 2011 e-mail between government aides and the public relations firm that included recommendations to use public opinion polls of Syrians to elicit reform ideas and to create what was called an "echo chamber" through using interviews and op-eds in international media through which President Assad could talk about wanting reform in a "non-chaotic, rational way." The e-mail memo, which Politico posted online, noted that a focus on Ms. Assad would be strategic:

> In our view, the President needs to communicate more often and with more finely-tuned messaging and the First Lady needs to get in

> the game. The absence of a public figure as popular, capable, and attuned to the hopes of the people as Her Excellency at such a critical moment is conspicuous. The key is to show strength and sympathy at once.

BLJ partner, Mike Holtzman, later told reporters that the agency had not been paid for the memorandum and that it had been sent in hopes the public relations advice might be used to help quell violence in Syria.

Criticism of Agency's Clients

The chair and chief executive of the PRSA, Rosanna M. Fiske, wrote a letter to the editor of *The Financial Times* on September 1, 2011, in response to an article that had featured the president of Lloyd Brown James defending the firm's work for the Libyan and Syrian regimes. In the letter, she noted:

> We believe every person or organisation has the right to have its voice heard in the global marketplace of ideas. But for PR firms to represent dictatorships that do not afford that same freedom to their own people is disingenuous toward the liberties of a democracy and to democratic societies' reputations as marketplaces for dissenting ideas.

An op-ed in The Hill on August 16, 2011, written by Ms. Fiske that included much of the content of the letter to the editor noted that she found "their work to be not the best representation of my profession." Similarly, in an April 1, 2011, post on the PRSA Web site, Thomas E. Eppes, chair of the PRSA Board of Ethics and Professional Standards, asked, "Can a public relations professional represent a dictator or an authoritarian government and remain faithful to the PRSA Code of Ethics?"

Other Agencies Questioned about Clients

In an October 3, 2011, article, *Mother Jones* magazine listed six Middle Eastern regimes that had hired public relations firms to foster more positive images. The list included Hosni Mubarak, the former Egyptian president, and the rulers in Bahrain, Saudi Arabia and Yemen, who engaged Qorvis; the Syrian Assad family, who worked with Brown Lloyd James; and Muammar Qaddafi, the former Libyan ruler, who used the firms of Brown Lloyd James, Hopps & Associates, and The Monitor Group. The magazine also noted that Brown Lloyd James had represented a group lobbying to have a State Department-listed organization Mujahideen-e-Khalq taken off the list of terrorist organizations.

Questions about public relations representation of international clients rose again when it was revealed that the American firm Ketchum was paid \$1.9 million in the first six months of 2013 for its consulting services for the Russian government that helped Russian President Vladimir Putin place an opinion piece in *The New York Times* on September 12, 2013, cautioning the United States to avoid a military strike against Syria. Ketchum also represented the Russian oil and gas company Gazprom, earning about \$3.7 million, according to CBS News reports drawn from Justice Department records.

Questions for Reflection

1. How would you answer the question posed by PRSA official Mr. Eppes: Can a public relations professional represent a dictator or an authoritarian government and remain faithful to the PRSA Code of Ethics?
2. What are the legal obligations of a U.S. public relations firm hired to represent an international government as a client?
3. How has the growth of social media changed the ways in which governments can communicate with their citizens—or citizens' communication with or about their governments?
4. Should public relations agencies publicly disclose all their clients? What are the advantages and disadvantages offered by such an approach?

Information for this course was drawn from Al Arabiya English. (July 25, 2012). Syria leads: Al Arabiya English reports on Assad's PR firm. *The World Post.* http://www.huffingtonpost.com/2012/07/25/syria-leaks-al-arabiya-assad_n_1701352.html: Alpert, Emily. (July 7, 2012). WikiLeaks: PR firm tried to buff Syria's image after crackdown. *Los Angeles Times.* http://latimesblogs.latimes.com/world_now/2012/07/wikileaks-syria-email-pr-firm.html#sthash.LeVyJC8W.dpuf: Carter, Bill, & Chozick, Amy. (11 June 11, 2012). Syria's Assads turned to west for glossy P.R. *The New York Times,* A1; CBS News. (September 13, 2013). Selling the message: How PR firm helped place controversial Putin op-ed. http://www.cbsnews.com/news/selling-the-message-how-pr-firm-helped-place-controversial-putin-op-ed/; Eppes, Thomas E. (April 1, 2011). Can ethical PR practitioners represent dictators? *PRSay.* http://prsay.prsa.org/index/php/2011/04/01/ethics-of-pr-working-with-dictators; Fiske, Rosanna. (August 15, 2011). Destroying America's reputation by rebuilding Libya's. The Hill. http:thehill.com/blogs/congress-blogs/politics-176879-destroying-americas-reputation-by-rebuilding-libyas#ixzz2zNIYsR5Q; Hamed, Aleaziz. (October 3, 2011). Extreme makeover: Mideast autocrat edition. *Mother Jones.* http:www.motherjones.com/politics/2011/09/pr-qaddafi-mubarak-saudi-yemen; Lynch, Colum. (March 20, 2012). The ambassador's daughter.

Foreign Policy Passport Blog. http://blog.foreignpolicy.com/posts/2012/03/20/the_ambassadors_daughter; Memorandum to Fares Kallas from Brown Lloyd James. Available at http://www.foreignpolicy.com/files/fp_uploaded_documents/120706_320303_Political%20Communications%202.0-1.pdf; Putin, Vladimir V. (September 12, 2013). A plea for caution from Russia. *The New York Times,* A31; Suebsaeng, Awasin. (October 3, 2011). Brown Lloyd James: Lobbying for backers of a terrorist group. *Mother Jones.* http:www.motherjones.com/politics/2011/09/mujahedin-iran-mek-lobby-brown-lloyd-james; Tau, Byron, & Drusch, Andrea. (September 3, 2013). Syria's U.S. efforts focused on PR, not lobbying . . . Politico.com. *http://www.politico.com/politicoinfluence/0913/politicoinfluence11542.html.*

CASE 42: STARBUCKS EXPANDS SUSTAINABLE PROGRAMS TO TEAMUP WITH OPRAH

Figure 10.4 Starbucks promotes its new Teavana Oprah Chai Tea.

The name around the mermaid insignia stamped on every eco-friendly cup and exotic bag of Starbucks coffee was meant to recall seafaring coffee traders who might have been contemporaries of the coffee company's namesake, Starbuck, the first mate in the epic novel *Moby Dick*. So, it may seem that coffee farmers from distant lands were fated to be a part of the story of Starbucks Coffee Company.

According to the company's Web site, it is "wholeheartedly committed to making a positive difference in the lives of farmers and their communities [by] promoting the sustainability of [supply chain] production." In order to make that positive difference and participate in the international fair trade conversation, the company began a program called "Coffee and Farmer Equity Practices" (C.A.F.E.) in 2001 to promote mutually beneficial relationships with farmers, workers and communities; to protect the environment; and to guarantee the production of high-quality coffee. Some 13 years later, the program is still in place but has branched off to include tea producers in what Starbucks is calling Ethical Tea Partnerships to "TEAmUp" with smallholder tea farmers around the world on one end and U.S. mega-brand Oprah Winfrey on the other.

Thus far, Starbucks has invested more than $70 million in collaborative (coffee and tea) farmer programs and activities. The activities include building farmer support centers, educating farmers on adjustments needed for farming as climate change dries leaves on the plants, providing farmer loans, and creating and maintaining forest carbon projects, which redouble their efforts to improve farmers' livelihoods and support their own long-term supply of high-quality tea.

"Tea"-ing Up for a Global Marketing Hole-in-One

As the health benefits of tea become public knowledge, some experts predict by 2017 tea drinkers will outnumber coffee drinkers in the United States. Therefore, as Starbucks' numbers begin to level off, a new product may invigorate the brand. In a press release, former CEO Howard Schultz said with Oprah's assistance, Starbucks is "going to elevate the tea experience in the same way we did for coffee."

At the coffee company's annual meeting in early 2014, Winfrey joined her friend Schultz to announce a new product, the Teavana Oprah Chai Tea, and a philanthropic partnership where proceeds from sales will go toward education-focused nonprofits, including the Oprah Winfrey Leadership Academy for girls, the media mogul's South African girls' boarding school.

"Elevating the tea experience" goes beyond the Oprah Chai Tea. It's a chance to perfect the approach to sustainable sourcing the company tried to deliver with coffee sourcing. The company Web site tells customers they are "committed to long-term strategy of ethical tea sourcing, which includes helping farmers and their communities throughout our tea supply chain."

They have been working with Ethical Tea Partnership, a nonprofit trade association that includes tea producers and companies. The trade association has existed since 1997 and has concentrated on improving "the sustainability of tea production, the lives of tea workers and the environment in which tea is produced." Starbucks also included tea leave farmers from the existing C.A.F.E program. They have also supported tea-growing communities in India and Guatemala with Mercy Corps through the Community Health and Advancement Initiative project or CHAI since 2003. The collaboration between Tazo Tea—the tea traditionally sold in Starbucks stores—and Mercy Corps has assisted 80,000 people in more than 200 farming communities in India and Guatemala, providing mostly education and health assistance.

"Tea"-ing Off Ethically

While Starbucks' sustainability programs reach beyond coffee and tea production, the C.A.F.E. program focuses on the supply chain of beans and leaves in their version of "farm to table" practices. The program asks farmers and, in some cases, their country officials to adhere to "critical social, environmental, economic and quality aspects of growing, processing and selling [products] for Starbucks." Farmers in countries such as Guatemala, Tanzania, Colombia, Kenya, and Ethiopia must meet minimum requirements, which include 28 specific tenets in five areas: product quality, economic accountability (transparency), social responsibility, and environmental leadership in growing and processing beans and leaves. High scoring suppliers are rewarded with contracts that will guarantee higher prices for their agricultural product and better contract terms altogether.

In 2006, Ethiopian coffee growers and the Ethiopian government wanted to trademark coffee in the United States, as they had in Canada and the European Union, so they could become bigger players in the coffee marketplace. Rumor had it that Starbucks was opposing that effort, although Starbucks denied the rumor. Even though Starbucks and the Ethiopian government brokered an understanding that Starbucks was not the one blocking the trademarks, Starbucks was still called upon to clarify and re-enforce its commitment to coffee farmers around the world.

Starbucks said it didn't block Ethiopia's trademark bid and claimed the dispute was between Ethiopia and U.S. regulators. America's National Coffee Association (NCA), the industry lobby group, was opposed to the trademark. But NCA exists to represent the interests of the big coffee marketers, and there is no coffee marketer bigger than Starbucks. Furthermore, the chair of the NCA's Government Relations Committee happened to be Dub Hay, Starbucks' senior vice president of coffee and global procurement.

Starbucks learned a lesson about transparency and public expectation from the global backlash of the Ethiopian trademark incident. Schultz wrote in his 1997 autobiography, *Pour your Heart into It*, "Running a company, while keeping to high ethical standards presents [a] dilemma: Sometimes you can't figure out how to live up to them."

"Tea"-ing Up With a Partner

As Starbucks launched its tea initiative, it had the benefit of understanding the company's responsibilities and the public's expectation of sustainability. From the beginning, Starbucks approached smallholder farmers with the mission of sustainable farming and the C.A.F.E program fully realized. This time they worked with a well-established global association that works with non-governmental organizations to fulfill certification, quality assurance, and fair trade goals. Additionally, teaming up with Winfrey adds another layer of accountability as her brand could well be affected by any missteps. With part of the money made with each cup of Teavana Oprah Chai Tea going back to Winfrey's education projects in Africa, it seems that the process comes full circle.

As many international companies have come to realize, it is difficult to "brew the right blend of global ambition and ethical trade." Corporations in capitalist countries need the great equalizer of public relations and non-governmental organizations when working in a global market to manage their relationships and responsibilities. And it doesn't hurt when a mega brand known for prudent and mindful control over its associations, such as Oprah Winfrey, endorses the product because of the care the company shows to the small, local farmer in mostly African nations, as well as the promise to give back to the community from which those profitable tea leaves originated.

Questions for Reflection

1. How should corporations balance their "triple bottom line" commitments to profitability, social responsibility, and sustainability?
2. What advantages and disadvantages does an association with non-governmental organizations, grassroots or trade associations have? Discuss the ethical dilemma between grassroots affiliations and corporations with a high stakes economic interest.
3. What is the strategic purpose of corporate philanthropic strategies?
4. Does Starbucks "brew the right blend of global ambition and ethical trade"?

Information for this case was drawn from the following: Bain, Simon, & MacDermid, Alan. (August 28, 2007). The coffee may be hot and sweet . . . but do you know if it is fair?: Starbucks defends plan to promote African farms. *The Glasgow Herald*, p. 3; Clark, Taylor. (2007). *Starbucked: A double tall tale of caffeine, commerce and culture.* New York: Little, Brown and Company; Ethical Tea Partnership (n.d.). The importance of tea smallholder farming. http://www.ethicalteapartnership.org/team-2014/importance-tea-smallholder-farming/; *The Ethiopian Herald* (February 15, 2007). Oxfam—Starbucks needs to change. *Africa News*; MercyCorp (November 4, 2004). CHAI program in India launches new initiatives (November 4, 2004). http://www.mercycorps.org/articles/india/chai-program-india-launches-new-initiatives; National Coffee Association Web site, Oxfam Web site, Starbucks Web site, and Voice of America Web site; O'Connor, Clare. (March 19, 2014). Oprah partners with billionaire buddy Howard Schultz for her own Starbucks tea. Forbes.com. http://www.forbes.com/sites/clareoconnor/2014/03/19/oprah-partners-with-billionaire-buddy-howard-schultz-for-her-own-starbucks-tea/; O'Rourke, P.J. (December 15, 2007). The frothy side of a corporate behemoth. *The International Herald Tribune*, p. 8; Pagnamenta, Robin. (December 11, 2006). Starbucks seeks the right blend of global ambition and ethical trade. *The London Times*, p. 44; Schultz, Howard, & Jones-Young, Dori. (1997). *Pour your heart into it.* New York: Hyperion; Starbucks (n.d.). Tea. http://www.starbucks.com/responsibility/sourcing/tea

PROFESSIONAL INSIGHT How do practitioners act as the champions of social responsibility?

Figure 10.5 James E. Grunig, Professor Emeritus, University of Maryland

Organizational theorists tell us that different types of expertise become important in management when people with that expertise are able to solve problems that are crucial to that organization at a particular time. Public relations professionals are becoming empowered today because of their ability to solve problems of relationships, trust, and responsibility that threaten the survival of many organizations and result in poor performance by most others.

The public relations function provides a voice for publics when management makes critical, strategic decisions. Too often, management makes decisions without considering the consequences of those decisions on publics who have no say in the decisions. When management makes such decisions, many publics develop into activist groups who actively oppose the organization. Opposition typically results in litigation, legislation, regulation, and negative publicity that cost the organization a great deal of money.

Even if publics do not organize to oppose decisions, management has a responsibility to alleviate negative consequences of its actions—such as pollution, risky products, discrimination, economic hardship, or a dangerous workplace. Recognizing and alleviating these consequences is the essence of social responsibility, and the public relations function is the management champion of social responsibility.

Public relations managers are the voice of management to explain its decisions; but, more importantly, they also are the voice of publics. I have described this relationship between public relations, other managers, and publics as two-way symmetrical public relations. Others have called it collaborative advocacy. Still others have called the public relations professional an in-house activist. All of these terms suggest that the public relations professional has a duty to the organization that employs him or her, a duty to the publics that make up society, and to himself or herself. Increasingly, public relations professionals are the chief ethics officers of their organizations. This role is a challenging one, but it makes public relations one of the most relevant and interesting professions today.

James E. Grunig is an emeritus professor of public relations in the Department of Communication at the University of Maryland. He holds a Ph.D. in Mass Communication from the University of Wisconsin. He has written or edited five books and over 260 articles and chapters about public relations.

APPENDIX A

IABC Code of Ethics for Professional Communicators

PREFACE

Because hundreds of thousands of business communicators worldwide engage in activities that affect the lives of millions of people, and because this power carries with it significant social responsibilities, the International Association of Business Communicators developed the Code of Ethics for Professional Communicators.

The Code is based on three different yet interrelated principles of professional communication that apply throughout the world. These principles assume that just societies are governed by a profound respect for human rights and the rule of law; that ethics, the criteria for determining what is right and wrong, can be agreed upon by members of an organization; and, that understanding matters of taste requires sensitivity to cultural norms.

These principles are essential:

- Professional communication is legal.
- Professional communication is ethical.
- Professional communication is in good taste.

Recognizing these principles, members of IABC will:

- Engage in communication that is not only legal but also ethical and sensitive to cultural values and beliefs;
- Engage in truthful, accurate and fair communication that facilitates respect and mutual understanding;
- Adhere to the following articles of the IABC Code of Ethics for Professional Communicators.

Because conditions in the world are constantly changing, members of IABC will work to improve their individual competence and to increase the body of knowledge in the field with research and education.

ARTICLES

1. Professional communicators uphold the credibility and dignity of their profession by practicing honest, candid and timely communication and by fostering the free flow of essential information in accord with the public interest.
2. Professional communicators disseminate accurate information and promptly correct any erroneous communication for which they may be responsible.
3. Professional communicators understand and support the principles of free speech, freedom of assembly, and access to an open marketplace of ideas and act accordingly.
4. Professional communicators are sensitive to cultural values and beliefs and engage in fair and balanced communication activities that foster and encourage mutual understanding.
5. Professional communicators refrain from taking part in any undertaking which the communicator considers to be unethical.
6. Professional communicators obey laws and public policies governing their professional activities and are sensitive to the spirit of all laws and regulations and, should any law or public policy be violated, for whatever reason, act promptly to correct the situation.
7. Professional communicators give credit for unique expressions borrowed from others and identify the sources and purposes of all information disseminated to the public.
8. Professional communicators protect confidential information and, at the same time, comply with all legal requirements for the disclosure of information affecting the welfare of others.
9. Professional communicators do not use confidential information gained as a result of professional activities for personal benefit and do not represent conflicting or competing interests without written consent of those involved.
10. Professional communicators do not accept undisclosed gifts or payments for professional services from anyone other than a client or employer.
11. Professional communicators do not guarantee results that are beyond the power of the practitioner to deliver.
12. Professional communicators are honest not only with others but also, and most importantly, with themselves as

individuals; for a professional communicator seeks the truth and speaks that truth first to the self.

ENFORCEMENT AND COMMUNICATION OF THE IABC CODE OF ETHICS

IABC fosters compliance with its Code by engaging in global communication campaigns rather than through negative sanctions. However, in keeping with the sixth article of the IABC Code, members of IABC who are found guilty by an appropriate governmental agency or judicial body of violating laws and public policies governing their professional activities may have their membership terminated by the IABC executive board following procedures set forth in the association's bylaws.

IABC encourages the widest possible communication about its Code.

The IABC Code of Ethics for Professional Communicators is published in several languages and is freely available to all: Permission is hereby granted to any individual or organization wishing to copy and incorporate all or part of the IABC Code into personal and corporate codes, with the understanding that appropriate credit be given to IABC in any publication of such codes. The IABC Code is published on the association's web site. The association's bimonthly magazine, *Communication World*, publishes periodic articles dealing with ethical issues. At least one session at the association's annual conference is devoted to ethics. The international headquarters of IABC, through its professional development activities, encourages and supports efforts by IABC student chapters, professional chapters, and regions to conduct meetings and workshops devoted to the topic of ethics and the IABC Code.

New and renewing members of IABC sign the following statement as part of their application: "I have reviewed and understand the IABC Code of Ethics for Professional Communicators."

As a service to communicators worldwide, inquiries about ethics and questions or comments about the IABC Code may be addressed to members of the IABC Ethics Committee. The IABC Ethics Committee is composed of at least three accredited members of IABC who serve staggered three-year terms. Other IABC members may serve on the committee with the approval of the IABC executive committee. The functions of the Ethics Committee are to assist with professional development activities dealing with ethics and to offer advice and assistance to individual communicators regarding specific ethical situations.

While discretion will be used in handling all inquiries about ethics, absolute confidentiality cannot be guaranteed. Those wishing more information about the IABC Code or specific advice about ethics are encouraged to contact IABC World Headquarters (601 Montgomery Street, Suite 1900, San Francisco, CA 94111 USA; phone, +1 415.544.4700; fax, +1 415.544.4747).

APPENDIX B

Public Relations Society of America Member Code of Ethics (2000)

PREAMBLE

- Professional Values
- Principles of Conduct
- Commitment and Compliance

This Code applies to PRSA members. The Code is designed to be a useful guide for PRSA members as they carry out their ethical responsibilities. This document is designed to anticipate and accommodate, by precedent, ethical challenges that may arise. The scenarios outlined in the Code provision are actual examples of misconduct. More will be added as experience with the Code occurs.

The Public Relations Society of America (PRSA) is committed to ethical practices. The level of public trust PRSA members seek, as we serve the public good, means we have taken on a special obligation to operate ethically.

The value of member reputation depends upon the ethical conduct of everyone affiliated with the Public Relations Society of America. Each of us sets an example for each other - as well as other professionals - by our pursuit of excellence with powerful standards of performance, professionalism, and ethical conduct.

Emphasis on enforcement of the Code has been eliminated. But, the PRSA Board of Directors retains the right to bar from membership or expel from the Society any individual who has been or is sanctioned by a government agency or convicted in a court of law of an action that is not in compliance with the Code.

Ethical practice is the most important obligation of a PRSA member. We view the Member Code of Ethics as a model for other professions, organizations, and professionals.

PRSA MEMBER STATEMENT OF PROFESSIONAL VALUES

This statement presents the core values of PRSA members and, more broadly, of the public relations profession. These values provide the foundation for the Member Code of Ethics and set the industry standard for the professional practice of public relations. These values are the fundamental beliefs that guide our behaviors and decision-making process. We believe our professional values are vital to the integrity of the profession as a whole.

Advocacy

We serve the public interest by acting as responsible advocates for those we represent.

We provide a voice in the marketplace of ideas, facts, and viewpoints to aid informed public debate.

Honesty

We adhere to the highest standards of accuracy and truth in advancing the interests of those we represent and in communicating with the public.

Expertise

We acquire and responsibly use specialized knowledge and experience. We advance the profession through continued professional development, research, and education. We build mutual understanding, credibility, and relationships among a wide array of institutions and audiences.

Independence

We provide objective counsel to those we represent. We are accountable for our actions.

Loyalty

We are faithful to those we represent, while honoring our obligation to serve the public interest.

Fairness

We deal fairly with clients, employers, competitors, peers, vendors, the media, and the general public. We respect all opinions and support the right of free expression.

PRSA CODE PROVISIONS

Free Flow of Information

Core Principle Protecting and advancing the free flow of accurate and truthful information is essential to serving the public interest and contributing to informed decision making in a democratic society.

Intent:
To maintain the integrity of relationships with the media, government officials, and the public.

To aid informed decision-making.

Guidelines:
A member shall:

Preserve the integrity of the process of communication.

Be honest and accurate in all communications.

Act promptly to correct erroneous communications for which the practitioner is responsible.

Preserve the free flow of unprejudiced information when giving or receiving gifts by ensuring that gifts are nominal, legal, and infrequent.

Examples of Improper Conduct Under this Provision:
A member representing a ski manufacturer gives a pair of expensive racing skis to a sports magazine columnist, to influence the columnist to write favorable articles about the product.

A member entertains a government official beyond legal limits and/or in violation of government reporting requirements.

Competition

Core Principle Promoting healthy and fair competition among professionals preserves an ethical climate while fostering a robust business environment.

Intent:
To promote respect and fair competition among public relations professionals.

To serve the public interest by providing the widest choice of practitioner options.

Guidelines:
A member shall:

Follow ethical hiring practices designed to respect free and open competition without deliberately undermining a competitor.

Preserve intellectual property rights in the marketplace.

Examples of Improper Conduct Under This Provision:
A member employed by a "client organization" shares helpful information with a counseling firm that is competing with others for the organization's business.

A member spreads malicious and unfounded rumors about a competitor in order to alienate the competitor's clients and employees in a ploy to recruit people and business.

Disclosure of Information

Core Principle Open communication fosters informed decision making in a democratic society.

Intent:

To build trust with the public by revealing all information needed for responsible decision making.

Guidelines:

A member shall:

Be honest and accurate in all communications.

Act promptly to correct erroneous communications for which the member is responsible.

Investigate the truthfulness and accuracy of information released on behalf of those represented.

Reveal the sponsors for causes and interests represented.

Disclose financial interest (such as stock ownership) in a client's organization.

Avoid deceptive practices.

Examples of Improper Conduct Under this Provision:

Front groups: A member implements "grass roots" campaigns or letter-writing campaigns to legislators on behalf of undisclosed interest groups.

Lying by omission: A practitioner for a corporation knowingly fails to release financial information, giving a misleading impression of the corporation's performance.

A member discovers inaccurate information disseminated via a website or media kit and does not correct the information.

A member deceives the public by employing people to pose as volunteers to speak at public hearings and participate in "grass roots" campaigns.

Safeguarding Confidences

Core Principle Client trust requires appropriate protection of confidential and private information.

Intent:

To protect the privacy rights of clients, organizations, and individuals by safeguarding confidential information.

Guidelines:
A member shall: Safeguard the confidences and privacy rights of present, former, and prospective clients and employees.

Protect privileged, confidential, or insider information gained from a client or organization.

Immediately advise an appropriate authority if a member discovers that confidential information is being divulged by an employee of a client company or organization.

Examples of Improper Conduct Under This Provision:
A member changes jobs, takes confidential information, and uses that information in the new position to the detriment of the former employer.

A member intentionally leaks proprietary information to the detriment of some other party.

Conflicts of Interest

Core Principle Avoiding real, potential or perceived conflicts of interest builds the trust of clients, employers, and the publics.

Intent:
To earn trust and mutual respect with clients or employers.

To build trust with the public by avoiding or ending situations that put one's personal or professional interests in conflict with society's interests.

Guidelines:
A member shall:

Act in the best interests of the client or employer, even subordinating the member's personal interests.

Avoid actions and circumstances that may appear to compromise good business judgment or create a conflict between personal and professional interests.

Disclose promptly any existing or potential conflict of interest to affected clients or organizations.

Encourage clients and customers to determine if a conflict exists after notifying all affected parties.

Examples of Improper Conduct Under This Provision:
The member fails to disclose that he or she has a strong financial interest in a client's chief competitor.

The member represents a "competitor company" or a "conflicting interest" without informing a prospective client.

Enhancing the Profession

Core Principle Public relations professionals work constantly to strengthen the public's trust in the profession.

Intent:

To build respect and credibility with the public for the profession of public relations.

To improve, adapt and expand professional practices.

Guidelines:

A member shall: Acknowledge that there is an obligation to protect and enhance the profession.

Keep informed and educated about practices in the profession to ensure ethical conduct.

Actively pursue personal professional development.

Decline representation of clients or organizations that urge or require actions contrary to this Code.

Accurately define what public relations activities can accomplish.

Counsel subordinates in proper ethical decision making.

Require that subordinates adhere to the ethical requirements of the Code.

Report practices not in compliance with the Code, whether committed by PRSA members or not, to the appropriate authority.

Examples of Improper Conduct Under This Provision:

A PRSA member declares publicly that a product the client sells is safe, without disclosing evidence to the contrary.

A member initially assigns some questionable client work to a non-member practitioner to avoid the ethical obligation of PRSA membership.

INDEX